HARBRACE
COLLEGE
HANDBOOK
CANADIAN EDITION

HARBRACE
COLLEGE
HANDBOOK
CANADIAN EDITION

John C. Hodges and Mary E. Whitten

Editorial Consultants: David Perlman
Trinity College, University of Toronto
Thomas O'Hanley

Longman Canada Limited

Copyright © 1979 by Longman Canada Limited
55 Barber Greene Road, Don Mills, Ontario

Copyright 1941, 1946, 1951, © 1956, 1962, 1967, 1972,
1977 by Harcourt Brace Jovanovich, Inc.

ISBN: 0-7747-3039-0

Printed in Canada

1 2 3 4 5 6 7 8 9 87 86 85 84 83 82 81 80 79

To the Instructor

The Canadian edition of the *Harbrace College Handbook* is based on the American eighth edition by John C. Hodges, late of the University of Tennessee, and Mary E. Whitten of North Texas State University. In preparing the Canadian edition we have attempted to preserve the organization and methodology of the American original (which have been tested and refined over the course of several editions), while at the same time making the book more responsive to the specific needs of Canadian students and more reflective of the Canadian cultural environment. In particular, we have included the work of Canadian writers in many of the examples, inserted a new term paper on a Canadian studies subject, added Canadian works to the lists of reference books, adopted metric units, and Canadianized the spelling. In choosing among the various spelling options which are current in Canada, we have followed the preferred spellings of the *Gage Canadian Dictionary* (Toronto: Gage, 1967), except in the case of words such as *colour* and *neighbour* where we have opted for the *-our* instead of the *-or* ending. In quoted examples, however, we have retained the spellings used in the original sources.

The *Harbrace College Handbook* is intended both as a guide for the individual writer and as a textbook for use in class. The book begins with a section on **Sentence Sense** and ends with a **Glossary of Grammatical Terms**. The former may be used, whenever needed, as an introduction to the other sections; the latter may be used for reference throughout the course. Some instructors may wish to begin with Section **32, Planning and Writing the Whole Composition**. Others may prefer to begin with Section **31, The Paragraph**, or with Sections **19–30**.

Exercises are provided for every section of the book. The number, the scope, and the variety of these exercises make it possible for instructors to select those activities that best suit the needs of their students. (Additional exercises keyed to this handbook are provided in the *Harbrace College Workbook* by Sheila Y. Graham.)

John C. Hodges originated this handbook in 1941. He died soon after its sixth edition was published in 1967. The basic approach of the *Harbrace College Handbook* is his and has been carried forward in subsequent editions by Mary C. Whitten.

To the Student

Contemporary Usage / The Canadian edition of the *Harbrace College Handbook* attempts to describe the usual practice of good contemporary writers and to state that practice as simply as possible. The rules given in colour are to be interpreted as descriptions of usage, and they have authority only to the extent that they describe usage. In your reading you should observe the practices of good writers so that you may gain the confidence that comes from firsthand knowledge of what good writing is.

Numbers or Symbols / A number or a symbol written in the margin of your paper indicates a need for correction or improvement and calls for revision. If a number is used, turn directly to the corresponding number at the top of the page in the handbook. If a symbol is used, first consult the alphabetical list of symbols inside the front cover to find the number of the section to which you should turn. An appropriate letter after a number or symbol (such as **2c** or **frag/c**) will refer you to a specific part of a section.

References / Your instructor will ordinarily refer you to the number or symbol (**2** or **frag**, **9** or **cap**, **18** or **sp**, **28** or **ref**) appearing at the head of one of the thirty-four sections of the handbook. The rule given in colour at the beginning of each section covers the whole section. One of the more specific rules given within the section will usually be needed to guide you in revision. Study the section to which you have been referred—the whole of the section if necessary—and master the specific part of the section that applies to your writing.

Additional Help / The general section on **Sentence Sense** at the beginning of the book may provide the background you need to understand later sections of the book. If you do not understand any grammatical term used in the text, consult the **Glossary of Grammatical Terms** at the end of the book.

Correction and Revision / After you have studied the rules called to your attention, revise your paper carefully, as directed by your instructor. One method of revision is explained and illustrated in Section **8**, page 84.

Contents

GRAMMAR

1

Sentence Sense   2

Contents

5
Case 45

6
Agreement 52

Contents

7

Verb Forms   61

MECHANICS

8

Manuscript Form   76

9
Capitals

10
Italics

Contents

11

Abbreviations and Numbers   97

PUNCTUATION

12

The Comma   104

13
Superfluous Commas 122

14
The Semicolon 126

15

The Apostrophe

16

Quotation Marks

17

The Period and Other Marks 146

SPELLING AND DICTION

18

Spelling and Hyphenation

19

Good Use—Glossary 174

20

Exactness 205

24

Subordination   245

25

Coherence: Misplaced Parts, Dangling Modifiers   250

Contents

28
Reference of Pronouns

29
Emphasis

30
Variety

LARGER ELEMENTS

31
The Paragraph

32
Planning and Writing the Whole Composition

Contents

34
Business Letters 415

HARBRACE
COLLEGE
HANDBOOK
CANADIAN EDITION

GRAMMAR

Sentence Sense **1**

Sentence Fragment **2**

Comma Splice and Fused Sentence **3**

Adjectives and Adverbs **4**

Case **5**

Agreement **6**

Verb Forms **7**

Sentence Sense

1

Master the essentials of the sentence as an aid to clear thinking and effective writing.

A key to good writing is to possess or develop sentence sense. With sentence sense, you can recognize the grammatical essentials of the written sentence.

Below are three simple sentences. In each, the line separates the two basic grammatical parts of the sentence.

Humanity | will survive.

Many dangers | threaten the human race.

We | are intelligent creatures.

The first part of each sentence above functions as the subject; the second part functions as the predicate. Most simple sentences follow this pattern: **subject + predicate**.

Speakers and writers combine sentences and in the process rearrange, add, delete, and substitute words:

The saying is old.   It has a new meaning.

VARIOUS COMBINATIONS

The saying is old, but it has a new meaning.
Although it has a new meaning, the saying is old.
The saying, which is old, has a new meaning.
The old saying has a new meaning.
It is an old saying with a new meaning.

A study of Sections **1** through **7** of this handbook should help you understand how words are related to one another and what order they take in sentences. For explanations of any unfamiliar grammatical terms, see the Glossary of Grammatical Terms beginning on page 423.

1a

Learn to recognize verbs.

You can learn to recognize a verb by observing its function in a sentence, its meaning, and its form.

Function   A verb may function as the predicate of a sentence or as a part of the predicate.

> **SUBJECT + PREDICATE.**

William	*drives.*
William	*drives* carefully in heavy traffic.
William	always *drives* his car to work.

Meaning   Verbs are words that express action, occurrence, or existence (a state of being).

| *Play* ball! | The rain *stopped.* |
| They *exist.* | *Am* I right? |

Form   When converted from the present to the past tense, nearly all verbs change form (*eat—ate*). In the present tense, all verbs change form to indicate a singular subject in the third person (I *eat*—he *eats*).

PRESENT   I *ski.* He *skis.* We *win.* He *wins.* BUT I *quit.* He *quits.*
PAST   Shirley *skied.* They *won.*   He *quit* early.

In addition, certain suffixes, such as *-ize* and *-ify*, often indicate that a word is a verb (*legalize, classify*).

3

Verb phrases A verb may consist of two or more words (*may see, have been eaten, will be helping*), a unit called a *verb phrase*. When used with *have, has,* or *had,* most verbs end in *-d* or *-ed* (*have moved, had played*), but many have a special ending (*has eaten*). Used with a form of *be,* all progressive verbs end in *-ing,* as in *was eating* (see page 63).

> Tom *has moved.*   They *have taken* the tests.
> He *is moving.*   We *had been taking* lessons.

Auxiliary verbs A verb phrase like *has moved* or *was taking* follows this pattern: **auxiliary verb + main verb.** The following words are commonly used as auxiliaries: *have, has, had, am, is, are, was, were, be, been, do, does, did, will, shall, can, may, must, would, could, should, might.* Word groups like *am going to, is about to, ought to, used to, had better,* and *have to* may function as auxiliary verbs:

> He *had gone* to London.
> We *were enjoying* the game.
> Ruth *is going to try.*   [Compare "Ruth *will try.*"]

Other words may intervene between the auxiliary and the main verb:

> Television *will* never completely *replace* the radio. [The auxiliary *will* signals the approach of the verb *replace.*]

The contraction for *not* may be added to many auxiliaries: *haven't, doesn't, aren't, can't.*

Verbs with particles Many verbs are used with particles like *away, across, in, off, on, down, for, out,* and *up with.* Notice how meaning can be changed by the addition of one of these uninflected words.

SINGLE-WORD VERBS

He *passed.* (succeeded)
I *put* his picture on my desk. (placed)

VERBS WITH PARTICLES

He *passed away.* (died)
I *put up with* his picture on my desk. (tolerated)

Other words may intervene between the verb and the particle:

> We *looked* Bill *up*.   Millie *handed* her report *in*.

■ **Exercise 1**   Write sentences (1) using *left* and *flies* as single-word predicates, (2) using *experimenting* and *taken* as main verbs in phrases, (3) using *did* and *have* as auxiliary verbs, and (4) using *up* or *on* as a particle with a verb.

■ **Exercise 2**   Underline the verbs, including any auxiliaries, in the following paragraph.

¹ Jim angrily called himself a fool, as he had been doing all the way to the swamp. ² Why had he listened to Fred's mad idea? ³ What did ghosts and family legends mean to him, in this age of computers and solar-energy converters? ⁴ He had mysteries enough of his own, of a highly complex sort, which involved an intricate search for values. ⁵ But now he was chasing down ghosts, and this chase in the middle of the night was absurd. ⁶ It was lunacy! ⁷ The legends that surrounded the ghosts had horrified him as a child, and they were a horror still. ⁸ As he approached the dark trail which would lead him to the old mansion, he felt almost sick. ⁹ The safe, sure things of every day had become distant fantasies. ¹⁰ Only this grotesque night—and whatever ghosts might be lurking in the shadows—seemed hideously real.

1b
Learn to recognize subjects and objects of verbs.

In the sentence below, the line separates the complete subject (the subject as well as the words associated with it) from the complete predicate (the verb and the words associated with it). The italics single out the subject (also called the simple subject or headword) and the objects of the verb:

> A persuasive *clerk*   quickly sold *me* an expensive *desk*.

You can learn to recognize subjects and objects of verbs by observing their meaning, their form, and their position in sentences.

Meaning　To identify a subject, find the verb; then use the verb in a question beginning with *who* or *what*, as shown in the following examples:

The dog in the cage ate.
Verb: *ate*
WHO or WHAT ate? *The dog* (not the cage) *ate.*
Subject: *dog*

The hut was built by Al.
Verb: *was built*
WHAT was built? *The hut* (not Al) *was built.*
Subject: *hut*

To identify a direct object, find the subject and the verb; then use them in a question ending with *whom* or *what* as shown in the following example:

Karen graciously invited the reporters to lunch.
Subject and verb: *Karen invited*
Karen invited WHOM or WHAT? *the reporters*
Direct object: *reporters*

A verb that has a direct object to complete its meaning is called a *transitive* verb. Notice that a direct object in a sentence like the following is directly affected by the action of the verb:

High winds levelled a *town* in Manitoba.

Some verbs (such as *give, offer, bring, take, lend, send, buy,* and *sell*) may have both a direct object and an indirect object. An indirect object states *to whom* or *for whom* (or *to what* or *for what*) something is done.

Richard sent *Mildred* an invitation. [Richard sent an invitation *to whom? Mildred* is the indirect object.]

Form　Although other words or word groups may function as subjects or objects, nouns and pronouns are most frequently used in this way.

Many nouns (words used to name persons, places, things, ideas, animals, and so on) change their form to indicate number (*movement, movements; city, cities; woman, women*) and to indicate the possessive case (*John's* car, the *boys'* dogs, the *men's* job). Such suffixes as *-ance, -ation, -ence, -ment, -ness,* and *-ship* frequently indicate that a word is a noun (*appearance, determination, reference, atonement, boldness, hardship*). The articles *a, an,* and *the* regularly signal that a noun is to follow (a *chair,* an *activity,* the last *race*).

Form makes it a simple matter to recognize some pronouns. Pronouns such as *I, we, she, he, they,* and *who* function as subjects; when used as objects, these words change to the forms *me, us, her, him, them,* and *whom.* Other pronouns—such as *you, it, mine, ours, yours, hers, his, theirs, that, which*—resemble nouns in that they function as either subjects or objects without a change in form.

Position　　Becoming thoroughly aware of the importance of the position of words in a sentence can help you recognize subjects and objects. Not every arrangement of words is possible in an English sentence.

> NONSENSICAL　　An girls John St. two man old in had robbed the.
>
> SENTENCE　　An old man had robbed the two girls in St. John.

The transposition of words makes a difference in meaning:

> The two girls had robbed an old man in St. John.

The following sentence patterns and examples show the usual word order of English sentences. (For patterns with subject and object complements, see **4b** and **5f**.)

> SUBJECT—VERB.

They disappeared.
The youngest *boy did* not *smile* very often.

SUBJECT—VERB—OBJECT.

Mice frighten elephants.
Many *fans were hanging placards* in the stadium.

SUBJECT—VERB—INDIRECT OBJECT—DIRECT OBJECT.

Mary baked Timothy a *cake.*
The *company will* probably *send you* a small *refund.*

Remember, however, that subjects and objects of verbs do not always take the position indicated by these basic patterns:

There *were* no *objections.*   [Verb precedes subject. *There* used as an introductory word or filler is an expletive, which is never the subject.]

Over the door *were sprigs* of mistletoe.   [Verb precedes subject. Compare "Sprigs of mistletoe were over the door."]

His last *question I did* not *answer.*   [Object precedes subject. Compare "I did not answer his last question."]

The following sentences show a basic pattern and several variations:

STATEMENT   Her *secretary typed* the *letters.*
 [SUBJECT—VERB—OBJECT.]

COMMAND OR REQUEST   *Type* the *letters.* **[VERB—OBJECT.]**

EXCLAMATION   What *letters* her *secretary typed!*
 [OBJECT—SUBJECT—VERB!]

QUESTIONS   *Has* her *secretary typed* the *letters?*
 [AUXILIARY—SUBJECT—VERB—OBJECT?]

 What *letters should* her *secretary type?*
 [OBJECT—AUXILIARY—SUBJECT—VERB?]

A test for an object Knowing how to change an active verb to the passive voice can also help you to identify an object, since the object of an active verb can usually be made the subject of a passive verb:

ACTIVE   The Canucks finally *defeated* the *Bruins.* [*Bruins* is the direct object of *defeated.*]
PASSIVE   The *Bruins were* finally *defeated* by the Canucks. [*Bruins* is the subject of *were defeated.*]

Notice above that a form of *be* is added when an active verb is changed to the passive.

Note: Subjects, verbs, and objects may be compound.

Cobras and *pythons* both lay eggs. [Compound subject]
A capable *student can face* and *solve* these *problems* or *difficulties.* [Compound verb and compound object]

■ **Exercise 3** Label all subjects of verbs, direct objects, and indirect objects in the quotations below. Prepare for a class discussion of the basic sentence patterns and the variations used.

1. All energy except atomic energy originates within the sun. —DAVID G. LEE
2. Raise less hell and more wheat.   —W. C. VAN HORNE
3. Scarcely anything awakens attention like a tale of cruelty. —SAMUEL JOHNSON
4. Down the lake, mile by mile over the calm water, steamed the Mariposa Belle. —STEPHEN LEACOCK
5. Only a moral idiot with a suicidal mania would press the button for a nuclear war. —WALTER LIPPMANN
6. Signs of the future float in our smoggy skies and on our greasy surf. —GEORGE B. LEONARD
7. On the south side of the highway, beyond the barn and the pastures, the South Mountain rose. —ERNEST BUCKLER
8. In the *Odyssey,* Homer gives us detailed information of wind and stars. —MAURICIO OBREGÓN
9. On his land there were three straw-stacks.
   —SINCLAIR ROSS
10. Neither intelligence nor integrity can be imposed by law. —CARL BECKER

1c

Learn to recognize all the parts of speech.

Two methods of classifying words in a sentence are shown below:

Waitresses usually offer us free coffee at Joe's cafe.

1. SUBJECT—MODIFIER—VERB—INDIRECT OBJECT—
   MODIFIER—DIRECT OBJECT—PREPOSITION—
   MODIFIER—OBJECT OF PREPOSITION.

2. NOUN—ADVERB—VERB—PRONOUN—ADJECTIVE—
   NOUN—PREPOSITION—NOUN—NOUN.

The first method classifies words according to their function in a sentence; the second, according to their part of speech. Notice here that one part of speech—the noun (a naming word with a typical form)—is used as a subject, a direct object, a modifier, and an object of a preposition.

Words are traditionally grouped into eight classes or parts of speech: *verbs, nouns, pronouns, adjectives, adverbs, prepositions, conjunctions,* and *interjections.* Verbs, nouns, adjectives, and adverbs (called vocabulary or content words) make up more than 99 per cent of all words listed in the dictionary. But pronouns, prepositions, and conjunctions—although small in number—are important because they are used over and over in our speaking and writing. Prepositions and conjunctions (called function or structure words) connect and relate other parts of speech.

Of the eight word classes, only three—prepositions, conjunctions, and interjections—do not change their form. For a summary of the form changes of the other parts of speech, see **inflection**, page 435.

Carefully study the forms, meanings, and functions of each of the eight parts of speech listed on the following pages.

VERBS   *notify, notifies, are notifying, notified*
             write, writes, is writing, wrote, has written

A verb can function as the predicate of a sentence or as a part of the predicate: see **1a**.

> Herman *writes.*
> He *has written* five poems.
> He *is* no longer *writing* those dull stories.

One frequently used verb-forming suffix is *-ize:*

> *terror, idols* (nouns)—*terrorize, idolize* (verbs)

Note: Verb forms classified as participles, gerunds, or infinitives (verbals) cannot function as the predicate of a sentence: see **1d**.

PARTICIPLES	The man *writing* the note is Bill. [Modifier]
	She gave him *written* instructions. [Modifier]
GERUND	His *writing* all night long disturbed his whole family. [Subject]
INFINITIVES	Herman wants *to write.* [Direct object]
	The urge *to write* left him. [Modifier]

NOUNS   *man, men; kindness, kindnesses*
nation, nations; nation's, nations'
Montreal, United States, William, RCMP
prudence, the *money,* an *understanding*

In sentences, nouns function as subjects, objects, complements, appositives, modifiers, and in direct address and in absolute constructions. Nouns name persons, places, things, ideas, animals, and so on:

> *Marilyn* drives a *truck* for the *Salvation Army.*

Endings such as *-ation, -ism, -ity, -ment, -ness,* and so on are called noun-forming suffixes:

> *relax, starve* (verbs)—*relaxation, starvation* (nouns)
> *kind, happy* (adjectives)—*kindness, happiness* (nouns)

Compound nouns   Words such as *father-in-law, Salvation Army, swimming pool, dropout,* and *breakthrough* are generally classified as compound nouns. Regardless of spelling, the first part of the compound is usually stressed.

PRONOUNS   *I, me, my, mine, myself; they, you, him, it
this, these; who, whose, whom; which, that
one, ones, one's; everybody, anyone*

Pronouns serve the function of nouns in sentences:

They bought *it* for *her*.   *Everyone* knows *this*.

ADJECTIVES   *shy, sleepy, attractive, famous
three men, this class, another one
young, younger, youngest*

The articles *a, an,* and *the* are variously classified as adjectives, determiners, or function words. Adjectives modify or qualify nouns and pronouns (and sometimes gerunds) and are generally placed near the words they modify:

Although *beautiful* and *famous,* cathedrals no longer interest *homesick* tourists.

Suffixes such as *-al, -able, -ant, -ative, -ic, -ish, -less, -ous,* and *-y* may be added to certain verbs or nouns to form adjectives:

accept, repent (verbs)—*acceptable, repentant* (adjectives)
angel, effort (nouns)—*angelic, effortless* (adjectives)

Predicate adjectives A <u>predicate adjective</u> (subject complement) <u>is a word that helps to complete the meaning of a linking verb</u> (*be, am, is, are, was, were, been, seem, become, feel, look, smell, sound, taste,* and so on) <u>and that modifies the subject:</u> see **4b.**

The cathedrals were *beautiful* and *famous.*
The tourists soon became *homesick.*

ADVERBS   *rarely* saw, call *daily, soon* left, left *sooner
very* short, *too* angry, *never* shy, *not* fearful
practically never loses, *nearly always* cold

As the examples show, adverbs modify verbs, adjectives, and other adverbs. In addition, an adverb may modify a verbal, a phrase, a clause, or even the rest of the sentence in which it appears:

> I noticed a plane *slowly* circling overhead.
> *Honestly,* Clarence lies about his age.

The *-ly* ending nearly always converts adjectives to adverbs:

> *rare, honest* (adjectives)—*rarely, honestly* (adverbs)

PREPOSITIONS   *on* a shelf, *between* us, *because of* rain
                     to the door, *by* them, *before* class

Words commonly used as prepositions are *across, after, as, at, because of, before, between, by, for, from, in, in front of, in regard to, like, near, of, on, over, through, to, together with, under, until, up, with.* A preposition, a function word, always has an object, which is usually a noun or a pronoun; the preposition with its object (and any modifiers) is called a *prepositional phrase:*

> Byron expressed *with great force* his love *of liberty*.

The preposition may follow rather than precede its object, and it may be placed at the end of the sentence:

> What are you selling it *for?*   Faith is what we live *by*.

CONJUNCTIONS   Ida *and* Bill, in *or* out, long *but* witty
                     She acts *as if* she cares.
                     I left *because* I had finished the job.

Conjunctions function as connectors. They fall into two classes: the coordinating conjunctions (*and, but, or, nor, for*), used to connect words or phrases or to connect clauses that are of equal rank; and the subordinating conjunctions (such as *after, as if, because, if, since, till, when, where, while*), used to connect subordinate clauses with main clauses:

According to one biographer, Bacon did not look at friends *when* he talked with them, *for* he was concerned chiefly with ideas, not people.

INTERJECTIONS   *Wow!*   *Oh,* that's a surprise.

Interjections are exclamations, which may be followed by an exclamation point or by a comma: see **12b** and **17c**.

A dictionary labels words according to their part of speech. Some words have only one classification—for example, *notify* (verb), *sleepy* (adjective), *practically* (adverb). Other words have more than one label. The word *living,* for instance, is first treated as a form of the verb *live* and is then listed separately and defined as an adjective and as a noun. The actual classification depends on the use of the word in a given sentence:

They were *living* wretchedly. [Verb]
She is a *living* example of patience. [Adjective]
He barely makes a *living.* [Noun]

Another example is the word *up:*

Look *up!* [Adverb]
They dragged the sled *up* the hill. [Preposition]
The *up* escalator is jerking again. [Adjective]
He follows the *ups* and downs of the market. [Noun]
"They will *up* the rent again," he complained. [Verb]

■ **Exercise 4** Using your dictionary as an aid if you wish, classify each word in the following sentences according to its part of speech.

1. He struts with the gravity of a frozen penguin. —TIME
2. Men are often taken, like rabbits, by the ears. And though the tongue has no bones, it can sometimes break millions of them. —F. L. LUCAS
3. Awesome is the tyranny of the fixed idea. —ERIC LARABEE

4. Of all persons, adolescents are the most intensely personal; their intensity is often uncomfortable to adults.

—EDGAR Z. FRIEDENBERG

5. They pick a President and then for four years they pick on him.   —ADLAI STEVENSON

1d

Learn to recognize phrases and subordinate clauses.

PHRASES

A phrase is often defined as a group of related words without a subject and a predicate. Phrases are generally classified as follows:

VERB PHRASES   The rose *has wilted.   Did* you *see* it?
Mr. Kelly *may run up* the bill.   The roof *used to leak.*

NOUN PHRASES   *The severe drought* struck *all the prairie provinces.*

PREPOSITIONAL PHRASES   A special program *on the growth of flowers* fascinated audiences everywhere.

PARTICIPIAL PHRASES   A person *seeing an accident* should stay on the scene.   *Seen by three men,* the accident was reported at once.

GERUND PHRASES   *Riding a horse* takes skill.   I prefer *riding a bicycle.*

INFINITIVE PHRASES   Does James like *to swim in the ocean?* That is the problem *to be solved now.*

Notice in the examples above that the gerund *riding,* like the present participle *seeing,* ends in *-ing,* and that the two are distinguished only by their use in the sentence: the participle functions as an adjective and the gerund functions as a noun.

Participles, gerunds, and infinitives are derived from verbs. (See also the Glossary of Grammatical Terms.) They are much like verbs in that they have different tenses, can take subjects and objects, and can be modified by adverbs. But they cannot serve as the only verb form in the predicate of a sentence. Participial, gerund, and infinitive phrases function as adjectives, nouns, or adverbs and are therefore only parts of sentences, as the following examples illustrate.

SENTENCES

Dr. Ford explained the process.   He drew simple illustrations.

PHRASES IN SENTENCES

Explaining the process, Dr. Ford drew simple illustrations.
OR
Simple illustrations *drawn by Dr. Ford* explained the process. [Participial phrases]

Dr. Ford explained the process by *drawing simple illustrations.* [Gerund phrase]

Dr. Ford drew simple illustrations *to explain the process.* [Infinitive phrase]

(1) Phrases used as nouns

Gerund phrases are always used as nouns. Infinitive phrases are often used as nouns (although they may also function as modifiers). Occasionally a prepositional phrase functions as a noun.

NOUNS	PHRASES USED AS NOUNS
The *decision* is important.	*Choosing a major* is important. [Gerund phrase—subject]
She likes the *job.*	She likes *to do the work.* [Infinitive phrase—direct object]
His *action* prompted the *change.*	*His leaving the farm* prompted *her to seek a job in town.* [Gerund phrase—subject; infinitive phrase—direct object]

He uses my room for *storage*.	He uses my room for *storing all his auto parts*. [Gerund phrase—object of a preposition]
That *hour* is too late.	*After supper* is too late. [Prepositional phrase—subject]

■ **Exercise 5** Make a list of the gerund phrases and the infinitive phrases used as nouns in the following sentences (selected from *Time*).

1. Merely to argue for the preservation of park land is not enough.
2. Successfully merchandising a product is creative.
3. "We just want to take some of the blindness out of blind dates," explains the founder of Operation Match.
4. He insisted on calling every play from the bench; he tried installing a radio receiver in his quarterback's helmet, and when other teams started tuning in on his broadcast, he switched to shuttling "messenger guards" back and forth with his orders.

(2) Phrases used as modifiers

Prepositional phrases nearly always function as adjectives or adverbs. Infinitive phrases are also used as adjectives or adverbs. Participial phrases are used as adjectives.

ADJECTIVES	PHRASES USED AS ADJECTIVES
It is a *significant* idea.	It is an idea *of significance*. [Prepositional phrase]
Appropriate language is best.	Language *to suit the occasion* is best. [Infinitive phrase]
Destructive storms lashed Southern Ontario.	*Destroying many crops of corn and oats*, storms lashed Southern Ontario. [Participial phrase containing a prepositional phrase]

17

The *icy* bridge was the narrow one.

The bridge *covered with ice* was the narrow one. [Participial phrase containing a prepositional phrase]

ADVERBS

Drive *carefully*.

Certainly Mary Ann radiates good will.

PHRASES USED AS ADVERBS

Drive *with care on wet streets.* [Prepositional phrases]

To be sure, Mary Ann radiates good will. [Infinitive phrase]

The preceding examples demonstrate how phrases function in the same way as single-word modifiers. Remember, however, that phrases are not merely substitutes for single words. Many times phrases express more than can be packed into a single word:

> The gas gauge fluttered *from empty to full.*
> He telephoned his wife *to tell her of his arrival.*
> The firefighters *hosing down the adjacent buildings* had very little standing room.

■ **Exercise 6**   Underline each phrase used as a modifier in the following sentences. Then state whether the phrase functions as an adjective or as an adverb.

1. A moment like that one should last forever.
2. The fans blinded by the sun missed the best plays.
3. Crawling through the thicket, I suddenly remembered the box of shells left on top of the truck.
4. The people to watch closely are the ones ruling behind the political scenes.
5. A motorcycle racing along the beach zoomed over our big sand castle.

SUBORDINATE CLAUSES

A clause is often defined as a group of related words that contains both a subject and a predicate. Like a phrase, a subordinate (or dependent) clause is not a sentence. The subordinate clause functions as a single part of speech—as a noun, an adjective, or an adverb. Notice the relationship of the sentences below to the clauses that follow.

SENTENCES

That fact I must admit.
Ralph was my first and only blind date.
I married him.

SUBORDINATE CLAUSES IN SENTENCES

I must admit *that Ralph was my first and only blind date.*
[Noun clause—direct object]

The first blind date *that I ever had* was Ralph.
[Adjective clause]

Ralph was my first and only blind date *because I married him.* [Adverb clause]

In the examples above, *that* and *because* are used as *subordinators:* they subordinate the clauses they introduce, making these clauses dependent. The following words are commonly used to mark subordinate clauses.

RELATIVE PRONOUNS *that, what, which, who, whoever, whom, whomever, whose*

SUBORDINATING CONJUNCTIONS *after, although, as, because, before, if, once, since, that, though, till, unless, until, when, whenever, where, wherever, while*

Subordinators may consist of more than one word:

as if, as soon as, as though, even though, in order that, in that, no matter how, so that

No matter how hard I try, I cannot float with my toes out of the water.
We bought three dozen doughnuts *so that everyone would be sure to have enough.*

19

(3) Subordinate clauses used as nouns

NOUNS	NOUN CLAUSES
The *news* may be false.	*What the newspapers say* may be false. [Subject]
I do not know his *address*.	I do not know *where he lives*. [Direct object]
Give the tools to *Rita*.	Give the tools to *whoever can use them best*. [Object of a preposition]
That fact—Karen's *protest*— amazed me.	The fact *that Karen protested* amazed me. [Appositive]

The conjunction *that* before a noun clause may be omitted in some sentences:

> I know *she is right*. [Compare "I know *that she is right*."]

(4) Subordinate clauses used as modifiers

Two types of subordinate clauses, the adjective clause and the adverb clause, are used as modifiers.

Adjective clauses   Any clause that modifies a noun or a pronoun is an adjective clause. Adjective clauses, which nearly always follow the words modified, are most frequently introduced by a relative pronoun but may begin with such words as *when, where,* or *why*.

ADJECTIVES	ADJECTIVE CLAUSES
Everyone needs *loyal* friends.	Everyone needs friends *who are loyal*.
The *golden* window reflects the sun.	The window, *which shines like gold*, reflects the sun.
Peaceful countrysides no longer exist.	Countrysides *where I found peace of mind* no longer exist.

If it is not used as a subject, the relative pronoun in an adjective clause may sometimes be omitted:

> He is a man *I admire.*
> [Compare "He is a man *whom I admire.*"]

Adverb clauses   An adverb clause may modify a verb, an adjective, an adverb, an infinitive, a gerund, a participle, or even the rest of the sentence in which it appears. Many adverb clauses can take various positions in a sentence: see **12b** and **12d**. Adverb clauses are ordinarily introduced by subordinating conjunctions.

ADVERBS	ADVERB CLAUSES
Soon the lights went out.	*When the windstorm hit,* the lights went out.
No alcoholic beverages are sold *locally.*	No alcoholic beverages are sold *where I live.*
Speak *distinctly.*	Speak *so that you can be understood.*

Some adverb clauses may be elliptical. See also **25b**.

> If I can save enough money, I'll go to Alaska next summer. *If not,* I'll take a trip to the Maritimes.   [Omitted words are clearly implied.]

■ **Exercise 7**   Find each subordinate clause in the following sentences (selected from the *New York Times Magazine*) and label it as a noun clause, an adjective clause, or an adverb clause.

1. Food manufacturers contend that modern processing often robs food of its natural color.
2. What my son wants to wear or be or try to be is now almost entirely his business.
3. Grocers today must deal with shoppers whose basic attitudes are drastically changed.
4. As I talked to my neighbors, I found that all of them did depend on a world that stretched far beyond their property lines.

5. Bloodhounds do not follow tracks as people often believe. . . . Because a trail so often hangs several inches or
sometimes feet above the ground, hounds can follow a
person even if he wades through water.

1e

Learn to recognize main clauses and the various types of sentences.

A main clause can stand alone as a sentence, a grammatically
independent unit of expression, although it may require
other sentences to complete its meaning. Coordinating
conjunctions (*and, but, or, nor, for*) often connect and relate
main clauses.

MAIN CLAUSES IN SENTENCES

I had lost my passport, but *I did not worry about it.*
[A coordinating conjunction links the two main clauses.]
Although I had lost my passport, *I did not worry about it.*
[A subordinate clause precedes the main clause.]

MAIN CLAUSES CONVERTED TO SENTENCES

I had lost my passport.
I did not worry about it.   OR   *But I did not worry about it.*

Unlike main clauses, subordinate clauses become fragments
if isolated and written as sentences: see **2b.**

Sentences, which are grammatically independent units of
expression, may be classified as *simple, compound, complex,*
or *compound-complex.*

1. A simple sentence has only one subject and one predicate
(either or both of which may be compound):

Dick started a coin collection.   [**SUBJECT—VERB—OBJECT.**
See also the various patterns of the simple sentence on
pages 7–8.]

22

2. A compound sentence consists of at least two main clauses:

> Dick started a coin collection, and his wife bought a set of antique china. [**MAIN CLAUSE,** *and* **MAIN CLAUSE.** See 12a.]

3. A complex sentence has one main clause and at least one subordinate clause:

> As soon as Dick started a coin collection, his wife bought a set of antique china. [**ADVERB CLAUSE, MAIN CLAUSE.** See 12b.]

4. A compound-complex sentence consists of at least two main clauses and at least one subordinate clause:

> As soon as Dick started a coin collection, his wife bought a set of antique china; on Christmas morning they exchanged coins and dishes. [**ADVERB CLAUSE, MAIN CLAUSE; MAIN CLAUSE.** See 14a.]

Sentences may also be classified as *statements, commands* or *requests, questions,* or *exclamations.* Notice differences in the punctuation of the following examples:

STATEMENT   He refused the offer.

COMMAND OR REQUEST   Refuse the offer.

QUESTIONS   Did he refuse the offer? He refused, didn't he? He refused it?

EXCLAMATIONS   What an offer! He refused it! Refuse it!

■ **Exercise 8** Classify each of the following sentences (selected from *Maclean's* and *Natural History*) as simple, compound, complex, or compound-complex.

1. So far in their campaign, none of the three national leaders has come up with an economic policy that would deal, in any real way, with the devastating effects of inflation.
2. In 1942 they rebelled against the combined will of federal and provincial governments and the church by voting against military conscription.

3. Later, the marketplace becomes a whirlpool of movement as performers and audience mingle and chase each other about.
4. Nature is his passion in life, and colleagues say he is a skilled naturalist and outdoorsman.
5. Silt, the most widespread pollutant in North America, is one byproduct of strip mining, but the general public remains unaware of the extent to which ecosystems are harmed by silt pollution.

■ **Exercise 9** Observing differences in emphasis, convert each pair of sentences below to (*a*) a simple sentence, (*b*) a compound sentence consisting of two main clauses, and (*c*) a complex sentence with one main clause and one subordinate clause.

EXAMPLE
Male sperm whales occasionally attack ships. These whales jealously guard their territory.

a. *Jealously guarding their territory, male sperm whales occasionally attack ships.*
b. *Male sperm whales occasionally attack ships; these whales jealously guard their territory.*
c. *Since male sperm whales jealously guard their territory, they occasionally attack ships.*

1. The men smuggled marijuana into Spain. They were sentenced to six years in prison.
2. The council first condemned the property. Then it ordered the owner's eviction.
3. Uncle Oliver applied for a patent on his invention. He learned of three hundred such devices already on the market.
4. The border guards delayed every tourist. They carefully examined passports and luggage.

Sentence Fragment

2

As a rule, do not write a sentence fragment.

A fragment is a part of a sentence—such as a phrase or a subordinate clause—written with the capitalization and punctuation appropriate to a sentence:

FRAGMENTS   My father always planting a spring garden. Because he likes fresh vegetables.
SENTENCES   My father always plants a spring garden. He likes fresh vegetables.
OR
My father always plants a spring garden because he likes fresh vegetables.

Some types of fragments are not only standard but desirable. Exclamations, as well as questions and their answers, are often single words, phrases, or subordinate clauses written as sentences:

Why? *Because governments cannot establish heaven on earth.*
Where does Peg begin a mystery story? *On the last page. Always!*

Written dialogue that mirrors speech habits often contains grammatically incomplete sentences or elliptical expressions within the quotation marks:

frag

"So kind of you," fluted Miss Marple. *"Oh, yes, and my
little blue muffler. Yes, as I say, so kind of you to ask me here.*
I've been picturing, you know, just what your home was like,
so that I can visualize dear Lucy working here."

"Perfect home conditions, with murder thrown in," said
Cedric.

—AGATHA CHRISTIE

Occasionally, professional writers deliberately use fragments
for rhetorical effect:

It spotted the boat and took to flight. A *slow unhurried
takeoff, the vast wings spreading, the slender elongated legs
gracefully folding up under the creature's body. Like a ptero-
dactyl, like an angel, like something out of the world's dawn.*
—MARGARET LAURENCE [The reader can readily supply omitted words in the italicized fragments. Note the use of repetition and parallel structure.]

Despite their suitability for some purposes, sentence fragments are comparatively rare in formal expository writing.
In formal papers, sentence fragments are to be used—if at
all—sparingly and with care. If you have difficulty recogniz-
ing fragments as you proofread your compositions, review
1d and **1e**.

Test for Sentence Completeness

Before handing in a composition, proofread each word group
written as a sentence. Test each one for completeness. First,
be sure that it has at least one subject and one predicate.

FRAGMENTS WITHOUT BOTH A SUBJECT AND A PREDICATE

And for days tried to change my mind. [No subject]
Water sparkling in the moonlight. [No predicate]

Next, be sure that the word group is not a dependent clause
beginning with a subordinating conjunction or a relative
pronoun (see page 19).

FRAGMENTS WITH SUBJECTS AND PREDICATES

When he tried for days to change my mind. [Subject and
  verb: *he tried*. Subordinating conjunction: *When*.]
Which sparkles in the moonlight. [Subject and verb: *Which
  sparkles*. Relative pronoun: *Which*.]

Revision of the Sentence Fragment

Since a fragment is often an isolated, mispunctuated part of
an adjacent sentence, <u>one way to revise a fragment is to
make it a part of the complete sentence</u>.

FRAGMENT Henry smiled self-consciously. *Like a politician
  before a camera.* [An isolated phrase]

REVISED Henry smiled self-consciously, like a politician
  before a camera. [Phrase included in sentence]
  OR
  Henry smiled self-consciously—like a politician
  before a camera. [The use of the dash instead of
  the comma tends to emphasize the material that
  follows.]

FRAGMENT *A few minutes later.* A news bulletin interrupted
  the show.

REVISED A few minutes later, a news bulletin interrupted
  the show.

<u>Another way to revise a fragment is to make it into a sen-
tence</u>.

FRAGMENT The children finally arrived at camp. *Many
  dancing for joy, and some crying for their
  parents.* [Isolated phrases containing parti-
  ciples]

REVISED The children finally arrived at camp. Many
  danced for joy, and some cried for their parents.
  [Substitution of past-tense verbs for participles]
  OR
  Many were dancing for joy, and some were crying for their parents. [Insertion of the auxiliary
  were]

27

2a

Do not carelessly capitalize and punctuate a phrase as you would a sentence.

FRAGMENT　Soon I began to work for the company. *First in the rock pit and later on the highway.* [Prepositional phrases]

REVISED　Soon I began to work for the company, first in the rock pit and later on the highway. [Fragment included in the preceding sentence]

FRAGMENT　Astronauts venturing deep into space may not come back to earth for fifty years. *Returning only to discover an uninhabitable planet.* [Participial phrase]

REVISED　Astronauts venturing deep into space may not come back to earth for fifty years. They may return only to discover an uninhabitable planet. [Fragment made into a sentence]

FRAGMENT　He will have a chance to go home next weekend. *And to meet his new stepfather.* [Infinitive phrase]

REVISED　He will have a chance to go home next weekend and to meet his new stepfather. [Fragment included in the preceding sentence]

■ **Exercise 1** Eliminate each fragment below by including it in the adjacent sentence or by making it into a sentence.

1. I enjoy reading a few types of novels. Like science fiction.
2. The pampered Dennis finally left home. Earnestly seeking to become an individual in his own right.
3. I think that it is wise to ignore her sarcasm. Or to make a quick exit.
4. I did not recognize Gary. His beard gone and hair cut.
5. Louise likes to pretend that she is very old. And to speak of the "days of her youth" during the "Vietnam War Age."

2b

Do not carelessly capitalize and punctuate a subordinate clause as you would a sentence.

FRAGMENT Thousands of young people became active workers in the community. *After this social gospel had changed their apathy to concern.* [Subordinate clause]

REVISED Thousands of young people became active workers in the community after this social gospel had changed their apathy to concern. [Fragment included in the preceding sentence]

FRAGMENT I didn't know where he came from. *Or who he was.* [Subordinate clause]

REVISED I didn't know where he came from or who he was. [Fragment included in the preceding sentence]

FRAGMENT I was trying to read the directions. *Which were confusing and absurd.* [Subordinate clause]

REVISED I was trying to read the directions, which were confusing and absurd. [Fragment included in the preceding sentence]

OR

I was trying to read the directions. They were confusing and absurd. [Fragment made into a sentence]

■ **Exercise 2** Eliminate each fragment below by including it in the adjacent sentence or by making it into a sentence.

1. I decided to give skiing a try. After I had grown tired of watching other people fall.
2. Pat believes that everyone should go to university. And that all tests for admission should be abolished.
3. Many students were obviously victims of spring fever. Which affected class attendance.

4. Paul faints whenever he sees blood. And whenever he climbs into a dentist's chair.
5. I stopped trying to read my assignment. As soon as she started imitating my favorite comedian.

2c

Do not carelessly capitalize and punctuate any other fragment (such as an appositive or a part of a compound predicate) as you would a sentence.

FRAGMENT Mrs. Carter was looking for a new secretary. *A secretary with youth and experience.*

REVISED Mrs. Carter was looking for a new secretary—a secretary with youth and experience. [The use of the dash tends to emphasize the material that follows.]

FRAGMENT He lost the gold watch. *The one which had belonged to his grandfather.*

REVISED He lost the gold watch, the one which had belonged to his grandfather. [Fragment included in the preceding sentence]

FRAGMENT She studied cello at school. *And played in the orchestra at the opening of the Montreal Olympics.* [Detached part of a compound predicate]

REVISED She studied cello at school and played in the orchestra at the opening of the Montreal Olympics.

■ **Exercise 3** Eliminate each fragment below by including it in the preceding sentence or by making it into a sentence.

1. My roommate keeps all her cosmetics, books, papers, and clothes in one closet. The worst disaster area on campus.
2. According to Chesterton, realism is a kind of romanticism. The kind that has lost its mind.
3. The group met during the summer and made plans. And decided on the dates for action in the fall.

4. The hydraulic lift raises the ploughs out of the ground. And lowers them again.
5. I had a feeling that some sinister spirit brooded over the place. A feeling that I could not analyze.

■ **Exercise 4** Find the nine fragments in the following paragraph. Revise each fragment by attaching it logically to an adjacent sentence or by rewriting the fragment so that it stands by itself as a sentence.

[1] The little paperback almanac I found at the newsstand has given me some fascinating information. [2] Not just about the weather and changes in the moon. [3] There are also intriguing statistics. [4] A tub bath, for example, requires more water than a shower. [5] In all probability, ten or twelve gallons more, depending on how dirty the bather is. [6] And one of the Montezumas downed fifty jars of cocoa every day. [7] Which seems a bit exaggerated to me. [8] To say the least. [9] I also learned that an average beard has thirteen thousand whiskers. [10] That, in the course of a lifetime, a man could shave off more than nine yards of whiskers, over twenty-seven feet. [11] If my math is correct. [12] Some other interesting facts in the almanac. [13] Suppose a person was born on Sunday, February 29, 1976. [14] Another birthday not celebrated on Sunday until the year 2004. [15] Because February 29 falls on weekdays till then—twenty-eight birthdays later. [16] As I laid the almanac aside, I remembered that line in *Slaughterhouse-Five:* ''And so it goes.''

Comma Splice and Fused Sentence

3

Do not carelessly link two sentences with only a comma (comma splice) or run two sentences together without any punctuation (fused sentence).

Carefully observe how three sentences have been linked to make the one very long sentence below.

SENTENCES SEPARATED   These are mysteries performed in broad daylight before our very eyes. We can see every detail. And yet they are still mysteries.

SENTENCES LINKED   These are mysteries performed in broad daylight before our very eyes; we can see every detail, and yet they are still mysteries.   —ANNIE DILLARD

[**MAIN CLAUSE; MAIN CLAUSE,** *and* **MAIN CLAUSE.**]

When you link the end of one sentence to the beginning of another, be especially careful about punctuation.

NOT   The current was swift, he could not swim to shore. [Comma splice—sentences are linked with only a comma]

NOT   The current was swift he could not swim to shore. [Fused sentence—sentences are run together with no punctuation]

VARIOUS METHODS OF REVISION

Because the current was swift, he could not swim to shore. [First main clause subordinated: see **12b**]

The current was so swift that he could not swim to shore. [Second main clause subordinated]

Because of the swift current he could not swim to shore. [First clause reduced to an introductory phrase]

The current was swift. He could not swim to shore. [Each main clause converted to a sentence]

The current was swift; he could not swim to shore. [Main clauses separated by a semicolon: see **14a**]

The current was swift, so he could not swim to shore. [Comma preceding the connective *so*: see **12a**]

He could not swim to shore, for the current was swift. [Comma preceding the coordinating conjunction *for*]

The choice of a method of correction depends on the emphasis you wish to achieve.

If you cannot always recognize a main clause and distinguish it from a phrase or from a subordinate clause, review **1d** and **1e**.

3a

Use a comma between main clauses *only* when they are linked by *and, but, or, for, nor, so,* or *yet*. See also **12a**.

COMMA SPLICE   Our country observed its Centennial in 1967, my hometown celebrated its fiftieth anniversary the same year.

REVISED   Our country observed its Centennial in 1967, *and* my hometown celebrated its fiftieth anniversary the same year. [The coordinating conjunction *and* added after the comma]

33

COMMA SPLICE   The old tree stumps grated against the bottom of our boat, they did not damage the propeller.

REVISED   The old tree stumps grated against the bottom of our boat **,** *but* they did not damage the propeller. [The coordinating conjunction *but* added after the comma]

OR

Although the old tree stumps grated against the bottom of our boat **,** they did not damage the propeller. [Addition of *although* makes the first clause subordinate: see **12b**]

Caution: Do not omit punctuation between main clauses not linked by *and, but, or, for, nor, so,* and *yet.*

FUSED SENTENCE   She wrote him a love letter he answered it in person.

REVISED   She wrote him a love letter **.** He answered it in person. [Each main clause written as a sentence]

OR

She wrote him a love letter **;** he answered it in person. [Main clauses separated by a semicolon: see **14a**]

Variation of 3a

Either a comma or a semicolon may be used between short main clauses not linked by *and, but, or, for, nor, so,* or *yet* when the clauses are parallel in form and unified in thought:

School bores them **,** preaching bores them **,** even television bores them.   —ARTHUR MILLER

One is the reality **;** the other is the symbol.   —NANCY HALE

Note 1: The comma is optional between such balanced *the . . . the* structures as those below. (A semicolon would not be appropriate.)

The more it rained **,** the worse they suffered.

—JOSEPH HELLER

The greater the fool the better the dancer.

—THEODORE EDWARD HOOK

Note 2: The comma is used to separate a statement from a tag question:

He votes, doesn't he? [Affirmative statement, negative question]

You can't change it, can you? [Negative statement, affirmative question]

■ **Exercise 1** Link each pair of sentences below in two ways, first with a semicolon and then with [and, but, for, or, nor, so, or yet.

EXAMPLE

I could have walked up the steep trail. I preferred to rent a horse.

a. *I could have walked up the steep trail; I preferred to rent a horse.*

b. *I could have walked up the steep trail, **but** I preferred to rent a horse.*

1. Dexter goes hunting. He carries his Leica instead of his Winchester.
2. The stakes were high in the political game. She played to win.
3. The belt was too small for him. She had to exchange it.
4. At the drive-in, they watched the musical comedy on one screen. We enjoyed the horror movie on the other.

■ **Exercise 2** Use a subordinating conjunction (see the list on page 19) to combine each of the four pairs of sentences in Exercise 1. For the use of the comma, refer to **12b**.

EXAMPLE

Although *I could have walked up the steep trail, I preferred to rent a horse.*

■ **Exercise 3** Proofread the following sentences (selected and adapted from *National Geographic*). In the left margin by the number, place a checkmark to indicate a comma splice or a fused sentence. Do not mark correctly punctuated sentences.

1. The second-home craze has hit hard, everyone wants a piece of the wilderness.
2. Man can easily unmake a wilderness he cannot make one.
3. Parting is an unsweet sorrow, for it connotes a lack of loyalty.

4. Attempts to extinguish such fires have often failed some have been burning for decades.
5. Some of them had never seen an automobile, the war had bred familiarity with aircraft.
6. When the mining machines rumbled away, the ruined mountain was left barren and ugly.
7. The winds lashed our tents all night, by morning we had to dig ourselves out from under a snowdrift.

■ **Exercise 4** Use various methods of revision (see page 33) as you correct the comma splices or fused sentences in Exercise 3.

3b

Be sure to use a semicolon before a conjunctive adverb or transitional phrase placed between main clauses. See also **14a**.

> COMMA SPLICE TV weather maps have various symbols, for example, a big apostrophe means drizzle.
>
> REVISED TV weather maps have various symbols; for example, a big apostrophe means drizzle. [**MAIN CLAUSE;** *for example,* **MAIN CLAUSE.**]
>
> FUSED SENTENCE The tiny storms cannot be identified as hurricanes therefore they are called neutercanes.
>
> REVISED The tiny storms cannot be identified as hurricanes; therefore they are called neutercanes.
> [**MAIN CLAUSE;** *therefore* **MAIN CLAUSE.**]

Note: Use a comma *after* a conjunctive adverb or transitional phrase placed between main clauses only when you consider the connective parenthetical: see **12d(3)** .

Below is a list of frequently used conjunctive adverbs and transitional phrases; they function as both an adverb and a conjunctive:

> CONJUNCTIVE ADVERBS *also, anyway, besides, consequently, finally, furthermore, hence, however, incidentally, indeed, instead, likewise, meanwhile, moreover, nevertheless, next, otherwise, still, then, therefore, thus*

TRANSITIONAL PHRASES *after all, as a result, at any rate, at the same time, by the way, for example, in addition, in fact, in other words, in the second place, on the contrary, on the other hand*

Expressions such as *that is* and *what is more* also function as adverbials connecting main clauses:

> The new members have paid their dues **;** *what is more,* they are all eager to work hard for our organization.

Conjunctive adverbs and transitional phrases are not grammatically equivalent to coordinating conjunctions. A coordinating conjunction has a fixed position between the main clauses it links, but many conjunctive adverbs and transitional phrases may either begin the second main clause or take another position in it:

> She doubted the value of daily meditation, *but* she decided to try it. [The coordinating conjunction has a fixed position.]
>
> She doubted the value of daily meditation; *however,* she decided to try it. [The conjunctive adverb begins the second main clause.]
>
> She doubted the value of daily meditation; she decided, *however,* to try it. [The conjunctive adverb appears later in the clause.]

■ **Exercise 5** Link each pair of sentences below, following the pattern of the example.

EXAMPLE
At first the slogan shocked. After a year or two, however, it became a platitude.
*At first the slogan shocked**;** however**,** after a year or two it became a platitude.*

1. The art company sent a sample collection of famous Canadian paintings. The work of A. Y. Jackson, however, was inexplicably omitted.
2. Her loud arguments sounded convincing. The majority, therefore, voted for her motion.

3. I don't mind lending him money. He is, after all, my favourite cousin.
4. India is not poor. It has, as a matter of fact, a huge amount
   of coal and iron reserves.

Caution: Do not let a divided quotation trick you into making a comma splice.

COMMA SPLICE	"Marry her," Martin said, "after all, she's very rich."
REVISED	"Marry her," Martin said. "After all, she's very rich."
COMMA SPLICE	"Who won?" Elizabeth asked, "what was the score?"
REVISED	"Who won?" Elizabeth asked. "What was the score?"

■ **Exercise 6** Divide the following quotations without creating a
comma splice, as shown in the example below.

EXAMPLE

W. L. Mackenzie King once said, "Some countries have too
  much history. Canada has too much geography."
*"Some countries have too much history," W. L. Mackenzie
  King once said. "Canada has too much geography."*

1. "I never saw her again. In fact, no one ever saw her again,"
   wrote Kenneth Bernard.
2. W. C. Fields once said, "I am free of all prejudice. I hate
   everyone equally."
3. "To generalize is to omit. It is in the details of things where
   the truth lies," Dr. Peter Beter commented.
4. Irving Layton has observed, "You can sing about life or you
   can try to understand it. You can't do both."
5. The student asked ironically, "What use are credit cards?
   Who needs an accurate list of debts?"

■ **Exercise 7** Correct the comma splices and fused sentences in
the following paragraph. Do not revise a correctly punctuated
sentence.

[1] "Nothing is impossible," Mr. Connell always tells us, "you can do anything if you want to badly enough." [2] We just look at him, an old man in a dingy store, and smile indulgently, at least we used to until we heard more about his life. [3] "I left the old country some seventy years ago," he told us, "I was only thirteen at the time." [4] He met his first wife, Nellie, while he was working as a longshoreman in Halifax, he was only eighteen then. [5] They were happily married for about three years however she died of typhus. [6] A couple of months later he pulled up roots, left the Maritimes, and headed out West. [7] "I'd heard there was work for men not afraid to work," he says, "I figured sweating in B.C. was better than crying in Nova Scotia." [8] He was on the road for twenty years, "I never made a fortune, but I never ate anything I didn't earn," he told us. [9] He met his second wife, Sarah, in Alberta, he farmed there for twenty years. [10] She died in the sixties, he got itchy feet again and headed back towards the Maritimes. [11] But he never got farther than Toronto. [12] He settled in Toronto, built up his hardware business from nothing, and lives very simply. [13] "I do it for a reason," he says, "you never know when I'll decide to move on again." [14] We don't smile when he says it, there's a lifetime of experience behind his words. [15] Maybe anything is possible if you want it badly enough.

Adjectives and Adverbs

4

Distinguish between adjectives and adverbs and use the appropriate forms.

Adjectives and adverbs function as modifiers; that is, they qualify or restrict the meaning of other words. Adjectives modify nouns and pronouns. Adverbs modify mainly verbs (or verbals), adjectives, and other adverbs.

ADJECTIVES	ADVERBS
the *sudden* change	changed *suddenly*
a *probable* cause	*probably* caused
an *unusual, large* one	an *unusually* large one

The -*ly* ending can be an adjective-forming suffix as well as an adverb-forming one.

NOUNS TO ADJECTIVES	earth—earthly, ghost—ghostly
ADJECTIVES TO ADVERBS	rapid—rapidly, lucky—luckily

A number of words ending in -*ly* (such as *deadly, cowardly*), as well as many not ending in -*ly* (such as *far, fast, little, well*), may function either as adjectives or as adverbs. Some adverbs have two forms (such as *loud, loudly; quick, quickly; slow, slowly*).

4a

Use adverbs to modify verbs, adjectives, and other adverbs.

His clothes fit him *perfectly*. [The adverb modifies the verb *fit*.]

We have a *reasonably* secure future. [The adverb modifies the adjective *secure*.]

Jean eats *exceptionally* fast. [The adverb *exceptionally* modifies the adverb *fast*.]

Most dictionaries still label (1) *sure* for *surely*, (2) *real* for *really*, (3) *bad* for *badly*, and (4) *good* for the adverb *well* as informal usage.

INFORMAL   I played *bad*, but I *sure* tried hard.

GENERAL   I played *badly*, but I *surely* tried hard. [Appropriate in both formal and informal usage]

■ **Exercise 1**   In the items below, convert adjectives into adverbs, following the pattern of the examples.

EXAMPLE
abrupt reply   *replied abruptly* [OR *abruptly replied*]

1. vague answer
2. safe travel
3. fierce battle
4. quick refusal
5. hearty welcome
6. blind conformity

EXAMPLE
real happiness   *really happy*

7. clear possibility
8. unusual anger
9. sudden popularity
10. strange sadness

4b

Use the appropriate modifiers after such verbs as *feel, look, smell, sound,* **and** *taste.*

Either an adjective or an adverb may be used after such verbs as *feel, look, smell, sound,* and *taste.*

ADJECTIVES	ADVERBS
He felt *nervous*.	He felt *nervously* for the key.
Jo looked *angry* to me.	Jo looked *angrily* at me.
The beans tasted *salty*.	He tasted the beans *reluctantly*.

Each adverb above refers to the action of the verb. Each adjective above modifies the subject of the sentence and functions as a subject complement (predicate adjective). The sentences with adjectives follow this pattern:

SUBJECT—LINKING VERB—SUBJECT COMPLEMENT.

Verbs like *feel, look, smell, sound,* and *taste* are called *linking verbs* when they connect the subject with the subject complement.

Note: Similarly, either an adverb or an adjective may follow a direct object; the choice depends on meaning, on the word modified:

He considered Jane *happily*. [The adverb *happily* modifies the verb *considered*.]

He considered Jane *happy*. [The adjective *happy* modifies the noun *Jane*, the direct object.]

In the example above, *happy* functions as the object complement. The sentence follows this pattern:

SUBJECT—VERB—OBJECT—OBJECT COMPLEMENT.

■ **Exercise 2**   Using adjectives as subject complements, write five sentences that illustrate the pattern
   SUBJECT—LINKING VERB—SUBJECT COMPLEMENT.

4c

Use the appropriate forms for the comparative and the superlative.

In general, the shorter adjectives (and a few adverbs) form the comparative degree by adding *-er* and the superlative by adding *-est*. The longer adjectives and most adverbs form the comparative by the use of *more* (*less*) and the superlative by the use of *most* (*least*). A few modifiers have an irregular comparison.

Positive	Comparative	Superlative
warm	warmer	warmest
warmly	more warmly	most warmly
helpful	less helpful	least helpful
good, well	better	best
bad, badly	worse	worst

Many writers prefer to use the comparative degree for two persons or things and the superlative for three or more:

COMPARATIVE   Was Monday or Tuesday *warmer?*
James was the *taller* of the two.

SUPERLATIVE   Today is the *warmest* day of the year.
William was the *tallest* of the three.

Be sure to make your comparisons complete: see **22c**.

4d

Avoid awkward or ambiguous use of a noun form as an adjective.

Many noun forms are used effectively to modify other nouns (as in *boat* race, *show* business, *opera* tickets, and so on), especially when appropriate adjectives are not available. But such forms should be avoided when they are either awkward or confusing.

AWKWARD	He is a medicine student.
BETTER	He is a medical student.
CONFUSING	There were four candidates in the Muskoka Parliament by-election.
BETTER	There were four candidates in the Parliamentary by-election in Muskoka.

■ **Exercise 3** Choose the adjective or adverb within the parentheses in each sentence to reflect formal usage.

1. The (older, oldest) of the three brothers has the (brighter, brightest) red hair.
2. She wants someone who will do the work (prompt and efficient, promptly and efficiently) and still be courteous (consistent, consistently).
3. I feel (glum, glumly) when I read his (nightmare, nightmarish) tales.
4. The magazine has been published (continuous, continuously) since 1951, and it has the (most funny, funniest) cartoons that you can (possible, possibly) imagine.
5. Canadian skaters often perform (good, well) enough to win medals in international competition.

Case

5

Choose the case form that shows the function of pronouns or nouns in sentences.

Case refers to the form of a word that indicates its use in a sentence as the subject of a verb, the object of a preposition, and so on. The English language has just three cases: subjective, possessive, objective. Most nouns, many indefinite pronouns, and *it* and *you* have a distinctive case form only for the possessive: *Rebecca's* coat, *someone's* dog, *its* colour, *your* hands. See **15a** But six common pronouns—*I, we, he, she, they, who*—have distinctive forms in all three cases:

SUBJECTIVE   *I, we, he, she, they, who*

> *He* and *I* travelled together in France.   [Subjects]
> The only ones in the group against the change are Lola and *she*.   [Subject complement]

POSSESSIVE   *my, our, his, her, their, whose*
                  mine, ours, hers, theirs

> *Theirs* broke down.   [Possessors—noun position]
> *Whose* car did you drive?   [Before a noun]
> *His* telling the story was a good idea.   [Before a gerund]

OBJECTIVE   *me, us, him, her, them, whom*

Fran likes Pat and *him.* [Object of a verb]
For you and *me* this is no problem. [Object of a preposition]
Leaving *them* at home, Eleanor drove to the airport to meet *us* girls. [Objects of verbals]
I wanted Bill and *her* to leave. [Subject of an infinitive]

5a

Take special care with pronouns in compound constructions.

Observe that the form of each pronoun below does not change when it is made a part of a compound construction; the function of the pronoun remains the same:

Her brother played golf. She did too.
Her brother and she played golf.

Clara may ask you about it. Or she may ask me.
Clara may ask *you or me* about it.

The form of the pronoun used as an appositive depends on the function of the noun (or pronoun) that the appositive explains or identifies:

Two clerks, Bruce and *I,* were promoted. [The appositive *Bruce and I* identifies *clerks,* the subject of the verb.]
Sandra Miles promoted two clerks, Bruce and *me.* [The appositive *Bruce and me* identifies *clerks,* the object of the verb.]

Be sure to use objective pronouns as objects of prepositions: *between you and me, to Kate and him.* Remember, too, that *me* is the correct pronoun form in the expression "Let's you and *me.* . . ."

Note: In your formal writing, do not substitute *myself* for *I* or *me:* see **19i,** page 200. Use expressions like *we freshmen* and *us freshmen* with care. The addition of a plural noun after the pronoun does not affect the form of the pronoun in such sentences as these:

> *We* registered late.   *We* freshmen registered late.
> Walter helped *us*.   Walter helped *us* girls.

■ **Exercise 1** Choose the correct pronoun within the parentheses in each sentence below.

1. Her cousin and (she, her) shared expenses.
2. Between Charlotte and (I, me) there is a friendly rivalry.
3. Mr. Rodriguez will hire a new foreman, either Williams or (he, him).
4. Study in Paris did not appeal to Tim or (I, me).
5. (We, Us) students get reduced rates at the theatre.
6. All of (we, us) guides were confused.
7. The birdwatchers, Vern and (he, him), spotted the Canada geese.
8. Let's you and (I, me) donate to the blood bank.
9. Leaving James and (I, me) at home, they went to the airport to meet the actor and (she, her).

5b

Determine the case of each pronoun by its use in its own clause.

(1) *Who* or *whoever* as the subject of a clause

The subject of a verb in a subordinate clause takes the subjective case, even when the whole clause is used as an object:

> I remember who won the Stanley Cup in 1968. [In its own clause, *who* is the subject of the verb *won*. The complete clause *who won the Stanley Cup in 1968* is the object of the verb *remember*.]
> He has respect for *whoever* is in power. [*Whoever* is the subject of *is*. The complete clause *whoever is in power* is the object of the preposition *for*.]

(2) *Who* or *whom* before *I think, he says,* and so on

Such expressions as *I think, he says, she believes,* and *we know* may follow either *who* or *whom.* The choice depends on the use of *who* or *whom* in its own clause:

> Gene is a man *whom* we know well. [*Whom* is the direct object of *know.*]
> Gene is a man *who* we know is honest. [*Who* is the subject of the second *is.* Compare "We know that Gene is a man *who* is honest."]

(3) Pronoun after *than* or *as*

In sentences such as the following, which have implied (rather than stated) elements, the choice of the pronoun form is important to meaning:

> She admires Kurt more than *I.* [Meaning "more than I do."]
> She admires Kurt as much as *me.* [Meaning "as much as she admires me."]

Formal usage still requires the use of the subjective case of pronouns in sentences such as the following:

> Mr. Ames is older than *I.* [Compare "older than I am."]
> Aristotle is not so often quoted as *they.* [Compare "as they are."]

■ **Exercise 2** In sentences 1, 2, and 3 below, insert *I think* after each *who;* then read each sentence aloud. Notice that *who,* not *whom,* is still the correct case form. In sentences 4 and 5, complete each comparison by using first *they* and then *them.* Prepare to explain the differences in meaning.

1. George Eliot, who was a woman, wrote *Adam Bede.*
2. It was Elizabeth Holland who served as the eighth president of the university.
3. Maugham, who was an Englishman, died in 1965.

4. The professor likes you as much as _____ .
5. The director praised her more than _____ .

5c

In formal writing use *whom* for all objects.

> The artist *whom* she loved has gone away. [*Whom* is the direct object of *loved.*]
>
> For *whom* did the board of directors vote? [*Whom* is the object of the preposition *for.*]

 Speakers tend to use *who* rather than *whom*, except immediately after a preposition:

> INFORMAL Who did they vote for?

Both speakers and writers may avoid *whom* by omitting it in sentences such as the following:

> The artist she loved has gone away.

■ **Exercise 3** Using the case form in parentheses, convert each pair of sentences below into a single sentence.

> EXAMPLES
>
> I understand the daredevil. He motorcycled across the Grand Canyon. (*who*)
>
> *I understand the daredevil who motorcycled across the Grand Canyon.*
>
> Evelyn consulted an astrologer. She had met him in San Francisco. (*whom*)
>
> *Evelyn consulted an astrologer whom she had met in San Francisco.*

1. Hercule Poirot is a famous detective. Agatha Christie finally kills him in *Curtain.* (*whom*)
2. Some parents make an introvert out of an only child. They think they are protecting their offspring. (*who*)

3. Does anyone remember the name of the Frenchman? He built a helicopter in 1784. (*who*)
4. One of the officials called for a severe penalty. The players had quarreled with the officials earlier. (*whom*)

5d

Review

As a rule, use the possessive case immediately before a gerund.

I resented *his* criticizing our every move. [Compare "I resented his criticism, not him."]

Harry's refusing the offer was a surprise. [Compare "Harry's refusal was a surprise."]

The *-ing* form of a verb can be used as a noun (gerund) or as an adjective (participle). The possessive case is not used before participles:

Caroline's radioing the Coast Guard solved our problem. [*Radioing* is a gerund. Compare "*Her action* solved our problem."]

The *man* eating a hamburger solved our problem. [*Eating* is a participle. Compare "*He* solved our problem."]

Note: Do not use an awkward possessive before a gerund.

AWKWARD   The board approved of something's being sent to the poor overseas.

BETTER   The board approved of sending something to the poor overseas.

5e

Use the objective case for the subject or the object of an infinitive.

They expected Nancy and *me* to do the scriptwriting. [Subject of the infinitive *to do*]

I did not want to challenge Victor or *him*. [Object of the infinitive *to challenge*]

5f

Use the subjective case for the complement of the verb *be*.

The man who will get all the credit is no doubt Blevins or *he*.

The main clause in the sentence above follows this pattern:

SUBJECT—LINKING VERB *BE*—SUBJECT COMPLEMENT.

---

man	is	Blevins (or) he

Speakers often use *me, him, her, us,* and *them* as subject complements. But many writers avoid the structure:

Blevins or he is no doubt the man who will get all the credit.

■ **Exercise 4** Find and revise in the sentences below all case forms that would be inappropriate in formal writing. Put a checkmark after each sentence that needs no revision.

1. I soon became acquainted with Ruth and her, whom I thought were agitators.
2. It was Doris and she who I blamed for me not making that sale.
3. Jack's racing the motor did not hurry Tom or me.
4. Between you and I, I prefer woodblock prints.
5. Who do you suppose will ever change Earth to Eden?
6. Since Joan eats less than I, I weigh more than she.
7. Let's you and I plan the curriculum of an ideal university.
8. The attorney who I interviewed yesterday is going to make public the records of three men who she believes are guilty of tax evasion.
9. We players always cooperate with our assistant coach, who we respect and who respects us.
10. The librarian wanted us—Kirt Jacobs and I—to choose Schlesinger's *The Bitter Heritage*.

Agreement

6

Make a verb agree in number with its subject; make a pronoun agree in number with its antecedent.

In sentences such as those below, the forms of the verb and the subject (a noun or a noun substitute) agree grammatically:

SINGULAR The *list* of items *was* long.
PLURAL The *lists* of items *were* long.

Singular subjects take singular verbs (*list was*), and plural subjects take plural verbs (*lists were*).

As a rule, a pronoun and its antecedent (the word the pronoun refers to) also agree grammatically:

SINGULAR Even an *animal* has *its* own territory.
PLURAL Even *animals* have *their* own territory.

Singular antecedents are referred to by singular pronouns (*animal* ← *its*), and plural antecedents are the referents of plural pronouns (*animals* ← *their*).

The -*s* (or -*es*) suffix

Remember that -*s* (or -*es*) is (1) a plural-forming suffix for most nouns and (2) a singular-forming suffix for verbs—those present-tense verbs taking third-person singular subjects.

SINGULAR	A bell *rings*.	The rope *stretches*.	It *does*.
PLURAL	The *bells* ring.	*Ropes* stretch.	They *do*.

Probably the best way for you to eliminate errors in subject–verb agreement in your writing is to proofread carefully. But if you find it difficult to distinguish verbs and relate them to their subjects, review **1a** and **1b**

6a
Make a verb agree in number with its subject.

(1) Do not be misled by nouns or pronouns intervening between the subject and the verb; do not carelessly drop the -s suffix from a subject or verb ending in -sk or -st.

The *repetition* of these sounds *stirs* the emotions.
Watermelons sold by the roadside usually *taste* good.

Her *interests* are wide and varied.
A good detective *asks* pertinent questions.

Most writers feel that the grammatical number of the subject is not changed by the addition of expressions beginning with such words as *with, along with, including, in addition to,* and *as well as*:

Unemployment as well as taxes *influences* votes.
Taxes, along with unemployment, *influence* votes.

(2) Subjects joined by *and* are usually plural.

Her typewriter and my radio *were stolen*.
The doctor and the minister *have* much in common.

Exceptions: Occasionally, such a compound subject takes a singular verb because the subject denotes one person or a single unit.

My best friend and adviser *has changed* his mind again.

The flesh and blood of the world *was* dead. —VIRGINIA WOOLF

Every or *each* preceding singular subjects joined by *and* calls for a singular verb:

> Every member and officer in the club *was* upset.
> Each cat and each dog *has* its own toy.

Placed after a plural subject, *each* does not affect the verb form. Some writers use a singular verb when *each* follows a compound subject:

> The cat and the dog each *have* their own toys.
> [Or, sometimes, "The cat and the dog each *has* its own toy."]

(3) Singular subjects joined by *or, either . . . or,* or *neither . . . nor* usually take a singular verb.

> Paula or her secretary *answers* the phone on Saturday.
> Either the mayor or the premier *is* the keynote speaker.
> Neither criticism nor praise *affects* them. [Informal "Neither criticism nor praise affect them."]

If one subject is singular and one is plural, the verb usually agrees with the nearer subject:

> Neither the quality nor the prices *have* changed.
> Neither the prices nor the quality *has* changed.

(When revising a subject–verb agreement error involving this structure, you may wish to substitute *and . . . not* for *neither . . . nor:* "The prices and the quality have not changed.")

(4) Do not let inverted word order (VERB + SUBJECT) or the structure *there*—VERB—SUBJECT cause you to make a mistake in agreement.

> In the upper branches *was* a *nest* made of twigs and mud.
> There *are* no poisonous *snakes* in the area.
> There *remains* an unanswered *question*, as well as an unasked one.

Sometimes *there is* precedes a singular part of a plural compound subject:

> There are the Clarks in *The Master of the Mill* . . . . *There is* John Elliott in *Our Daily Bread* and Abe Spaulding in *The Fruits of the Earth*.   —MARGARET ATWOOD

(5) A relative pronoun (*who, which, that*) used as a subject takes a singular or plural verb to accord with its antecedent.

It is the *pharmacist who* often *suggests* a new brand.
Tonsillitis is among those *diseases that are* curable.
This is the only *one* of the local papers *that prints* a daily horoscope. [*That* refers to *one* because only one paper prints a daily horoscope; the other papers do not.]

(6) When used as subjects, such words as *each, either, neither, one, everybody,* and *anyone* regularly take singular verbs.

Neither likes the friends of the other.
Each of them *does have* political ambitions.
Everybody in the office *has* tickets.

Subjects such as *all, any, half, most, none,* and *some* may take a singular or a plural verb; the context generally determines the choice of the verb form.

Evelyn collects stamps; *some are* worth a lot.   [Compare "Some of them are worth a lot."]
The honey was marked down because *some was* sugary. [Compare "Some of it was sugary."]

(7) Collective nouns, as well as noun phrases denoting a fixed quantity, frequently take a singular verb because the group or quantity is usually regarded as a unit.

The majority *has made* its decision.
A committee *was investigating* the charges.

The number of board members *is* very small.
Ten dollars *seems* too much for dues.
A thousand bushels *is* a good yield.

Sometimes, a plural verb is used because the group or quantity is regarded as individuals or parts rather than as a unit:

A number of the board members *were* absent.
A thousand bushels of apples *were crated.*

(8) A linking verb usually agrees with its subject, not with its complement.

Excessive absences *were* the reason for his failure.
The reason for his failure *was* excessive absences.

(By recasting such sentences, you may avoid this problem in subject–verb agreement: "He failed because of excessive absences.")

(9) Nouns plural in form but singular in meaning usually take singular verbs. In all doubtful cases, consult a good dictionary.

News *is traveling* faster than ever before.
Physics *has fascinated* my roommate for months.

Nouns which are regularly treated as singular include *economics, electronics, measles, mumps, news, physics,* and *tactics.*

Some nouns ending in *-ics* (such as *athletics, politics,* and *statistics*) are considered singular when referring to an organized body of knowledge and plural when referring to activities, qualities, or individual facts:

Athletics *is required* of every student. [Compare "Participation in games *is required* of every student."]

Athletics *provide* good recreation. [Compare "Various games *provide* good recreation."]

56

(10) The title of a single work or a word spoken of as a word, even when plural in form, takes a singular verb.

Bowser's "The Eggomaniacs" *describes* an egg fad.
The *New York Times* still *has* a wide circulation.
They, a personal pronoun, *has* an interesting history.

■ **Exercise 1** The following sentences are all correct. Read them aloud, stressing the italicized words. If any sentence sounds wrong to you, read it aloud two or three more times so that you will gain practice in saying and hearing the correct forms.

1. The *timing* of these strikes *was* poorly planned.
2. There *are* a few *cookies* and *pickles* left.
3. A *wrench* and a *hubcap were* missing.
4. *Every one* of my cousins, including Larry, *has* brown eyes.
5. Sandy was the *only one* of the singers *who was* flat.

■ **Exercise 2** Choose the correct form of the verb within parentheses in each sentence below. Make sure that the verb agrees with its subject according to the rules of formal English.

1. Neither Anita nor Juan (feels, feel) that the evidence is circumstantial.
2. Tastes in reading, of course, (differs, differ).
3. Every one of the figures (was, were) checked at least twice.
4. A fountain and a hanging basket (adorns, adorn) the entrance.
5. Neither of them ever (asks, ask) for a second helping.
6. There (comes, come) to my mind now the names of the two or three people who were most influential in my life.
7. The booby prize (was, were) green apples.
8. A rustic lodge, as well as a game refuge and fishing waters, (is, are) close by.
9. Hidden cameras, which (invades, invade) the privacy of the unwary few, (provides, provide) entertainment for thousands.
10. The study of words (is, are) facilitated by breaking them down into prefixes, suffixes, and roots.

6b

Make a pronoun agree in number with its antecedent.

A singular antecedent (one that would take a singular verb) is referred to by a singular pronoun; a plural antecedent (one that would take a plural verb) is referred to by a plural pronoun:

SINGULAR An *actor* during early rehearsals often *forgets his* lines.

PLURAL *Actors* during early rehearsals often *forget their* lines.

(1) As a rule, use a singular pronoun to refer to such antecedents as *each, either, neither, one, anyone, everybody, a person*, and so on.

Each of these companies had *its* books audited.   [NOT *their*]
One has to live with *oneself*.   [NOT *themselves*]

Usage varies regarding the choice of pronoun referring to such antecedents as *everyone* or *a person* when the meaning includes both sexes or either sex:

A person needs to see *his* dentist twice a year.   [OR *his or her*]

Every man and woman shows his/her essence by reaction to the soil.   —ROBERT S. De ROPP

So everybody gets married—unmarried—and married, but they're all married to somebody most of the time.
—MARGARET MEAD

In fact, the fear of growing old is so great that every aged person is an insult and a threat to the society. They remind us of our own death. . . .   —SHARON CURTIN

(2) Two or more antecedents joined by *and* are referred to by a plural pronoun; two or more singular antecedents joined by *or* or *nor* are referred to by a singular pronoun.

Leon and Roger lost *their* self-confidence.
Did *Leon or Roger* lose *his* self-confidence?

<u>If one of two antecedents joined by *or* or *nor* is singular
and one is plural, the pronoun usually agrees with the nearer
antecedent:</u>

Neither the *package nor* the *letters* had reached *their* destina-
tion. [*Their* is closer to the plural antecedent *letters*.]
Stray kittens or even an abandoned grown *cat* has *its* problems finding enough food to survive long. [*Its* is closer to
the singular antecedent *cat*.]

**(3) Collective nouns are referred to by singular or plu-
ral pronouns, depending on whether the collective
noun is used in a singular or plural sense.** See also
6a(7).

Special care should be taken to avoid inconsistency by treating a collective noun as *both* singular and plural within the
same sentence.

INCONSISTENT The choir is writing their own music.
[Singular verb, plural pronoun]

CONSISTENT The choir *is* writing *its* own music.
[Both singular]

CONSISTENT The group of students *do* not agree on methods, but *they* unite on basic aims.
[Both plural]

■ **Exercise 3** Choose the correct pronoun or verb form within
parentheses in each sentence below; follow the rules of formal
English usage.

1. A number of people, such as Kate Swift and Warren Farrell,
(has, have) offered (his, her and his, their) suggestions for a
''human'' singular pronoun, like *te* for *he or she* to refer to
the antecedent *a person*.
2. If any one of the sisters (needs, need) a ride to church, (she,
they) can call Trudy.

3. Neither the pilot nor the flight attendants mentioned the incident when (he, they) talked to reporters.
4. The Edmonton team (was, were) opportunistic; (it, they) took advantage of every break.
5. If the board of directors (controls, control) the company, (it, they) may vote (itself, themselves) bonuses.

■ **Exercise 4** All the following sentences are correct. Change them as directed in parentheses, revising other parts of the sentence to secure agreement of subject and verb, pronoun and antecedent.

1. Everyone in our Latin class thoroughly enjoys the full hour. (Change *Everyone* to *All students*.)
2. Every activity in that class seems not only instructive but amusing. (Change *Every activity* to *All activities*.)
3. Since the students eat their lunch just before the class, the Latin professor keeps coffee on hand to revive any sluggish thinkers. (Change *the students* to *nearly every student*.)
4. Yesterday one of the students was called on to translate some Latin sentences. (Change *one* to *two*.)
5. We were busily following the oral translation in our textbooks. (Change *We* to *Everyone else*.)
6. One or perhaps two in the class were not paying attention when the student, Jim Melton, said, ''Who do you see?'' (Use *Two or perhaps only one* instead of *One or perhaps two*.)
7. The Latin professor ordered, ''Look at those inflections that indicate case! *Whom! Whom* do you see! Not *who!*'' (Change *those inflections* to *the inflection*.)
8. Nobody in the room was inattentive as Jim translated the sentence again: ''*Whom* do *youm* see?'' (Change *Nobody* to *Few*.)
9. All students in the class were laughing as the professor exclaimed, ''*Youm!* Whoever heard of *youm!*'' (Change *All students* to *Everyone*.)
10. Jim, a student who sometimes gives a reply that provokes the professor, said, ''Well now *youm* have.'' (Change *a reply* to *replies*.)

Verb Forms

7

Use the appropriate form of the verb. (See also **6a**.)

Tense

Tense is the form of the verb that indicates time. Single-word verbs indicate the simple present tense or the simple past.

PRESENT   allow (allows), see (sees)
PAST   allowed, saw

Note: The *-s* form of the verb (*allows, sees*) is used only with third-person singular subjects. Auxiliaries like *be, do,* and *have* indicate tense in verb phrases like *was blowing, did try, had become.*

When we consider certain verb phrases along with the form changes of single-word verbs, there are six tenses.

PRESENT	allow (allows), see (sees)
PAST	allowed, saw
FUTURE	will allow, shall allow; will see, shall see
PRESENT PERFECT	have (has) allowed, have (has) seen
PAST PERFECT	had allowed, had seen
FUTURE PERFECT	will have allowed, shall have allowed; will have seen, shall have seen

There are three main divisions of time—present, past, and future. Various verb forms and verb phrases refer to divisions of actual time.

PRESENT

At last I *see* what you meant by that remark.
Right now he is *seeing* double. He *does see* double now.

PAST

We *saw* the accident this morning.   [At a definite time]
They *have* already *seen* much of the West.
   [At some time before now]
Nancy *had seen* the play before she received our invitation.
   [Before a given time in the past]
We *were to see* the dean on Monday.
We *were going to see* great changes.
I *was about to see* Paris for the first time.
I *used to see* him daily.   I *did see* him daily.
In the sixteenth century the Spaniards *see* their Armada
   defeated.   [Historical present]
Shakespeare writes about what he *sees* in the human heart.
   [Literary present]

FUTURE

I *will* (OR *shall*) *see* him.
Tomorrow I *see* my lawyer.
Pauline *is to see* Switzerland next summer.
He *is going to* (OR *will*) *see* justice done.
They *are about to see* their dreams in action.
   [Immediate future]
Mr. Yates *will have seen* the report by then.
   [Before a given time]

Note: A present-tense verb form may be used to express a
universal truth or a habitual action.

   People *see* that death *is* inevitable.   [Universal truth]
   My father *sees* his doctor every Tuesday.   [Habitual action]

The auxiliary *do*—which has only the present and past
forms, *do* (*does*) and *did*—is used for negations, questions,
and emphatic statements or restatements.

   He *pays* his bills on time.   [Positive statement]
   He *does* not *pay* his bills on time.   [Negation]

Does he *pay* his bills on time? [Question]
He *does pay* his bills on time. [Emphatic restatement]

Voice

Transitive verbs have voice. There are two voices, active and passive. A transitive active verb has a direct object.

ACTIVE   Burglars often *steal* small items.
[Subject—verb—object.]

The object of a transitive active verb can usually be converted to the subject of a transitive passive verb. When an active verb is made passive, a form of *be* is used with a past participle.

PASSIVE   Small items *are* often *stolen* by burglars. [The phrase "by burglars" could be omitted.]

Note: Intransitive verbs do not take objects.

Carol *became* an engineer. [Subject—linking verb— subject complement.]
The rookies *will* not *be going.*

Compare the active and passive verb forms below.

	Active	*Passive*
PRESENT	see (sees)	am (is, are) seen
PAST	saw	was (were) seen
FUTURE	will see	will be seen
PRESENT PERFECT	have (has) seen	have (has) been seen
PAST PERFECT	had seen	had been seen
FUTURE PERFECT	will have seen	will have been seen

Progressive Forms

The English language also has progressive verb forms, which are verb phrases consisting of a form of *be* plus an *-ing* verb (the present participle). These phrases denote an action in progress.

PRESENT	am (is, are) seeing
PAST	was (were) seeing
FUTURE	will be seeing
PRESENT PERFECT	have (has) been seeing
PAST PERFECT	had been seeing
FUTURE PERFECT	will have been seeing

Passive progressive forms include *am (is, are) being seen, was (were) being seen,* and so on.

Note: Infinitives, participles, and gerunds (verbals) also have progressive forms, as well as tense—but not all six tenses.

Infinitives

PRESENT	to see, to be seen, to be seeing
PRESENT PERFECT	to have seen, to have been seen, to have been seeing

Participles

PRESENT	seeing, being seen
PAST	seen
PRESENT PERFECT	having seen, having been seen

Gerunds

PRESENT	seeing, being seen
PRESENT PERFECT	having seen, having been seen

7a

Avoid misusing the principal parts of verbs and confusing similar verbs.

(1) Avoid misusing the principal parts of verbs.

The principal parts of a verb include the *present* form (which is also the stem of the infinitive), the *past* form, and the *past participle*.

Present stem (*infinitive*)	Past tense	Past participle
ask	asked	asked
begin	began	begun

The *present* form may function as a single-word verb or may be preceded by words such as *will, do, may, could, have to, ought to,* or *used to.*

> I *ask,* he *does ask,* we *begin,* it *used to begin*

The *past* form functions as a single-word verb.

> He *asked* questions.
> The show *began* at eight.

The *past participle,* when used as a part of a verb phrase, always has at least one auxiliary.

> they *have asked,* she *was asked,* he *has been asked*
> it *has begun,* the work *will be begun,* we *have begun*

Do not omit a needed *-d* or *-ed* because of the pronunciation. For example, although it is easy to remember a clearly pronounced *-d* or *-ed* (*faded, repeated*), it is sometimes difficult to remember to add a needed *-d* or *-ed* in such expressions as *hoped to* or *opened the.* As you read the following sentences aloud, observe the use of the *-d* or *-ed* ending:

> Yesterday he ask*ed* me.   Then he talk*ed* to her.
> Perhaps we had price*d* our vegetables too high.
> It had happen*ed* before.   She was not experience*d.*
> He use*d* to smoke.   I am not suppose*d* to do it.

When in doubt about the forms of a verb, consult a good dictionary. (If forms are not listed after an entry, the verb is generally a regular one, taking the *-d* or *-ed* ending.)

Note: Sometimes a verb has two forms for the past participle, both standard but one of which is used in a special way. Take, for example, *struck* and *stricken,* past participle forms of the verb *strike:*

> STANDARD   They *had struck* all their matches.
> ABSURD   They *had stricken* all their matches.
> STANDARD   Keith was *stricken* by paralysis.

The following list gives the principal parts of a number of verbs that are sometimes misused. Give special attention to any forms unfamiliar to you.

Principal Parts of Verbs

Present stem (infinitive)	Past tense	Past participle
become	became	become
begin	began	begun
blow	blew	blown
break	broke	broken
bring	brought	brought
choose	chose	chosen
cling	clung	clung
come	came	come
dive	dived OR dove	dived
do	did	done
draw	drew	drawn
drink	drank	drunk (*Informal:* drank)
drive	drove	driven
eat	ate	eaten
fall	fell	fallen
fly	flew	flown
forgive	forgave	forgiven
freeze	froze	frozen
give	gave	given
go	went	gone
grow	grew	grown
know	knew	known
ride	rode	ridden
ring	rang	rung
rise	rose	risen
shake	shook	shaken

Present stem (infinitive)	Past tense	Past participle
sing	sang OR sung	sung
sink	sank OR sunk	sunk
speak	spoke	spoken
spin	spun	spun
steal	stole	stolen
swear	swore	sworn
swim	swam	swum
swing	swung	swung
take	took	taken
tear	tore	torn
wear	wore	worn
write	wrote	written

Note: Mistakes with verbs sometimes involve spelling errors. Use care when you write troublesome verb forms such as *paid, studying, drowned, attacked, led, meant, lose, choose,* and so on.

■ **Exercise 1** Respond to the questions in the past tense with a past tense verb; respond to the questions in the future tense with a present perfect verb. Follow the pattern of the examples.

EXAMPLES
Did she criticize Don? *Yes, she criticized Don.*
Will they take that? *They have already taken it.*

1. Did he give it away?
2. Will she surprise him?
3. Did the man drown?
4. Will he pay the bill?
5. Did she know it?
6. Will they risk that?
7. Did it really happen?
8. Will she ask him?
9. Did he do that?
10. Will they announce it?
11. Did she mean that?
12. Will they freeze it?
13. Did they advertise it?
14. Will he break it?
15. Did they attack him?
16. Will they go?
17. Did she lead them?
18. Will he eat it?
19. Did he please Thelma?
20. Will she speak out?

(2) Do not confuse *set* with *sit* or *lay* with *lie.*

As you know, *sit* means "be seated," and *lie down* means "rest in or get into a horizontal position." To *set* or *lay* something is to place it or put it somewhere.

Learn the distinctions between the forms of *sit* and *set* and those of *lie* and *lay.*

Present stem (infinitive)	Past tense	Past participle	Present participle
(to) sit	sat	sat	sitting
(to) set	set	set	setting
(to) lie	lay	lain	lying
(to) lay	laid	laid	laying

To avoid confusing these troublesome verbs in your writing, remember as you proofread that, as a rule, the verbs (or verbals) *set* and *lay* take objects; *sit* and *lie* do not.

> She had *laid* the book aside. [*Book* is the object.]
> I wanted to *lie* in the sun. [*To lie* has no object.]
> After asking me to *sit* down, she seemed to forget I was there. [*To sit* has no object.]

Study the examples below, noting the absence of objects.

> I did not sit down.   You should lie down.
> Al sat up straight.   He lay down awhile.
> She had sat too long.   It has lain here a week.
> It was sitting here.   The coat was lying there.

Note: Unlike *sit* and *lie,* the verbs *set* and *lay* may be passive as well as active.

> Somebody *had set* the pup in the cart. [Active]
> The pup *had been set* in the cart. [Passive]
>
> We *ought to lay* our prejudices aside. [Active]
> Our prejudices *ought to be laid* aside. [Passive]

■ **Exercise 2** Substitute the correct forms of *sit* and *lie* for the italicized word in each sentence. Follow the pattern of the example. Do not change the tense of the verb.

> EXAMPLE
> I *remained* in that position for twenty minutes.
>
> *I **sat** in that position for twenty minutes.*
> *I **lay** in that position for twenty minutes.*

1. Herbie doesn't ever want to *get* down.
2. The drunk *parked* on the curb.
3. The toy soldier has been *rusting* in the yard.
4. He often *sleeps* on a park bench.
5. Has it *been* there all along?

7b
Use logical tense forms in sequence.

(1) Finite verbs

Notice in the examples below the relationship of each verb form to actual time:

> When the speaker *entered*, the audience *rose*. [Both actions took place at the same definite time in the past.]
>
> I *have ceased* worrying because I *have heard* no more rumours. [Both verb forms indicate action at some time before now.]
>
> When I *had been* at camp four weeks, I *received* word that my application *had been accepted*. [The *had* before *been* indicates a time prior to that of *received*.]

(2) Infinitives

Use the present infinitive to express action contemporaneous with, or later than, that of the main verb; use the present perfect infinitive for action prior to that of the main verb:

She wanted *to win*. She wants *to win*. [Present infinitives —for time later than *wanted* or *wants*]

I would like *to have won* that prize. [Present perfect infinitive—for time prior to that of the main verb. Compare "I wish I *had won*."]

I would have liked *to live* (NOT *to have lived*) in Shakespeare's time. [Present infinitive—for time contemporaneous with that of the main verb]

(3) Participles

Use the present form of participles to express action contemporaneous with that of the main verb; use the present perfect form for action prior to that of the main verb:

Walking along the streets, he met many old friends. [The walking and the meeting were contemporaneous.]

Having climbed that mountain, they felt a real sense of achievement. [The climbing took place first; then came their sense of achievement.]

■**Exercise 3** Choose the verb form inside parentheses that is the logical tense form in sequence.

1. When the fire sale (ended, had ended), the store closed.
2. Fans cheered as the goal (had been made, was made).
3. The team plans (to celebrate, to have celebrated) tomorrow.
4. We should have planned (to have gone, to go) by bus.
5. (Having finished, Finishing) the test, Leslie left the room.
6. (Having bought, Buying) the tickets, Mr. Selby took the children to the circus.
7. The president had left the meeting before it (had adjourned, adjourned).
8. It is customary for ranchers (to brand, to have branded) their cattle.
9. Marilyn had not expected (to see, to have seen) her cousin at the rally.
10. The pond has begun freezing because the temperature (dropped, has dropped).

7c

Use the subjunctive mood in the few types of expressions in which it is still appropriate.

Distinctive forms for the subjunctive mood (such as *they* **be**, *I* **were,** or *he* **do**) have been almost totally replaced by the indicative or by alternate structures:

Suppose he *were* to die.	OR	Suppose he dies.
I ask that he *do* this.	OR	I ask him to do this.
I wish I *were* rich.	OR	I wish I was rich. [Informal]
It is necessary that she *be* there on time.	OR	She must be there on time.

Especially in formal English, however, the subjunctive is still used to express a contrary-to-fact condition.

> Drive as if every other car on the road *were* out to kill you.
> —ESQUIRE

Standard English requires the use of the subjunctive in a few idiomatic expressions and in *that* clauses of recommendation, request, or demand:

> *Come* rain or shine, their dinner pail stays full.
> —ROBERT HELLER

> As a matter of fact, it is terribly shocking to see a man hit a woman and to hear him demand that she *wash* his pants.
> —BARBARA GARSON

Note: *Should* or *had* may be used to express a supposition or a contrary-to-fact condition:

> *Should* the careerist choose love he would cease to be a careerist. —PHILIP SLATER

> *Had* I been born on the banks of the Saskatchewan, I would myself have shouldered a musket to fight. —WILFRED LAURIER

Do not use *would have* as a substitute for *had:*

> If I *had* (NOT *would have*) been born on the banks of the Saskatchewan, I would myself have shouldered a musket to fight.

7d

Avoid needless shifts in tense or mood. See also **27a**.

INCONSISTENT   He walked up to me in the cafeteria and tries to start a fight.

BETTER   He *walked* up to me in the cafeteria and *tried* to start a fight.

INCONSISTENT   It is necessary to restrain an occasional foolhardy park visitor. If a female bear *were* to mistake his friendly intentions and *supposes* him a menace to her cubs, he would be in trouble. [Mood shifts improperly from subjunctive to indicative within the compound predicate.] But females with cubs *were* only one of the dangers. [A correct sentence if standing alone, but here inconsistent with present tense of preceding sentence and therefore misleading] One *has* to remember that all bears *were* wild animals and not domesticated pets. [Inconsistent and misleading shift of tense from present in main clause to past in subordinate clause] Though a bear *may seem* altogether peaceable and harmless, he *might* not *remain* peaceable, and he is never harmless. [Tense shifts improperly from present in introductory clause to past in main clause.] It *is* therefore an important part of the park ranger's duty *to watch* the tourists and above all *don't* let anyone try to feed the bears. [Inconsistent and needless shift in mood from indicative to imperative]

BETTER   It is necessary to restrain an occasional foolhardy park visitor. If a female bear *were* to mistake his friendly intentions and *suppose* him a menace to her cubs, he would be in trouble. But females with cubs *are* only one of the dangers. One *has* to remember that all bears *are* wild animals and not domesticated pets. Though a bear *may seem* altogether peaceable and harmless, he *may* not *remain* peaceable, and he is never harmless. It *is* therefore an important part of the park ranger's duty *to watch* the tourists and above all not *to let* anyone try to feed the bears.

■ **Exercise 4** Revise any incorrect verb forms in the sentences below. Put a checkmark after any sentence that needs no revision. Prepare to explain the reason for each change you make.

1. If he would have registered later, he would have had night classes.
2. If Terri enrolled in the class at the beginning, she could have made good grades.
3. A stone lying in one position for a long time may gather moss.
4. The members recommended that all delinquents be fined.
5. It was reported that there use to be very few delinquents.
6. After Douglas entered the room, he sat down at the desk and begins to write rapidly.
7. Until I received that letter, I was hoping to have had a visit from Marty.
8. Follow the main road for a mile; then you need to take the next road on the left.
9. The two suspects could not deny that they had stole the tapes.
10. I would have liked to have been with the team on the trip to Quebec.

■ **Exercise 5** In the following passage correct all errors and inconsistencies in tense and mood as well as any other errors in verb usage. Put a checkmark after any sentence that is satisfactory as it stands.

¹ Across the Thames from Shakespeare's London lay the area known as the Bankside, probably as rough and unsavoury a neighbourhood as ever laid across the river from any city. ²And yet it was to such a place that Shakespeare and his company had to have gone to build their new theatre. ³For the Puritan government of the City had set up all sorts of prohibitions against theatrical entertainment within the city walls. ⁴ When it became necessary, therefore, for the company to have moved their playhouse from its old location north of the city, they obtain a lease to a tract on the Bankside. ⁵ Other theatrical companies had went there before them, and it seemed reasonable to have supposed that Shakespeare and his partners would prosper in the new location. ⁶ Apparently the Puritans of the City had no law

against anyone's moving cartloads of lumber through the public streets. [7] There is no record that the company met with difficulty while the timbers of the dismantled playhouse are being hauled to the new site. [8] The partners had foresaw and forestalled one difficulty: the efforts of their old landlord to have stopped them from removing the building. [9] Fearing that his presence would complicate their task and would perhaps defeat its working altogether, they waited until he had gone out of town. [10] And when he came back, his lot was bare. [11] The building's timbers were all in stacks on the far side of the river, and the theatre is waiting only to be put together. [12] It is a matter of general knowledge that on the Bankside Shakespeare continued his successful career as a showman and went on to enjoy even greater prosperity after he had made the move than before.

MECHANICS

Manuscript Form

8

Put your manuscript in acceptable form. Divide words at the ends of lines according to standard practices. Proofread and revise with care.

8a
Use the proper materials.

Unless you are given other instructions, follow these general rules:

(1) Handwritten papers Use regular notebook paper, size 21 × 28 cm, with widely spaced lines. (Narrow spaces between lines do not allow sufficient room for corrections.) To make your handwriting more readable or to provide extra room for revisions, you may wish to write on every other line. Use black or blue ink. Write on only one side of the paper.

(2) Typewritten papers Use regular typing paper (not yellow second sheets or sheets torn from a spiral notebook), size 21 × 28 cm. Or use a good grade of bond paper (not onion skin or the kind that smears easily and resists inked-in revisions). Double-space between lines. Use a black ribbon. Type on only one side of the paper.

8b
Arrange your writing in clear and orderly fashion on the page. Divide a word at the end of a line only between syllables.

ARRANGEMENT

(1) Margins Leave sufficient margins—about an inch and a half at the left and top, an inch at the right and at the bottom—to prevent a crowded appearance. The ruled vertical line on notebook paper marks the left margin.

(2) Indention Indent the first lines of paragraphs uniformly, about an inch in handwritten copy and five spaces in typewritten copy.

(3) Paging Use Arabic numerals—without parentheses or periods—in the upper right-hand corner to mark all pages after the first.

(4) Title *Do not put quotation marks around the title or underline it* (unless it is a quotation or the title of a book), and use no period after the title. Centre the title on the page about an inch and a half from the top or on the first ruled line. Leave the next line blank and begin the first paragraph on the third line. In this way the title will stand off from the text. Capitalize the first and last words of the title and all other words except articles, short conjunctions, and short prepositions. See also **9c.**

(5) Poetry Quoted lines of poetry are ordinarily arranged and indented as in the original: see **16a(2)**

(6) Punctuation Never begin a line with a comma, a colon, a semicolon, or a terminal mark of punctuation; never end a line with the first of a set of brackets, parentheses, or quotation marks.

(7) Identification Papers are identified in the way prescribed by the instructor to facilitate handling. Usually papers carry the name of the student, the course, the date, and the number of the assignment. Often the name of the instructor is also given.

WORD DIVISION

When you need to divide a word at the end of a line, use a hyphen to mark the separation of syllables. (Of course, one-syllable words such as *through, twelfth,* and *beamed* are not divided.)

(8) Dictionary syllabication In college dictionaries, dots usually mark the divisions of the syllables of a word:

i · so · late   **re · peat · ed**   **set · ting**   **sell · ing**

(9) Conventional practices Not every division between syllables is an appropriate place for dividing a word at the end of a line. The following principles are useful guidelines:

  (a) Do not put a single letter of a word at the end or at the beginning of a line: **e · vade, perk · y**.

  (b) Do not put any two-letter ending at the beginning of a line: **dat · ed, tax · is**.

  (c) Do not make divisions that may temporarily mislead the reader: **re · ally, mag · ical, sour · ces**.

  (d) Divide hyphenated words only at the hyphen: mass‑produced, broken‑down, father‑in-law OR father-in‑law.

For easy readability, avoid having a series of word divisions at the ends of consecutive lines. Also try to avoid dividing proper names like *Mexico, Agnes,* or *T. E. Stowe.*

■ **Exercise 1** First list the words below that should not be divided at the end of a line; then, with the aid of your dictionary, write out the other words by syllables and insert hyphens to mark appropriate end-of-line divisions.

1. cross-examination
2. economic
3. fifteenth
4. Paris
5. combed
6. scrubbing
7. guessing
8. psychoanalyst
9. against
10. stick-in-the-mud

8c
Write or type the manuscript so that it can be read easily and accurately.

(1) Legible handwriting Form each letter clearly; distinguish between each *o* and *a*, *i* and *e*, *t* and *l*, *b* and *f*. Be sure that capital letters differ from lower-case letters. Use firm dots, not circles, for periods. Make each word a distinct unit. Avoid flourishes.

(2) Legible typing Before typing your final draft, check the quality of the ribbon and the cleanliness of the type. Do not forget to double-space between lines. Do not strike over an incorrect letter; make neat corrections. Leave one space after a comma or a semicolon, one or two after a colon, and two or three after a period, a question mark, or an exclamation point. To indicate a dash, use two hyphens without spacing before, between, or after. Use ink to insert marks that are not on your typewriter, such as accent marks, mathematical symbols, or brackets.

8d

Proofread and revise the manuscript with care.

(1) Proofread the paper and correct mistakes before submitting it to the instructor.

When doing in-class papers, use the last few minutes of the period for proofreading and making corrections. Changes should be made as follows:

(a) Draw one line horizontally through any word to be deleted. Do not put it within parentheses or make an unsightly erasure.

(b) In case of an addition of one line or less, place a caret (∧) at the point in the line where the addition is to come, and write just above the caret the word or words to be added.

Since you have more time for out-of-class assignments, write a first draft, put the paper aside for several hours or for a day, and then use the following checklist as you proofread and make changes.

Proofreader's Checklist

1. *Title.* Is there any unnecessary punctuation in the title? Is it centred on the first line? Are key words capitalized? See **8b(4)**.

2. *Logic.* Is the central idea of the paper stated clearly and developed logically? Does the paper contain any questionable generalizations? Does it contain any irrelevant material? See Section **23**.

3. *Shifts.* Are there any needless shifts in tense, mood, voice, person, number, type of discourse, tone, or perspective? See Section **27**.

4. *Paragraphs.* Is the first line of each paragraph clearly indented? Are ideas carefully organized and adequately developed? See **8b(2)**, **31a**, and **31c–d**.

5. *Transitions.* Do ideas follow one another smoothly? Do all conjunctions and transitional expressions relate ideas precisely? See **31b**.

6. *Sentences.* Are there any sentence fragments, comma splices, or fused sentences? Are ideas properly subordinated? Are modifiers correctly placed? Is there any faulty parallelism? Are the references of pronouns clear? Are sentences as effective as possible? See Sections **2–3**, **24–26**, and **28–30**.

7. *Grammar.* Are appropriate forms of modifiers, pronouns, and verbs used? Do subjects and verbs agree? See Sections **4–7**.

8. *Spelling and diction.* Is the spelling correct? Are words carefully chosen, appropriate, exact? Should any words be deleted? Should any be inserted? Should any be changed because of ambiguity? See Section **18**; **19i**; and Sections **20–22**.

9. *Punctuation.* Are apostrophes correctly placed? Are end marks appropriate? Is any one mark of punctuation overused? See Sections **12–17**.

10. *Mechanics.* Do word divisions at the ends of lines follow conventional practices? Are capitals and underlining (italics) used correctly? Should any abbreviations or numbers be spelled out? See **8b(9)** and Sections **9–11**.

To detect errors in spelling, try reading lines backward so that you will see each word separately. To proofread individual sentences, look at each one as a unit, apart from its context.

■ **Exercise 2** Proofread the following composition; circle mistakes. Prepare to discuss in class the changes that you as a proofreader would make.

Programmed People.

People over twenty is a machine—an insensitive, unhearing, unseeing, unthinking, unfeeling mechanism. They act like they are programmed, all their movements or responses triggered by clocks. Take, for example my brother. At 7:30 A.M. he automatically shuts off the alarm, then for the next hour he grumbles and sputter around like the cold, sluggish motor that he is.

On the way to work he did not see the glorious sky or notice ambulance at his neighbor's house. At 8:20 he unlocks his store and starts selling auto parts; however, all mourning long he never once really sees a customers' face. While eating lunch at Joe's cafe, the same music he spent a quarter for yesterday is playing again. he does not hear it. At one o'clock my bother is back working with invoices and punching an old comptometer; The clock and him ticks on and on.

When the hour hand hits five, it pushes the "move" button of my brother: lock store, take bus, pet dog at front door, kiss wife and baby, eat supper, read paper, watch TV, and during the 10-o'clock news he starts his nodding. His wife interrupts his heavy breathing to say that thier neighbour had a mild heart attach while mowing the lawn. My brother jerks and snorts.   Then he mumbles, "Tomorrow, honey, tomorrow.   I have got a year and a half to go before I am twenty

(2) Revise the paper after the instructor has marked it.

One of the best ways to learn how to write is to revise returned papers carefully. Give special attention to any comment on content or style, and become familiar with the numbers or abbreviations used by your instructor to indicate specific errors or suggested changes.

Unless directed otherwise, follow this procedure as you revise a marked paper:

(a) Find in this handbook the exact principle that deals with each error or recommended change.

(b) After the instructor's mark in the margin, write the letter designating the appropriate principle, such as **a** or **c**.

(c) Rather than rewrite the composition, make the corrections on the marked paper. To make the corrections stand out distinctly from the original, use ink of a different colour or a no. 2 pencil.

The purpose of this method of revision is to help you not only to understand why a change is desirable but to avoid repetition of the same mistakes.

On the following page are examples of a paragraph marked by an instructor and the same paragraph corrected by a student.

A Paragraph Marked by an Instructor

Those who damn advertising stress its

3 disadvantages, however, it saves consumers time,

labour, and money. Billboards can save travellers

12 time for many billboards tell where to find a meal

18 or a bed. TV commercials announce new labour—saving

2 products. Such as a spray or a cleaner. In

addition, some advertisers give away free samples

19 of shampoo, toothpaste, soap flakes, and etc.

24 These samples often last for weeks. They save the

consumer money. Consumers should appreciate

advertising, not condemn it.

The Same Paragraph Corrected by a Student

Those who damn advertising stress its

3b disadvantages; however, it saves consumers time,

labour, and money. Billboards can save travellers

12a time for many billboards tell where to find a meal

18c or a bed. TV commercials announce new labour—saving

2c products. such as a spray or a cleaner. In

addition, some advertisers give away free samples

19i of shampoo, toothpaste, soap flakes, etc.

24a These samples which often last for weeks, save the

consumer money. Consumers should appreciate

advertising, not condemn it.

The method of revision shown opposite works equally well if your instructor uses abbreviations or other symbols instead of numbers. In that case, instead of putting **c** after **18**, for example, you would put **c** after **sp**.

Individual Record of Errors

You may find that keeping a record of your errors will help you to check the improvement in your writing. A clear record of the symbols on your revised papers will show your progress at a glance. As you write each paper, keep your record in mind; avoid mistakes that have already been pointed out and corrected.

One way to record your errors is to write them down as they occur in each paper, grouping them in columns according to the seven major divisions of the handbook, as illustrated below. In the spaces for paper no. 1 are the numbers and letters from the margin of the revised paragraph on the opposite page. In the spelling column is the correctly spelled word rather than **18c**. You may wish to add on your record sheet other columns for date, grade, and instructor's comments.

RECORD OF ERRORS

r	Grammar 1–7	Mechanics 8–11	Punctuation 12–17	Words Misspelled 18	Diction 19–22	Effective- ness 23–30	Larger Elements 31–34
	3b 2c		12a	~~saving~~	19i	24a	

85

Capitals

9

**Capitalize words according to standard con-
ventions. Avoid unnecessary capitals.**[1]

A study of the principles in this section should help you use
capitals correctly. When special problems arise with individual words or phrases, consult a good recent college dictionary. Dictionary entries of words that are regularly capitalized begin with capitals:

| Calvinism | Milky Way | Big Dipper |
| Halloween | House of Commons | Dead Sea Scrolls |

Dictionaries also list capitalized abbreviations, along with
options if usage is divided:

| Mr., Ms. | Ph.D. | A.M., a.m., AM |
| P.E.I. | M.A. | UHF, U.H.F., uhf, u.h.f. |

A recent dictionary is an especially useful guide when a
trademark (such as *Band-Aid* or *Kleenex*) begins to function
as a common noun (*bandaid, kleenex*), and when a generally

---

[1]For a more detailed discussion of the capitalization of words and abbreviations, consult *A Manual of Style*, 12th ed. (Chicago: University of Chicago Press, 1969), pp. 149–94. This is the most influential reference on
matters of style and mechanics and is widely used by North American
publishers.

uncapitalized word is capitalized because of a specific meaning in a given sentence:

> Oh, my big brother thinks that he knows everything.
> Oh, Big Brother knows everything.   [The all-knowing authority]

Most capitalized words fall into three main categories: proper names, key words in titles, and the first words of sentences.

9a

Capitalize proper names, words used as an essential part of proper names, and, usually, derivatives and abbreviations of proper names.

Proper names begin with capitals, but names of classes of persons, places, or things do not:

T. H. Brady, Jr.	on Main Street	the Liberal Party
his junior	a main street	a liberal person

(1) Proper names

Capitalize the names of specific persons, places, and things; peoples and their languages; religions and their adherents; members of national, political, racial, social, civic, and athletic groups; geographical names and regions; organizations and institutions; historical documents, periods, and events; calendar designations; trademarks; holy books and words denoting the Supreme Being.

> Tom Evans, Europe, the Olympics, Jews, English
> Christianity, a Christian, Canadians, New Democrat
> a Presbyterian, an Albertan, Vancouver Canucks, Yellowknife
> Arctic Ocean, the Prairies, the Red Cross, Newman Club
> the U.S. Senate, McGill University, the Durham Report
> the Middle Ages, the Winnipeg Strike, Monday, August
> Canada Day, Masonite, Bible, Koran, God, Allah, Yahweh

Note 1: Some writers still capitalize pronouns (except *who, whom, whose*) referring to the Deity. Many writers capitalize such pronouns only when the capital is needed to prevent ambiguity, as in the following sentence:

> God commanded Moses to lead *His* people.

Note 2: Capitalize names of objects, animals, or ideas when they are personified. See also **20a(4)**

> People in the Thirties, Forties, and Fifties were hardly likely to believe that life was a bowl of cherries when *War, Famine, Pestilence,* and *Depression* were staring them in the face so much of the time. —ANDREW SARRIS

(2) Words used as an essential part of proper names

Words like *college, river, park, memorial, street,* and *company* are capitalized only when they are part of proper names:

Trent University	Bay of Fundy	Kicking Horse Pass
New York City	Abbey Road	AVS Food Service

[Compare Norwegian elkhounds, a Honda hatchback, Parkinson's disease, Alberta oil]

Note: In instances such as the following, capitalization depends on word placement:

> on the Erie and Huron lakes   on Lakes Erie and Huron

(3) Derivatives

Words derived from proper names are usually capitalized:

> Africanize   Torontonian   Darwinism   Orwellian

(4) Abbreviations

As a rule, capitalize abbreviations of (or acronyms formed from) capitalized words. See also **17a(2)**

> L. G. Savard   RMC   NATO   NDP   NASA

Note 1: Both *no.* and *No.* are correct abbreviations for *number.*

Note 2: When proper names and their derivatives become names of a general class, they are no longer capitalized.

malapropism   [Derived from *Mrs. Malaprop*]
chauvinistic   [Derived from *Nicolas Chauvin*]

9b

In ordinary writing, capitalize titles that precede a proper name, but not those that follow it.

Mayor Mike Stevens, Sergeant Bouchard, Aunt Edith
Mike Stevens, our mayor; Bouchard, the sergeant; Edith, my
   aunt

Note: Usage is divided regarding the capitalization of titles indicating high rank or distinction when not followed by a proper name, or of words denoting family relationship when used as substitutes for proper names.

Who was the President (OR president) of the United States?
"Oh, Dad (OR dad)!" I said. "Tell Mother (OR mother)."

9c

In titles of books, plays, student papers, and so on, capitalize the first and last words and all other words except articles (*a, an, the*), short conjunctions, and short prepositions.

Crime and Punishment, Lives of Girls and Women
The Man Without a Country   [In titles a conjunction or
   preposition of five or more letters is usually capitalized.]
"The Canadian Poet's Predicament," "A Code to Live By"

Note: In a title capitalize the first word of a hyphenated compound. As a rule, capitalize the word following the hyphen if it is a noun or a proper adjective or if it is equal ir importance to the first word.

> *A Substitute for the H-Bomb*   [Noun]
> *French-Canadian Music*   [Proper adjective]
> "Hit-and-Run Accidents"   [Parallel words]

Usage varies with respect to the capitalization of words following such prefixes as *anti-, ex-, re-,* and *self-*:

> *The Anti-Poverty Program,* "Re-covering Old Sofas"

9d

Capitalize the pronoun *I* and the interjection *O* (but not *oh*, except when it begins a sentence).

> David sings, "Out of the depths I cry to thee, O Lord."

9e

Capitalize the first word of every sentence (as well as the first word of a fragment in dialogue).

> My father asked me how I liked university.
> "It's OK," I said. Then I added, "On weekends."

Note: Be sure to quote a written passage accurately, using the exact words, punctuation, and capitalization of the original.

> As Youth Cult continues to collapse all around us, Instant Historians will spring forth to examine this little fragment of Instant History.   —MICHAEL HALBERSTAM

9f

Avoid unnecessary capitals.

If you have a tendency to overuse capitals, review **9a** through **9e** and study the following style sheet.

Style Sheet for Capitalization

Capitals	*No capitals*
Central High School	in high school
Dr. Freda E. Watts	my doctor
two Conservative MPs	a conservative approach
the Lord I worship	a lord among his peers
a Chihuahua, Saint Bernards	a beagle, fox terriers
Parkinson's disease	the flu, asthma, leukemia
the War of 1812	a space war in 1999
May, July, Friday, Sunday	summer, fall, winter, spring
the West, a Westerner	to fly west, a western wind
Zionism, Marxism	capitalism, socialism
the University Players	a university stadium

■ **Exercise 1**　Write brief sentences correctly using each of the following words.

(1) professor, (2) Professor, (3) college, (4) College, (5) south, (6) South, (7) avenue, (8) Avenue, (9) theatre, (10) Theatre.

■ **Exercise 2**　Supply capitals wherever needed below.

1. Trying to raise my average in both english and history, i spent my thanksgiving holiday writing a paper entitled "the historical development of english-canadian literature."
2. the west offers grand sights for tourists: banff and jasper national parks, the canadian rockies, the fraser river, vancouver island, and the pacific ocean.
3. at the end of his sermon on god's social justice as set forth in the bible, he said, "materialism is undermining the true individualism which is at the heart of christianity."
4. robert sherrill wrote a book, the full title of which is *the saturday night special and other guns with which americans won the west, protected bootleg franchises, slew wildlife, robbed countless banks, shot husbands purposely and by mistake, and killed presidents together with the debate over continuing same.*

Italics

10

To indicate italics, underline words and phrases (along with the punctuation) in accordance with customary practices. Use italics sparingly for emphasis.

In handwritten or typewritten papers, italics are indicated by underlining. Printers set underlined words in italic type.

TYPEWRITTEN

In <u>David Copperfield</u> Dickens writes of his own boyhood.

PRINTED

In *David Copperfield* Dickens writes of his own boyhood.

10a

Titles of books, newspapers, periodicals, pamphlets, plays, long poems, musical works, and movies are underlined (italicized) when mentioned in writing.

> I skimmed through William Goldman's *Marathon Man* and then decided to see the movie. [Note that the author's name is not italicized.]

According to the *Encyclopædia Britannica*, Arthur Miller wrote *The Misfits* for Marilyn Monroe. [An initial *a, an,* or *the* is italicized and capitalized when part of a title.]

Tickets to *Hello, Dolly!* were hard to find. [The italicized punctuation is part of the title.]

He subscribes to *Maclean's*, the *West Coast Review,* and the *New York Times* (OR the New York *Times*). [An initial *the* in titles of periodicals is usually not italicized; the name of the city in titles of newspapers is sometimes not italicized.]

Occasionally quotation marks are used instead of italics for titles of separate publications. The usual practice, however, is to reserve quotation marks for titles of television and radio programs, songs, short stories, essays, short poems, articles from periodicals, subdivisions of books, and unpublished dissertations or theses: see **16b**

"Canada and Its Poetry" is the second essay in Northrop Frye's book *The Bush Garden.*

Exception: Neither italics nor quotation marks are used in references to the Bible and its parts or to legal documents.

The Bible begins with the Book of Genesis.
The Foreign Investment Review Act, passed by the Canadian Parliament in 1973, was a controversial measure.

10b

Foreign words and phrases not yet Anglicized are usually underlined (italicized).

Ceramic highrises look down over the tin shanties of some of Rome's 60,000 *baraccati*—the poor and displaced, many of them immigrants from the south, who live without water or electricity. —MACLEAN'S

Pauli studied the formulas carefully, frowned, looked up and said, "*Das ist falsch.*" —SCIENTIFIC AMERICAN

Genuine simplicity is always a technical *tour de force.*
—NORTHROP FRYE

The first was karate v. *kung fu*—Little John Davis v. Sifu
James Lowe. —ANTHONY TUTTLE
[The italicized *kung fu,* from Chinese, is still considered
non-English; the unitalicized *karate,* from Japanese, is fully
Anglicized.]

Fully Anglicized words, such as the following, are not
italicized.

crevasse (French)
nucleus (Latin)
psyche (Greek)

Some dictionaries still label certain words and phrases as
foreign and are fairly dependable guides to the writer in
doubt about the use of italics. The labels, however, are not
always up-to-date, and writers must depend on their own
judgment after considering current practices.

10c

**Names of ships, aircraft, and spacecraft and titles of
works of art are underlined (italicized).**

The spacecraft *Pioneer 10* sent back evidence that there
are hydrogen atoms in the vicinity of one of Jupiter's 13
satellites, Io. —DONALD M. HUNTEN

A performance of Robert Aitken's *Spirals* was made memora-
ble by a torrent of boos and hisses, followed by letters the
likes of which he'd never seen. —KASPARS DZEGUZE

10d

**Words, letters, or figures spoken of as such or used
as illustrations are usually underlined (italicized).**

In no other language could a foreigner be tricked into pro-
nouncing *manslaughter* as *man's laughter.* —MARIO PEI

The letters *qu* replaced *cw* in such words as *queen, quoth,* and *quick.* —CHARLES C. FRIES

The first *3* and the final *0* of the serial number are barely legible.

10e

Use underlining (italics) sparingly for emphasis. Do not underline the title of your own paper.

Writers occasionally use italics to show stress, especially in dialogue:

> Out comes the jeer-gun again: "Whose side are *you* on?"
> —GEORGE P. ELLIOTT [Compare "Whose side *are* you on?"]

Sometimes italics are used to emphasize the meaning of a word, especially when the exact meaning might be missed without the italics.

> To *do* justice means to treat all men with respect and human dignity—Negroes, whites, cops, and all of creation.
> —DICK GREGORY

But overuse of italics for emphasis (like overuse of the exclamation point) defeats its own purpose. If you tend to overuse italics to stress ideas, study Section **29**. Also try substituting more specific or more forceful words for those you are tempted to underline.

Note: Writers occasionally substitute all capitals for italics in order to gain emphasis.

> The symbol is NOT the thing symbolized; the word is NOT the thing; the map is NOT the territory it stands for.
> —S. I. HAYAKAWA

A title is not italicized when it stands at the head of a book or article. Accordingly, the title at the head of a student's paper (unless the title happens to be also that of a book) should not be underlined. See also **8b(4)**

95

■ **Exercise 1** Underline all words in the following sentences that should be italicized.

1. While waiting for the dentist, I thumbed through an old issue of U.S. News & World Report and scanned an article on ''Changes in Grading Policies,'' read Psalms 50 and 52 in a Gideon Bible, and worked a crossword puzzle in an old newspaper.
2. On the Queen Mary from New York to London, Eleanor said that she was so bored she read all three books of The Divine Comedy. She has to be kidding!
3. Spelling errors involving the substitution of d for t in such words as partner and pretty reflect a tendency in pronunciation.
4. In Vienna my young cousin attended a performance of Mozart's opera The Magic Flute, which she characterized in her letter as très magnifique.
5. Michelangelo's Battle of the Centaurs and his Madonna of the Steps are among the world's finest sculptures.

■ **Exercise 2** Copy the following passage, underlining all words that should be italicized.

¹ I was returning home on the America when I read Euripides' Medea. ² The play was of course in translation, by Murray, I believe; it was reprinted in Riley's Great Plays of Greece and Rome. ³ I admire Medea the play and Medea the woman. ⁴ Both have a quality that our contemporary primitivism misses. ⁵ Characters in modern plays are neurotic; Medea was sublimely and savagely mad.

Abbreviations and Numbers

11

In ordinary writing use abbreviations only when appropriate, and spell out numbers that can be expressed simply.

Abbreviations and figures are desirable in tables, footnotes, and bibliographies (see the list on page 375) and in some kinds of special or technical writing. In ordinary writing, however, only certain abbreviations are appropriate, and numbers that can be expressed in one word or two (like *forty-two* or *five hundred*) are usually spelled out.

All the principles in this section apply to ordinary writing, which of course includes the kind of writing often required in college.

Abbreviations

11a

Use the abbreviations *Mr., Mrs., Ms., Dr.,* and *St.* (for *Saint*). Spell out *doctor* and *saint* when not followed by proper names.

Dr. Bell, Ms. Kay Gibbs, Mr. W. W. Kirtley, St. Francis

the young doctor, the early life of the saint

11b

Spell out names of provinces, countries, months, days of the week, and units of measurement.

On Sunday, October 10, we passed through Guy, Alberta.
Slightly over a metre tall, Susan weighs forty-two kilograms.

Note: When using SI metric units with numerals, SI abbreviations may be used. These are never pluralized and are written without a period. The standard reference on SI style is the *Canadian Metric Practice Guide* (Rexdale, Ontario: Canadian Standards Association, 1976).

The lake was 8.5 km long but only a few metres deep.

11c

Spell out *Street, Mount, River, Company,* and similar words used as an essential part of proper names.

Fifth Avenue is east of Central Park.
The Ford Motor Company does not expect a strike soon.

Note: Avoid the use of & (for *and*) and such abbreviations as *Bros.* or *Inc.*, except in copying official titles.

11d

Do not abbreviate the names of courses of study and the words for *page, chapter,* and *volume.*

I registered for psychology, math, and chemistry. [Not an abbreviation, *math* is a clipped form of *mathematics.*]
The model sales chart is on page 46 of chapter 3.

11e

Do not abbreviate first names.

George or William Price will be elected. [NOT Geo. or Wm.]

Permissible Abbreviations

In addition to the abbreviations listed in **11a**, the following abbreviations and symbols are permissible and usually desirable.

1. *For titles and degrees after proper names*: Jr., Sr., Esq., D.D., Ph.D., M.A., M.D., C.P.A.

   Mr. Sam Jones, Sr.; Sam Jones, Jr.; Alice Jones, M.D.

2. *For words used with dates or figures:* A.D., B.C.; A.M. OR a.m., P.M. OR p.m.; no. OR No.; $

   The city of Jerusalem fell in 586 B.C. and again in A.D. 70.

   At 8 A.M. (OR 8:00 A.M.) he paid the manager $14.25.
   [Compare "At eight o'clock the next morning he paid the manager over fourteen dollars."]

3. *For such terms as* British Columbia *or* United States *used adjectivally, for the names of organizations or agencies and things usually referred to by their capitalized initials:* Washington D.C.; the B.C. government; NDP, NORAD, RCMP, CIA, WHO, JFK, CP Telecommunications, CRTC

4. *For certain common Latin expressions, although the English term is usually spelled out in formal writing, as indicated in parentheses*: i.e. (that is), e.g. (for example), viz. (namely), cf. (compare), etc. (and so forth, and so on), vs. OR v. (versus), et al. (and others)

If you have any doubt about the spelling or capitalization of an abbreviation, consult a good dictionary.

■ **Exercise 1** Strike out any form below that is not appropriate in formal writing. (In a few items two forms are appropriate.)

1. Ms. Janet Hogan; a dr. but not a saint
2. in the U.S. Senate; in the United States; in the U.S.

3. on TV; in B.C. and Alta.
4. on Barrington St.; on Barrington Street
5. Victoria, B.C.; Winnipeg, Man.
6. FBI; Federal Bureau of Investigation
7. on Aug. 15; on August 15
8. for Jr.; for John Evans, Jr.
9. e.g.; for example
10. before 6 A.M.; before six in the A.M.

Numbers

11f

Although usage varies, writers tend to spell out numbers that can be expressed in one word or two; they regularly use figures for other numbers.

after twenty-two years	after 124 years
only thirty dollars	only $29.99
one fourth OR one-fourth	$56\frac{1}{4}$
five thousand voters	5,261 voters
ten million light years	10,402,317 light years

Special Usage Regarding Numbers

1. *Specific time of day*

   2 A.M.   OR   2:00 A.M.   OR   two o'clock in the morning
   4:30 P.M.   OR   half-past four in the afternoon

2. *Dates*

   May 7, 1977   OR   7 May 1977   [NOT May 7th, 1977]
   May sixth OR the sixth of May OR May 6 OR May 6th
   the thirties OR the 1930's OR the 1930s
   the twentieth century
   in 1900[1]   in 1975–1976 OR in 1975–76

---

[1] The year is never written out except in very formal social announcements or invitations.

from 1940 to 1945   OR   1940–1945   OR   1940–45
   [NOT from 1940–1945, from 1940–45]

3. *Addresses*

35 Wellington Street, London, Ontario, N6B 2K3
P.O. Box 14   Rural Route 2   Apartment 3   Room 19
16 Tenth Street   2 East 114 Street   OR   2 East 114th Street

4. *Identification numbers*

Channel 13   Highway 407   Henry VIII   *Skylab 3*

5. *Pages and divisions of books*

page 30   chapter 6   part 4   exercise 14

6. *Decimals and percentages*

a 72.5 average   .63 centimeters $12\frac{1}{2}$ per cent

7. *Numbers in series and statistics*

two cows, five pigs, and forty-two chickens
125 metres long, 20 metres wide, and 5 metres deep
scores of 17 to 13 and 42 to 3   OR   scores of 17–13 and 42–3
The members voted 99 to 23 against it.

8. *Large round numbers*

four billion dollars   OR $4 billion   OR $4,000,000,000
   [Figures are used for emphasis only.]
12,500,000   OR   12.5 million

9. *Numbers beginning sentences*

Six per cent of the students voted.   OR   Only 6 per cent of the
   students voted.   [NOT 6 per cent of the students voted.]

10. *Repeated numbers (in legal or commercial writing)*

The agent's fee will not exceed one hundred (100) dollars.
OR   The agent's fee will not exceed one hundred dollars
($100).

■ **Exercise 2** All items below are appropriate in formal writing. Using desirable abbreviations and figures, change each item to an acceptable shortened form.

> EXAMPLES
> Jude, the saint   *St. Jude*
> at two o'clock that afternoon   *at 2* P.M.

1. on the fifteenth of June
2. Ernest Threadgill, a doctor
3. thirty million dollars
4. Louise Perreault, a chartered accountant
5. the United Nations
6. one o'clock in the afternoon
7. by the first of December, 1977
8. at the bottom of the fifteenth page
9. the Royal Canadian Air Force
10. four hundred years before Christ

PUNCTUATION

The Comma

12

Use the comma (which ordinarily indicates a pause and a variation in voice pitch) where it is required by the structure of the sentence.

Just as pauses and variations in voice pitch help to convey the meaning of spoken sentences, commas help to clarify the meaning of written sentences.

> When the lightning struck, James Harvey fainted.
> When the lightning struck James, Harvey fainted.

The sound of a sentence can serve as a guide in using commas.

But many times sound is not a dependable guide. The use of the comma is primarily determined by the structure of the sentence. If you understand this structure (see Section 1), you can learn to apply the basic principles governing comma usage. The following rules cover the usual practices of the best modern writers:

Commas—

a   precede the coordinating conjunctions *and, but, or, nor, for* and the connectives *so* and *yet* between main clauses;

b   follow certain introductory elements;

c   separate items in a series (including coordinate adjectives);

d   set off nonrestrictive, parenthetical, and miscellaneous elements.

Main Clauses

12a

A comma precedes *and, but, or, nor, for, so,* and *yet* when they link main clauses.

Notice below how the coordinating conjunction *but* is used to connect and relate two simple sentences:

> Mr. Thomas let out an experimental yell. Nobody answered.

> Mr. Thomas let out an experimental yell, *but* nobody answered. —GRAHAM GREENE

[SUBJECT—PREDICATE, *but* SUBJECT—PREDICATE.
OR   MAIN CLAUSE, *but* MAIN CLAUSE.]

Study the sentence structure of the examples that follow the pattern below. Observe that each main clause could be written as a separate sentence because each contains both a subject and a predicate. (Without one of these seven connectives, the main clauses would be separated by a semicolon: see Sections **3** and **14**.)

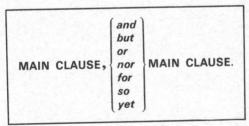

MAIN CLAUSE, { *and* / *but* / *or* / *nor* / *for* / *so* / *yet* } MAIN CLAUSE.

> We are here on the planet only once, and we might as well get a feel for the place.   —ANNIE DILLARD

> Justice stands upon Power, or there is no justice.
> —WILLIAM S. WHITE

> No one watches the performance, for everybody is taking part.   —JAN KOTT

They are hopeless and humble , so he loves them.
—E. M. FORSTER

Here is a great mass of people , yet it takes an effort of intellect and will even to see them. —MICHAEL HARRINGTON

Be sure to use the comma before the coordinating conjunction *and* (not before the *so* or *yet* following the *and*) in sentences such as the following:

The engine noises are not obtrusive , and so the visual experience is reinforced by the sounds of the water and the qualities of being outdoors. —DAVID HANDLIN

Linking sentences with *nor* involves the omission of *not* as well as a shift in word order:

FROM   A woman cannot hope to find a man who is free of sexist attitudes. She cannot make a man give up his privileges by arguing.

TO   A woman cannot hope to find a man who is free of sexist attitudes , *nor* can she make a man give up his privileges by arguing. —ELLEN WILLIS

As the example above illustrates, the connectives *and, but, or, nor, for, so,* or *yet* may be used to link various types of sentences, not just simple sentences.

Caution: Do not confuse the compound sentence with a simple sentence containing a compound predicate.

Colonel Cathcart had courage , and he never hesitated to volunteer his men for any target available. [Compound sentence—comma before *and*]

Colonel Cathcart had courage and never hesitated to volunteer his men for any target available. —JOSEPH HELLER [Compound predicate—no comma before *and*]

Exceptions to 12a and variations

1. The semicolon or the dash may be substituted for the comma, especially when the main clauses reveal a striking contrast or have internal punctuation.

Historically, French Canadians have not really believed in democracy for themselves **;** and English Canadians have not really wanted it for others.   —PIERRE ELLIOTT TRUDEAU

Hope springs eternal **—**but somehow or other troubles never stay long away.   —ARTHUR MEIGHEN

2. The comma may be omitted when there is no possibility of confusing the reader or when the comma is not needed to make reading easier.

Sometimes she went for walks but she didn't like dogs or cats or birds or flowers or nature or nice young men.
—FLANNERY O'CONNOR

3. Only occasionally, for special emphasis, is the comma used before a coordinating conjunction when the predicate that follows has no stated subject.

Artists always seek a new technique **,** and will continue to do so as long as their work excites them.   —E. M. FORSTER

4. The clause before *and* may not have a stated subject and may have the force of an introductory adverb clause.

Call an industrial chieftain incompetent, and he won't love you. Tell him he has laid a Grade A egg, and he will argue. But call his company a one-man band, and he will be furious—especially if it is.   —ROBERT HELLER   [Compare "If you call an industrial chieftain incompetent, he won't love you. If you tell him. . . ." See also **12b**.]

■ **Exercise 1**   Following the punctuation pattern of **12a**, link the sentences in the items below by relating the ideas with an appropriate *and, but, or, nor, for, so,* or *yet.*

EXAMPLE
We cannot win the battle. We cannot afford to lose it.
We cannot win the battle **,** *nor can we afford to lose it.*

1. A crisis strikes. The government cobbles together yet another Royal Commission.
2. The new leash law did not put all dogs behind bars. It did not make the streets safe for cats.

3. Motorists may admit their guilt and pay a fine immediately. They may choose to appear in court within thirty days and plead not guilty.
4. They decided not to take a vacation. They needed the money to remodel their kitchen.
5. The band leader can sing and dance and whistle. She cannot read music.

Introductory Elements

12b

Commas follow introductory elements such as adverb clauses, long phrases, transitional expressions, and interjections.

(1) Introductory adverb clauses

> **ADVERB CLAUSE, MAIN CLAUSE.**

If men could get pregnant, abortion would be a sacrament
—LAURA SABIA

Where modern science has achieved its mastery, there is no place for local cultures. —GEORGE P. GRANT

(2) Long introductory phrases

Except for an overalled man with a bandage around his head and one ear, the waiting room was empty. —W. O. MITCHELL

In Canada with its hostile winters and its total dependence on transportation for survival, the energy crisis of the early seventies was not punitive but prophetic. —PELHAM DAVI

Short introductory prepositional phrases, except when they are distinctly parenthetical expressions (such as *in fact* or *for example*), are seldom followed by commas:

In the Maritimes the Liberals were in fair shape.
—J. L. GRANATSTEIN

Through the Middle Ages the Church was not an agent of oppression. —RICHARD N. GOODWIN

(3) Introductory transitional expressions and interjections

Interjections, as well as transitional expressions (such as *for example, in fact, on the other hand, in the second place*), are generally considered parenthetical: see **12d(3)**. When used as introductory elements, they are ordinarily followed by commas:

In fact, the most obvious fact about the rebellion is how strong and immediate the resistance to it was.
—J. M. S. CARELESS

Well, I could, and did, and that is the way I am made.
—LOVAT DICKSON

Exceptions to 12b and variations

1. The comma may be omitted after an introductory adverb clause and a long introductory phrase if the omission does not make for difficult reading.

    As soon as I saw the elephant I knew with perfect certainty that I ought not to shoot him. —GEORGE ORWELL

    After months of listening for some meager clue he suddenly began to talk in torrents. —ARTHUR L. KOPIT

2. Introductory phrases, even though short, and introductory adverb clauses must sometimes be followed by a comma to prevent misreading. See also **12e**.

    As he spoke, a few heavy preliminary drops were already coming down. —MARGARET ATWOOD

    As we would expect, Freud's self-evaluation would hardly be agreed upon by everyone. —ERNEST BECKER

3. When the adverb clause *follows* the main clause, there is usually no pause and no need for a comma.

> MAIN CLAUSE ADVERB CLAUSE.

They squatted down as if they belonged to the land.
—FARLEY MOWAT

He stands amazed while she serenely twists her legs into the lotus position. —JOHN UPDIKE

Adverb clauses in this position, however, may be preceded by a comma if they are loosely connected with the rest of the sentence, especially if the subordinating conjunction seems equivalent to a coordinating conjunction.

Marine life is concentrated in about 4 per cent of the ocean's total body of water, whereas roughly 96 per cent is just about as poor in life as is a desert ashore. —THOR HEYERDAHL

Land ought not to be a commodity, because like air and water it is necessary to human existence.
—PHILLIPS THOMPSON

■ **Exercise 2** In each sentence below, find the main clause and identify the preceding element as an adverb clause or as a phrase. Then determine whether or not to use a comma after the introductory element.

¹In order to pay his way through university George worked at night in an iron foundry. ²During this time he became acquainted with all the company's operations. ³After four years of evaluating George's work the foundry owner offered George a position as manager. ⁴Although George had planned to attend medical school and become a psychiatrist he found now that the kind of work he had been doing had a far greater appeal for him. ⁵In fact he accepted the offer without hesitation. ⁶When asked later if he thought he had made the right decision George smiled and nodded.

Items in a Series

12c

Commas separate items in a series (including coordinate adjectives).

The punctuation of a series depends on its form:

> The air was *raw, dank, gray.* [*a, b, c*]
> The air was *raw, dank,* and *gray.* [*a, b,* and *c*]
> The air was *raw* and *dank* and *gray.* [*a* and *b* and *c*]

(1) Words, phrases, and clauses in a series

> He should be large, combative, swift, cool, and crafty.
> —IRWIN SHAW

> Life at the top is financially rewarding, spiritually draining, physically exhausting, and short.   —PETER C. NEWMAN

> What the camel is to desert tribes, what the horse is to the Arab, what the ship is to the colonizing Briton, what all modern means of locomotion are to the civilized world today, that the canoe was to the Indian.   —WILLIAM WOOD

The comma before the conjunction may be omitted in the series *a, b,* and *c* if there is no danger of misreading:

> The only safe, legal way to reproduce, adapt or translate copyright material is to get written permission from the copyright holder.   —CANADIAN WRITER'S GUIDE

(2) Coordinate adjectives

Use a comma between coordinate adjectives not linked by a coordinating conjunction:

> It is a waiting, silent, limp room.   —EUDORA WELTY

> She was a frowsy, middle-aged woman with wispy, drab-brown hair. She sat behind a long wooden table on a high platform overlooking her disciples with her narrow, piercing eyes.   —EVELYN KOSSOFF

Coordinate adjectives may modify one word (as in the preceding examples) or a word group:

> It is a silent , limp waiting room.
> She sat behind a long , rickety wooden table.

The word order of modifiers and the use of commas can make a difference in meaning as well as intonation:

> They are young , social , alert workers.
> They are young , alert social workers.

Exception to 12c and a variation

If the items in a series contain internal punctuation, semi-colons are used instead of commas for clarity: see **14b.** Occasionally the semicolon replaces the comma to mark a sharp separation of the items in a series, especially in a series of main clauses:

> Among scholars there are discoverers ; there are critics ; and there are teachers. —GILBERT HIGHET

■ **Exercise 3** Using commas as needed, supply coordinate adjectives to modify any six of the following twelve items.

EXAMPLE
metric system   *the familiar, sensible metric system*

1. apple pie
2. social climbers
3. electronic music
4. pop art
5. minimum wage
6. traveller's cheques
7. Canada goose
8. rhetorical question
9. apartment buildings
10. major oil companies
11. blue cheese
12. secondary school

Parenthetical and
Miscellaneous Elements

12d
Commas set off nonrestrictive clauses and phrases and other parenthetical and miscellaneous elements, such as transitional expressions, items in dates, words used in direct address, and so on. Restrictive clauses and phrases are not set off by commas.

To set off a word or a word group with commas, use two commas unless the element is placed at the beginning of the sentence or at the end:

> Darwin's *Origin of Species,* as Robert Ardrey points out, explains everything except the origin of species.
> —F. W. HOLIDAY

> Socially, death is as taboo as Victorian sex.
> —OSBORN SEGERBERGER, JR.

> Just take a look around El Barrio, the section where so many Puerto Ricans live. —OSCAR LEWIS

Caution: When two commas are needed to set off an element, do not forget one of the commas.

CONFUSING   An experienced driver generally speaking, does not fear the open road.

CLEAR   An experienced driver, generally speaking, does not fear the open road.

(1) Nonrestrictive clauses and phrases are set off by commas. Restrictive clauses and phrases are not set off.

NONRESTRICTIVE CLAUSES AND PHRASES

Adjective clauses and phrases are nonrestrictive when they are not essential to the meaning of the main clause and may be omitted. Such modifiers are parenthetical and are set off by commas.

> This intrigued Newton, *who sought knowledge in many strange places.* —JOSEPH F. GOODAVAGE [The *who* clause is nonessential to the meaning of "This intrigued Newton."]

> Major famines, *which were not infrequent earlier in the 1900s,* have ceased. —J. H. PLUMB [The *which* clause provides nonessential information.]

> He tossed the letter aside and pulled his apple pie, *topped with a melting scoop of vanilla ice cream,* toward him. —TRUMAN CAPOTE [The nonrestrictive phrase can be changed to a nonrestrictive clause: "*which was* topped with a melting scoop of vanilla ice cream."]

> Claud got up, *groaning and growling,* and limped off. —FLANNERY O'CONNOR [Compare "Claud got up (*he was* groaning and growling) and limped off."]

RESTRICTIVE CLAUSES AND PHRASES

Restrictive clauses and phrases follow and limit the words they modify. They are essential to the meaning of the main clause and are not set off by commas.

> The Tories *who opposed responsible government* hurled a stream of insult and abuse at the Reform leaders.
> —RAMSAY COOK
> [The *who* clause is essential to the meaning of the sentence; not all Tories acted this way, but only those who were opposed to responsible government.]

> Medical science has placed in their hands an instrument *that can determine the whole future of heredity.* —TORONTO LIFE [An adjective clause beginning with *that* is restrictive.]

> The two things *most universally desired* are power and admiration. —BERTRAND RUSSELL [The restrictive phrase can be expanded to a clause: "*that are* most universally desired."]

Sometimes a clause or phrase may be either nonrestrictive or restrictive. The writer signifies the meaning by using or by omitting commas.

NONRESTRICTIVE He spent hours caring for the Indian guides, *who were sick with malaria.* [He cared for all the Indian guides. They were all sick with malaria.]

RESTRICTIVE He spent hours caring for the Indian guides *who were sick with malaria.* [Some of the Indian guides were sick with malaria. He cared only for the sick ones.]

■ **Exercise 4** Use commas to set off nonrestrictive clauses and phrases in the following sentences. Put a checkmark after any sentence that needs no further punctuation.

1. I will interview Betty Lee who manages the bank.
2. I will interview the Betty Lee who manages the bank.
3. Freshmen who make a high verbal score are exempt from that English course.
4. The graduates of Clayton High School who always make a high verbal score are exempt from that English course.
5. My father always worrying about money wanted me to get a job.
6. The coach chewing gum and licking his fingers is George.

(2) Nonrestrictive appositives, contrasted elements, geographical names, and most items in dates and addresses are set off by commas.

NONRESTRICTIVE APPOSITIVES

But inertia, *the great minimizer,* provided them with the usual excuses. —MARY McCARTHY

The most visible victims of pollution, fish are only a link in a chain from microscopic life to man. —GEORGE GOODMAN [The appositive precedes rather than follows *fish.*]

The peaks float in the sky, *fantastic pyramids of flame.* —ARTHUR C. CLARKE [Notice that the appositive could be shifted to the beginning of the sentence.]

Was the letter from Frances Evans, *Ph.D.,* or from F. H. Evans, *M.D.?* [Abbreviations after names are treated like nonrestrictive appositives.]

Note: Commas do not set off restrictive appositives.

His son *James* is sick. [*James,* not his son William]
The word *malapropism* is derived from Sheridan's *The Rivals.*
Do you refer to Samuel Butler *the poet* or to Samuel Butler *the novelist?*

CONTRASTED ELEMENTS

Racing is supposed to be a test of skill, *not a dice game with death.* —SONNY KLEINFIELD

His phrases dribbled off, *but not his memories.*
—JAMES A. MICHENER

The goal was achievement, *not adjustment;* the young were taught to work, *not to socialize.* —ALLEN WHEELIS [Only one comma sets off an element before a semicolon.]

Note: Usage is divided regarding the placement of a comma before *but* in such structures as the following:

Other citizens who disagree with me base their disagreement, not on facts different from the ones I know, but on a different set of values. —RENÉ DUBOS

But I think I should prefer to go out laughing, not at death itself but at something irrelevantly funny enough to make me forget it. —JOSEPH WOOD KRUTCH

GEOGRAPHICAL NAMES, ITEMS IN DATES AND ADDRESSES

Edmonton, Alberta, was the site of the 1978 Commonwealth Games.

The letter was addressed to Mr. R. K. Haines, Topsail, Newfoundland A0A 3Y0. [The postal code is not separated by a comma from the name of the province.]

Leslie applied for the job in October, 1975, and accepted it on Thursday, May 13, 1976. OR
Leslie applied for the job in October 1975 and accepted it on Thursday, 13 May 1976.

[Note that commas may be omitted when the day of the month is not given or when the day of the month precedes rather than follows the month.]

■ **Exercise 5** Combine each pair of sentences by reducing the second sentence to an appositive or to a contrasted element set off by commas. Insert commas where needed to set off items in dates or addresses.

EXAMPLES

Roger Michel was born on January 7 1977 in Lachine. He is my only son.

Roger Michel, my only son, was born on January 7, 1977, in Lachine.

Margaret's social insurance number is 426-973-624. It is not 326-973-624.

Margaret's social insurance number is 426-973-624, not 326-973-624.

1. Termites really are insects. Termites are distant cousins of roaches.
2. Those are pill bugs. They are not insects.
3. On April 1 1976 his divorced wife married his lawyer. His lawyer was Bill Wynne.
4. The publisher's address is 450 King Street West Toronto Ontario M5S 1R7. It is not 490 King Street West.
5. We moved to Kelowna British Columbia on 30 September 1975. British Columbia is one of the popular skiing provinces.

(3) Use commas to set off parenthetical elements (inserted or appended expressions, asides), expressions like *I replied* with direct quotations, absolute constructions, words in direct address, and mild interjections.

PARENTHETICAL ELEMENTS

The term *parenthetical* is correctly applied to all nonrestrictive elements discussed under **12d** But it may also be applied to such transitional expressions as *on the other hand,* *first, in the first place, in fact, to tell the truth, however, that is, then, therefore,* and *for example* and to such expressions as *I hope, I believe,* and *he says* (sometimes called "interrupters"). Expressions that come at the beginning of a sentence are treated by both **12b** and **12d**.

Language, *then,* sets the tone of our society.

—EDWIN NEWMAN

The troubled moment, *in fact,* had its importance for them only in retrospect.   —MARY McCARTHY

To put it still more bluntly, we need a world government that can come to logical and humane decisions and can enforce them.   —ISAAC ASIMOV

Astronomy, *as nothing else can do,* teaches men humility.

—ARTHUR C. CLARKE

He disliked being categorized, *no matter what the category.*

—IRWIN SHAW

Yet standards there are, *timeless as the universe itself.*

—MARYA MANNES

Self-admissions or boasts like that, *I understand,* have special weight as testimony.   —PAUL A. SAMUELSON

Note: Expressions such as *also, too, of course, perhaps, at least, therefore,* and *likewise,* when they cause little or no pause in reading, are frequently not set off by commas.

"Involvement" is *perhaps* the key word to all that is happening in movies today.   —ARTHUR KNIGHT

A great many people *therefore* think of me as being so vigorously concerned with technology that I lack humanist considerations.   —R. BUCKMINSTER FULLER

EXPRESSIONS WITH DIRECT QUOTATIONS

With direct quotations, such expressions as *I replied, he said, she asked,* and *we shouted* are set off by commas. See also **16a(4)**.

He said, "Our rose-hips tea is really different."
"Our rose-hips tea," he said, "is really different."
"Our rose-hips tea is really different," he said.

ABSOLUTE CONSTRUCTIONS

(For a definition of *absolute construction,* see page 423.)

He was thumping at a book, *his voice growing louder and louder.* —JOYCE CAROL OATES

Jackson, *his forehead slashed by the glass in the riddled cockpit,* mopped away the blood that had poured into his eyes. —THOMAS HARRIS

His eyebrows raised high in resignation, he began to examine his hand. —LIONEL TRILLING

DIRECT ADDRESS AND MILD INTERJECTIONS

Animal lovers, write letters of protest now. [Direct address]
Oh, well, winning is not all that important. [Interjections]

12e

Occasionally a comma, although not called for by any of the major principles already discussed, may be needed to prevent misreading.

Use **12e** sparingly to justify your commas. In a general sense, nearly all commas are used to prevent misreading or to make reading easier. Your mastery of the comma will come through application of the more specific major principles (**a, b, c, d**) to the structure of your sentences.

CONFUSING   A few weeks before I had seen him in an off-Broadway play.

BETTER   A few weeks before, I had seen him in an off-Broadway play. [The comma clearly indicates intonation.]

,/

CONFUSING	Those who can pay and forego consumption of other essential goods.
BETTER	Those who can, pay and forego consumption of other essential goods. —ERIK P. ECKHOLM

■ **Exercise 6** All commas in the following paragraph are correctly used. Explain the reason for each comma by referring to one of the principles discussed in this section (**12a, 12b, 12c,** or **12d**).

[1]Speed of the various kinds of hawks has never been reliably measured, but experts claim that true falcons reach 180 mph during their electrifying earthward plunge when capturing smaller birds, and this remarkable speed would make the species among the fastest moving creatures on earth. [2]Released from her trainer's forearm with an upward thrust, a bird in "yarak" (the condition between aggressive hunger and perfect fitness) will climb steeply, use her fantastic eyesight to find a victim, hover in an on-target position above—then, with the wind shrilling in her bells, drop on the quarry like a thunderbolt and kill by striking a tremendous blow with an open foot (talons extended) or with a hard closed "fist." [3]A coup de grace, if necessary, is administered by the falcon's sharp beak—by biting the victim through the backbone near the skull. [4]Then she devours her prey on the ground, or on the hawker's gauntlet.
—JOAN HOBSON[1]

■ **Exercise 7** Insert commas where needed in the following sentences (selected and adapted from the works of modern writers). Be prepared to explain the reason for each comma used.

1. Police action in arresting drunks will never prevent drunkenness nor can it cure an alcoholic. —RAMSEY CLARK
2. Fifty years ago *Hazel Beverly Marian Frances* and *Shirley* were all perfectly acceptable boys' names.
   —ALLEEN PACE NILSEN

---

[1]From "Tower to Falcon One: Picking Up the Gauntlet for the USAF" by Joan Hobson, *Holiday*, April/May 1975. © 1975 The Curtis Publishing Company. Reprinted by permission of *Travel/Holiday* Magazine.

3. Thus the ocean floors far from being the oldest features on earth were relatively young. —ALLISON R. PALMER

4. Even today in Communist Yugoslavia they assert their difference clinging ostentatiously to the Roman Catholic religion. —SATURDAY NIGHT

5. Hooper said ''Look Chief you can't go off half-cocked looking for vengeance against a fish. That shark isn't evil.''
—PETER BENCHLEY

6. Thus expressed we need not offer love on command to people who are truly unlovable; we need not love others as much as ourselves which would be contrary to the laws of biology. —HANS SELYE

7. The crowd's answer was polite almost dainty applause the kind that has a lot of coughing at the end instead of a release of spirit. —ANTHONY TUTTLE

8. We do not always communicate with words. For instance when we are angry we can communicate our feelings physically—by hitting somebody. —AUSTIN REPATH

9. The earth breathes in a certain sense. —LEWIS THOMAS

10. December is the most violent month the time of murder robbery assault suicide and Christmas. —EARL SHORRIS

Superfluous Commas

13

Do not use superfluous commas.

Unnecessary or misplaced commas are false or awkward signals that may confuse the reader. If you tend to use too many commas, remember that although the comma ordinarily signals a pause (see Section 12), not every pause calls for a comma. As you read the following sentence aloud, for example, you may pause naturally at least once, but no commas are necessary:

> Here I was with a John Bunyan farmer for a father and a Queen Victoria housewife for a mother. —GEORGE P. ELLIOTT

13a
Do not use a comma to separate the subject from its verb or the verb from its object.

The encircled commas below should be omitted.

> Even people with unlisted telephone numbers ⊙ receive crank calls.
> [Needless separation of subject and verb]

> The man said ⊙ that the old tires were guaranteed.
> [Indirect quotation—needless separation of verb and object]

13b

Do not misuse a comma before or after a coordinating conjunction. See 12a.

The encircled commas below should be omitted:

The facts were selected ⊙ and organized with care.

The authorities debunk UFO sightings, but ⊙ millions of people don't listen to them.

13c

Do not use commas to set off words and short phrases (especially introductory ones) that are not parenthetical or that are very slightly so.

The encircled commas below should be omitted:

E. J. Pratt was born ⊙ in Newfoundland ⊙ in 1883.

Maybe ⊙ the battery cables needed cleaning.

13d

Do not use commas to set off restrictive (necessary) clauses, restrictive phrases, and restrictive appositives.

The encircled commas below should be omitted:

Everyone ⊙ who smokes cigarettes ⊙ risks losing about ten years of life.
[Restrictive clause: see **12d(1)**.]

For years she has not eaten anything ⊙ seasoned with onions or garlic.
[Restrictive phrase: see **12d(1)**.]

The word ⊙ *nope* ⊙ is an interesting substitute for *no*.
[Restrictive appositive: see **12d(2)**.]

13e

Do not use a comma before the first item or after the last item of a series (including a series of coordinate adjectives).

The encircled commas below should be omitted:

> Field trips were required in a few courses, such as ⊙ botany geology, and sociology.

> The company hires talented, smart, ambitious ⊙ women.

■ **Exercise 1** Study the structure of the sentence below; then answer the question that follows by giving a specific rule number (such as **13a**, **13d**) for each item. Be prepared to explain your answers in class.

> Now when you say "newly rich" you picture a middle-aged and corpulent man who has a tendency to remove his collar at formal dinners and is in perpetual hot water with his ambitious wife and her titled friends. —F. SCOTT FITZGERALD

Why is there no comma after (1) *Now,* (2) *say,* (3) *middle-aged,* (4) *man,* (5) *collar,* (6) *dinners,* or (7) *wife?*

■ **Exercise 2** Change the structure and the punctuation of the following sentences according to the pattern of the examples.

> EXAMPLE
> A motorcyclist saw our flashing lights**,** and he stopped to offer aid. [An appropriate comma: see **12a**.]
> *A motorcyclist saw our flashing lights and stopped to offer aid.* [Comma no longer needed]

1. The hail stripped leaves from trees, and it pounded early gardens.
2. Some science fiction presènts newly discovered facts, and it predicts the future accurately.
3. Carter likes the work, and he may make a career of it.

EXAMPLE

If any students destroyed public property, they were ex-
pelled.   [An appropriate comma: see **12b**.]
Any students who destroyed public property were expelled.
[Comma no longer needed]

4. When people lead rather than demand, they often get good
results.

5. If the woman is willing to work, she can earn her living
there.

The Semicolon

14

Use the semicolon (a) between main clauses not linked by *and, but, or, nor, for, so,* or *yet* and (b) between coordinate elements containing commas. Do not use the semicolon between parts of unequal grammatical rank.

Read aloud the following sentences; notice the way your voice reflects the differences in punctuation.

> The letters did not arrive until Thursday, although I had mailed them early Monday morning.
> The letters did not arrive until Thursday; however, I had mailed them early Monday morning.

A stronger mark of punctuation than the comma, the semicolon is sometimes called a weak period. The semicolon can be used to mark the connection of closely related sentences:

> SENTENCES SEPARATED If she continues to act aggressively, she provokes fear. If she returns to feminine values, she provokes laughter.

> SENTENCES LINKED If she continues to act aggressively, she provokes fear; if she returns to feminine values, she provokes laughter. —WARREN FARRELL

If you can distinguish between phrases and clauses, between main and subordinate clauses (see **1d** and **1e**), you should have little trouble using the semicolon.

14a

Use the semicolon between two main clauses not linked by a coordinating conjunction (*and, but, or, nor, for*) or by the connectives *so* and *yet*.

> ### MAIN CLAUSE; MAIN CLAUSE.

He liked her very much; of that she was quite sure; she could always tell.   —MORLEY CALLAGHAN

A community cannot stand still; it must develop or decline.
—CLINTON ROSSITER

Landscapes in poems are often interior landscapes; they are maps of a state of mind.   —MARGARET ATWOOD

Caution: Be sure to use a semicolon before conjunctive adverbs (*hence, however, therefore,* and so on) and conjunctive transitional phrases (*in fact, on the other hand,* and so on) placed between main clauses. See also **3b**.

The semicolon also separates main clauses not joined by *and, but, or, for, nor, so,* or *yet* in compound-complex sentences:

SENTENCES SEPARATED   They have not yet been molded by experience. Therefore, the immediate moment makes a great impression on them because that is all they know. [Simple sentence and complex sentence]

SENTENCES LINKED   They have not yet been molded by experience; therefore, the immediate moment makes a great impression on them because that is all they know.
—WILLIAM J. HARRIS

Caution: Do not overwork the semicolon. Often compound sentences are better revised according to the principles of subordination: see Section **24** and also **14c**.

Note: A number of writers prefer to use a semicolon before *so* and *yet* between main clauses. A semicolon (instead of the usual comma) is often used before *so*, *yet*, or a coordinating conjunction to mark the connection of sentences when they have internal punctuation or reveal a striking contrast. See also **12a**

Food is obviously necessary for survival **;** so you might pay more for it than you would for almost anything else.

—HARRY BROWNE

Wherever people celebrated Christmas, what was old was transformed **;** and often, following their new creeds and new thoughts, people created new forms of celebration.

—MARGARET MEAD

Profound experiences stimulate thought **;** but such thoughts do not look very adequate on paper.   —WALTER KAUFMANN

■ **Exercise 1** Change each of the following items to conform to pattern **14a** as shown in the examples below.

EXAMPLES

The new translation of the Bible is not poetic. Nor is its language really modern.
The new translation of the Bible is not poetic; its language is not really modern.

Students filled in forms in September. And then they had to answer the same questions in December.
Students filled in forms in September; then they had to answer the same questions in December.

1. An engagement is not a marriage. Nor is a family quarrel a broken home.
2. The team kept on losing. And, consequently, the morale of the whole school was low.
3. Tony himself cut and polished the turquoise. And it is a beauty.
4. He took a course in the art of self-defence. But later, during a class demonstration, he broke his wrist.
5. Carol was hired as a design assistant. But in two years she was promoted to fashion designer.

14b

Use the semicolon to separate a series of items which themselves contain commas.

This use of the semicolon instead of the comma in a series is for clarity. The semicolon sharply separates the items so that the reader can distinguish the main divisions of the series at a glance.

> A board is elected or appointed from each of three general categories of citizens: for example, a judge or lawyer of good repute; a professor of art, literature, or one of the humanities; and a social worker, psychologist, or clergyman.
> —GEORGE P. ELLIOTT

Note: Occasionally, for special emphasis, semicolons may divide a series of items that do not contain internal punctuation.

> What results from this in the mind of the student? Facts, perhaps; ideas; information; the techniques of the present; the traditions of the past.
> —NORTHROP FRYE

■ **Exercise 2** Combine the following sentences by deleting words and using a series of items separated by semicolons. Use the colon to introduce each series, as in the example.

EXAMPLE

On stage all set to fight were three debaters. One was Eric Dunn, a zero-population advocate. Another was Susan Miles, a theologian. And the third was K. C. Osborn, president of the first year committee.

On stage all set to fight were three debaters: Eric Dunn, a zero-population advocate; Susan Miles, a theologian; and K.C. Osborn, president of the first year committee.

1. On the talk show were three guests. One was T. J. Ott, a psychic. Another was Charles Shelton, a local ufologist. And the third was Abbish Ludah, a guru.

2. We sold everything at our benefit flea market. We sold many dishes and vases, old and cracked. We also sold fishing gear, garden tools, and half-used tubes of lipstick.

14c

Do not use a semicolon between parts of unequal grammatical rank, such as a clause and a phrase or a main clause and a subordinate clause.

> PARTS OF EQUAL RANK
> Then came the declaration of an emergency; this frightened the psychologically unprepared.
> [Two main clauses]

> PARTS OF UNEQUAL RANK
> Then came the declaration of an emergency, frightening the psychologically unprepared.
> [Main clause and a phrase, separated by a comma]
> Then came the declaration of an emergency, which frightened the psychologically unprepared.
> [Main clause and a subordinate clause, separated by a comma]

The semicolon may be followed by a main clause with elliptical elements. The author of each sentence below omitted the clearly implied words that have been inserted in brackets:

> At best the books engendered curiosity; at worst [they engendered] prejudice. —BASIL JOHNSTON

> He wrote him, then telephoned him; [there was] no answer.
> —MORLEY CALLAGHAN

Sometimes, as an aid to clarity, commas are used to mark omissions that avoid repetition:

> Family life in my parents' home was based upon a cosmic order: Papa was the sun; Mama, the moon; and we kids, minor satellites. —SAM LEVENSON

Exercise 3 Substitute commas for any semicolons standing between parts of unequal rank in the following sentences. Do not change a correctly placed semicolon.

1. Don went jogging one afternoon; never returning; then he was numbered among the tens of thousands who disappear every year.
2. Although the educational TV channel is sometimes a bore; at least tedious ads do not interrupt the programs.
3. Eric is studying psychology; Anna, languages; and Bob, forestry.
4. Alexandra took the motor apart; intending to overhaul it before the rally.
5. The tormented bull lowered his head in readiness for another charge; the one-sided contest not being over yet.

Exercise 4 Compose four sentences to illustrate various uses of the semicolon.

General Exercise on the Comma and the Semicolon

Exercise 5 First, review Sections **12** and **14**. Then, using the following examples as guides, punctuate sentences 1 through 10 appropriately.

12a Pat poured gasoline into the hot tank, for he had not read the warning in his tractor manual.

12b Since Pat had not read the warning in his tractor manual, he poured gasoline into the hot tank.
 In very large print in the tractor manual, the warning is conspicuous.

12c Pat did not read the tractor manual, observe the warning, or wait for the tank to cool.
 Pat was a rash, impatient young mechanic.

12d Pat did not read his tractor manual, which warned against pouring gasoline into a hot tank.
 Pat, a careless young man, poured gasoline into the hot tank of his tractor.

12e First, warnings should be read.

14a Pat ignored the warning in the tractor manual; he poured gasoline into the hot tank.

Pat poured gasoline into the hot tank; thus he caused the explosion.

14b At the hospital Pat said that he had not read the warning; that he had, of course, been careless; and that he would never again, under any circumstances, pour gasoline into a hot tank.

1. Many young people in the mid-1970s were bored or discouraged for their dreams of the 1960s had not become reality.

2. Dr. Felipe a visiting professor from Africa says that often it is not fun to learn but that it is always fun to know.

3. The stalls of the open market along the wharf were filled with tray after tray of glassy-eyed fish flat-topped pyramids of brussel sprouts slender stalks of pink rhubarb mounds of home-grown tomatoes and jars of bronze honey.

4. Two or three scrawny mangy-looking hounds lay sprawled in the shade of the cabin.

5. While Diana was unpacking the cooking gear and Grace was chopping firewood I began to put up our shelter.

6. Slamming the door of his four-wheel drive to cut short the argument with his wife Jerry grabbed the handful of food coupons from her and stalked into the supermarket.

7. Still in high school we had to memorize dates and facts such as 1066 the Battle of Hastings 1914–1918 World War I 1939–1945 World War II and 1969 the first moon landing.

8. The dream home that they often talk about is a retreat in the Rockies to tell the truth however they seem perfectly happy in their mobile home on the outskirts of Winnipeg.

9. The criminal was asking for mercy his victim for justice.

10. Chris and I felt that our blustery argument would never end however my weather-watching roommate reminded us that thunderstorms are usually of a short duration.

The Apostrophe

15

Use the apostrophe to indicate the possessive case (except for personal pronouns), to mark omissions in contracted words or numerals, and to form certain plurals.

15a
Use the apostrophe to indicate the possessive case of nouns and indefinite pronouns.

The possessive case expresses ownership or a comparable relationship, which may often be otherwise expressed by the substitution of an *of* phrase or another modifier.

Gloria's dogs	the dogs owned by Gloria
everybody's friend	the friend of everybody
for clarity's sake	for the sake of clarity
Al's pie	the pie that Al baked, bought, or ate
a girls' school	a school for girls
the Indians' interesting history	the interesting history of the Indians

A possessive noun or pronoun may be related to a word (or word group) that precedes it or that is clearly implied.

Is that old broken-down dune buggy *Frank's* or *Jane's?*

Children live in today's truth while parents cling to *yesterday's.* —RAMSEY CLARK

(1) For singular nouns and indefinite pronouns, add the apostrophe and *s.*

Laura's idea	somebody's coat
anyone's guess	a dime's worth
a week's work	one's choices

Option: If a singular noun ends in *s,* add the apostrophe and *s* or only the apostrophe.

Keats's poetry	OR	Keats' poetry
a waitress's tips	OR	a waitress' tips

(2) For plural nouns ending in *s,* add only the apostrophe. For plurals not ending in *s,* add the apostrophe and *s.*

boys' shoes (shoes for *boys*)	two dollars' worth
babies' toes (toes of *babies*)	the Joneses' reunion

BUT

men's clothing   women's jobs   children's rights

(3) For compounds or word groups, add the apostrophe and *s* only to the last word.

my sister-in-law's shop
the Governor General's residence
someone else's turn
John Bassett, Jr.'s reply.

(4) To indicate individual ownership, add the apostrophe and *s* to each name.

Al's and Sue's cars   [Note that *cars* is plural.]
the doctor's and the dentist's offices

Note: To indicate joint ownership, add the apostrophe and *s* only to the last name or to each name.

> Al and Sue's car   OR   Al's and Sue's car

Variations to 15a

1. The use of the apostrophe or the possessive form varies with proper names (organizations, geographical designations, and so on).

   > Devil's Island   Devils Tower   Devil Mountain

2. When a singular word ends in *s*, many writers use the apostrophe and *s* to reflect pronunciation, but they prefer to use only the apostrophe when the word following begins with an *s* or a *z* sound.

   > Chris's enthusiasm   BUT   Chris' zeal
   > the hostess's idea   BUT   for the hostess' sake

■ **Exercise 1**   Change the modifier after the noun to a possessive form before the noun, following the pattern of the examples.

> EXAMPLES
> the laughter of the crowd   *the crowd's laughter*
> suggestions made by James   *James's suggestions*
>   OR *James' suggestions*

1. the tape decks belonging to Johnny
2. the boat bought by the Weinsteins
3. the voices of Bess and Mary
4. the efforts of the editor-in-chief
5. the strategy that Doris uses

15b
Use an apostrophe to mark omissions in contracted words or numerals.

> didn't   he'll   they're   there's   class of '76

15c

Use the apostrophe and _s_ to form the plural of lower-case letters and of abbreviations followed by periods. When needed to prevent confusion, use the apostrophe and _s_ to form the plural of capital letters, of symbols, of abbreviations not followed by periods, and of words referred to as words.

> His _a_'s look like _o_'s. [The _'s_ is not italicized (underlined). See also **10d**.]
>
> Over half of the Ph.D.'s were still looking for desirable positions.
>
> Her _I_'s are illegible, and her _miss_'s appear to be _mess_'s.

Either _'s_ or _s_ may be used to form such plurals as the following:

> the 1970's OR the 1970s   his 7's OR his 7s
> two _B_'s OR two _Bs_   the &'s OR the &s
> her _and_'s OR her _ands_   the UFO's OR the UFOs

15d

Do not use the apostrophe with the pronouns _his, hers, its, ours, yours, theirs,_ or _whose_ or with plural nouns not in the possessive case.

> _His_ parents sent money; _ours_ sent food.
> A friend of _theirs_ knows a cousin of _yours_.
> The _sisters_ design _clothes_ for _babies_.

Caution: Do not confuse _its_ with _it's_ or _whose_ with _who's_:

> _Its_ motor is small. [The motor _of it_]
> _It's_ a small motor. [_It is_ a small motor.]
> _Whose_ is that? [_Who owns_ that?]
> _Who's_ that? [_Who is_ that?]

■ **Exercise 2** Insert apostrophes where needed in the following sentences. Put a checkmark after any sentence that needs no change in punctuation.

1. Many students attitudes changed completely in the mid-1970s.
2. Some students dropped these courses because of the stiff requirements.
3. Those newsstands sell Marian Rosss homemade candy.
4. Theyre not interested in hockey; its roughness repels them.
5. Snapshots of everyone in the class of 77 cover Jerrys bulletin board.
6. "Its just one C.A.s opinion, isnt it?" Otis commented.
7. Is that dog yours or theirs?
8. There are two es and two ds in Hildegardes name, but not any us.
9. The computer confused my account with somebody elses.
10. Marnie often quotes her Granddads favourite expression: "Everybodys useful, but nobodys indispensable!"

Quotation Marks

16

Use quotation marks to set off all direct quotations, some titles, and words used in a special sense. Place other marks of punctuation in proper relation to quotation marks.

Quotations usually consist of passages borrowed from the written work of others or the direct speech of individuals, especially in dialogue (conversation).

QUOTED WRITING Again Hopkins writes: "Take breath and read it with the ears, as I always wish to be read, and my verse comes all right." And Joyce never tired of explaining how in *Finnegans Wake* "the words the reader sees are not the words that he will hear." [The words and punctuation within quotation marks are exactly as they appear in Marshall McLuhan's *The Gutenberg Galaxy* (Toronto: University of Toronto Press, 1962), p. 104.]

QUOTED SPEECH "Sure enough, I'd like to own a slave," Donna explained. "A compact, push-button robot!" [Within quotation marks are the exactly recorded words of the speaker; the punctuation is supplied by the writer.]

Notice that quotation marks are used in pairs: the first one marks the beginning of the quotation, and the second marks the end. Be careful not to omit or misplace the second one. Remember that the speaker and the verb of saying (such as *Donna explained*) should be outside the quotation marks.

16a

Use double quotation marks to enclose direct (but not indirect) quotations; use single marks to enclose a quotation within a quotation.

> Making fun of Cooper, Mark Twain said, "He saw nearly all things as through a glass eye, darkly." [A directly quoted sentence]

> According to Mark Twain, Cooper "saw nearly all things as through a glass eye, darkly." [Part of a sentence quoted directly]

> Mark Twain said that Cooper saw nearly everything darkly, as if he were looking through a glass eye. [Indirect quotation—no quotation marks]

> She said, "Earl keeps calling my idea 'an impossible dream.'" [A quotation within a quotation]

(1) Long prose quotations (not dialogue) In printed matter, quoted material of ten or more lines is usually set off from the rest of the text by the use of smaller type. Quotation marks are used only if they appear in the original. In typewritten papers, lengthy quoted passages are single-spaced and indented from both sides five spaces. [1] The first line is indented ten spaces when it marks the beginning of a paragraph.

(2) Poetry In both printed matter and typewritten papers, except for very special emphasis, a single line of poetry or less is handled like other short quotations—run in with the text and enclosed in quotation marks. A two-line quotation may be handled in either of two ways. It

---

[1] When quotation marks—instead of the usual smaller type or indention—are used to set off a passage of two or more paragraphs, the quotation marks come before each paragraph and at the end of the last; they do not come at the ends of intermediate paragraphs.

may be run in with the text, with a slash marking the end of the first line. Or it may be set off from the text like longer quotations and quoted line by line exactly as it appears in the original:

```
The poet asks, "If there were dreams to

sell, / What would you buy?"


OR


The poet asks,

        If there were dreams to sell,
        What would you buy?
```

In printed matter, longer passages (sometimes italicized) are usually set off by smaller type. In typewritten papers, they are single-spaced and indented from the left five spaces. The numbers in parentheses indicate the line numbers of the poetry.

```
        Persons who angered the czar were

sent to Siberia. James Mangan describes

in "Siberia" the land and its effect on

the exiled:

        In Siberia's wastes
          Are sands and rocks.
        Nothing blooms of green or soft,
        But the snowpeaks rise aloft
          And the gaunt ice-blocks.

        And the exile there
          Is one with those;
        They are part, and he is part,
        For the sands are in his heart,
          And the killing snows.  (21-30)
```

(3) **Dialogue (conversation)** Written dialogue represents
the directly quoted speech of two or more persons talking together. Standard practice is to write each person's
speech, no matter how short, as a separate paragraph.
Verbs of saying, as well as closely related bits of narrative, are included in the paragraph along with the
speech:

> Through an interpreter, I spoke with a Bedouin man tend-
> ing nearby olive trees.
> "Do you own this land?" I asked him.
> He shook his head. "The land belongs to Allah," he said.
> "What about the trees?" I asked. He had just harvested a
> basket of green olives, and I assumed that at least the trees
> were his.
> "The trees, too, are Allah's," he replied.
> I marveled at this man who seemed unencumbered by
> material considerations . . . or so I was thinking when, as if in
> afterthought, he said, "Of course, I own the *olives!*"
> —HARVEY ARDEN[2]

(4) **Punctuation of dialogue** Commas are used to set off
expressions such as *he said* and *she asked* in quoted
dialogue: see **12d(3)**.

> He said, "Pro football is like nuclear warfare."
> "Pro football," he said, "is like nuclear warfare."
> "Pro football is like nuclear warfare," he said.

When the quoted speech is a question or an exclamation,
the question mark or exclamation point replaces the
usual comma.

> "Pro football?" she asked. "Like nuclear warfare!" she
> added.

[2] From "In Search of Moses" by Harvey Arden, *National Geographic*,
January 1976. Reprinted by permission.

When an expression such as *he said* introduces a quotation of two or more sentences, it is often followed by a colon: see **17d(1)**.

It is as Frank Gifford said: "Pro football is like nuclear warfare. There are no winners, only survivors."

■ **Exercise 1** In the following sentences, change each indirect quotation to a direct quotation and each direct quotation to an indirect one.

1. Doris said that she had a theory about me.
2. Allen announced that he had read "The Sunless Sea."
3. An ardent Weight Watcher, Laura explained that she could eat as much as she wanted—of foods like spinach, rhubarb, and celery!
4. Clyde asked, "Will you go with me to the opera?"
5. Last night Bill said that he thought that Joan's favourite quotation was "Tomorrow belongs to me."

16b

Use quotation marks for minor titles (short stories, essays, short poems, songs, articles from periodicals) and for subdivisions of books.

"The Bucks Start Here" in the May issue of *Maclean's* is a thought-provoking article.

Max Shulman's *Guided Tour of Campus Humor* contains numerous poems and short stories, including "Tears from One Who Didn't Realize How Good He Had It" and "Love Is a Fallacy."

Note: Quotation marks are sometimes used to enclose titles of books, periodicals, and newspapers, but italics are generally preferred: see **10a**.

16c
Words used in a special sense are sometimes enclosed in quotation marks.

Such **"**prophecy**"** is intelligent guessing.
His **"**castle**"** was in reality a cozy little rattrap.

Note: Either quotation marks or italics may be used in definitions such as the following. See also **10d**.

"Puritanical**"** means **"**marked by stern morality.**"**
Puritanical means **"**marked by stern morality.**"**
Puritanical means *marked by stern morality.*

16d
Do not overuse quotation marks.

Do not use quotation marks to enclose the title of your composition: see **8b(4)**. In general, do not enclose in quotation marks common nicknames, bits of humour, technical terms, or trite or well-known expressions. Instead of using slang and colloquialisms within quotation marks, use more formal English. Do not use quotation marks for emphasis.

NEEDLESS PUNCTUATION "Kitty" will not "cop out."
BETTER Kitty will not quit.

■ **Exercise 2** Add correctly placed quotation marks below.

1. In a poem entitled 2001, scientists turn one Einstein into three Einsteins.
2. Here, stoked means fantastically happy on a surfboard.
3. David enjoyed reading the short story A Circle in the Fire.
4. *Learning to Live Without Cigarettes* opens with a chapter entitled Sighting the Target.
5. Bernice replied, my grandfather once said, Never spend your money before you have it.

16e

When using various marks of punctuation with quoted words, phrases, or sentences, follow the conventions of Canadian printers.

(1) Place the period and the comma within the quotation marks.

"Gerald," he said, "let's organize."

Exception:

"Time alone reveals the just" (p. 471).

(2) Place the colon and the semicolon outside the quotation marks.

She spoke of "the protagonists"; yet I remembered only one in "The Tell-Tale Heart": the mad murderer.

(3) Place the dash, the question mark, and the exclamation point within the quotation marks when they apply only to the quoted matter; place them outside when they apply to the whole sentence.

Pilate asked, "What's truth?" [The question mark applies only to the quoted matter.]

What is the meaning of the term "half truth"? [The question mark applies to the whole sentence.]

Why did he ask, "What's truth?" [Both the quoted matter and the sentence as a whole are questions, but a second question mark does not follow the quotation marks.]

They chanted, "Hell no! We won't go!" [The exclamation points apply only to the quoted matter.]

Stop whistling "Frère Jacques"! [The whole sentence, not the song title, is an exclamation.]

■ **Exercise 3** Insert quotation marks where they are needed in the following sentences.

1. Helen's really out of it, I commented to Carl as we sat down to lunch in the cafeteria. Too bad she saw *The Rivals*. She's been acting like Mrs. Malaprop ever since.

2. Oh, cut it out about Helen! Carl snapped as he unrolled his napkin and sorted his silverware. I actually like Helen's bad jokes. Her word play—

3. Please pass the salt, I interrupted.

4. Ignoring my frown, Carl continued: I'll grant you that Helen's puns are usually as old and as bad as the joke ending with Huck'll bury Finn; but here she comes. Start talking about something else.

5. Clearing my throat noisily, I took his advice and said, Perhaps your parents should buy a perambulator.

6. A perambulator! Helen happily took up my cue as she plopped down in the chair near Carl. My parents bought me an eight-cup perambulator for my birthday. Just plug it in, and coffee is ready in four minutes!

7. Aren't you thinking of a percolator? I asked her in mock seriousness. An electric percolator heats quickly.

8. Sure, Helen replied, winking at Carl. It's the same thing as an incubator.

9. You don't mean *incubator!* I said sharply, and then I added a bit of my own nonsense. You mean *incinerator*. After a moment of silence, I yawned and said, Incinerator bombs are really fiery weapons.

10. As though admitting defeat at her own game, Helen grinned and said, with a blasé sigh, Oh, let's forget this game. It's time we had a new aversion.

The Period
and Other Marks

17

Use the period, the question mark, the exclamation point, the colon, the dash, parentheses, brackets, and the slash according to standard practices. (For the use of the hyphen, see **18f**.)

Read the following sentences aloud. Observe how the punctuation in colour serves as signals for intonation (pitch, stress, stops) and helps to reveal sentence meaning:

> Think—just think! Who controls everything?
>
> —SAUL BELLOW

> In *Lady Windermere's Fan* (1892) is this famous line: "I [Lord Darlington] can resist everything except temptation."

> Still he listened . . . and it seemed that all that would speak, in this world, was listening.   —EUDORA WELTY

> No day / night cycle exists there. The inhabitants have no way of measuring time—even years— by our standards.
>
> —JOHN A. KEEL

This section covers the main principles of usage of these punctuation marks in ordinary (rather than technical or special) writing.

The Period

17a

Use the period after declarative and mildly imperative sentences, after indirect questions, and after most abbreviations. Use the ellipsis mark (three spaced periods) to indicate omissions from quoted passages.

(1) Use the period to mark the end of a declarative sentence, a mildly imperative sentence, and an indirect question.

Everyone should drive defensively. [Declarative]

Learn how to drive defensively. [Mild imperative]

She asks *how drivers can cross the city without driving offensively.* [Indirect question]

Note: Courtesy questions, which sometimes replace imperatives (especially in business writing), may be followed by question marks but are usually followed by periods.

Will you write me again if I can be of further service. [Here *will you* is equivalent to the word *please.*]

(2) Use periods with most abbreviations.

Mr.	Mrs.	Ms.	Dr.	Ph. D.	N.H.L.
U.S.	I.R.A.	P.M.	A.M.	etc.	LL.D.

In current usage the period is frequently omitted after many abbreviations, especially for names of organizations and national or international agencies:

UBC	CBC	CTV	CRTC
OPEC	UN	CFL	RCAF

When in doubt about the punctuation of an abbreviation, consult a good dictionary. Dictionaries often list a range of choices (for example, *e.s.t.,* *E.S.T.,* or *EST*).

(3) Use the ellipsis mark (three spaced periods) to indicate the omission of one or more words within a quoted passage.

If a complete sentence precedes the omission (whether or not it was a complete sentence in the original), use a period before the ellipsis mark. It is generally considered unnecessary to use ellipsis periods at the beginning or the end of a quoted passage.

QUOTATION

No man is an island, entire of itself; every man is a piece of the continent, a part of the main. If a clod be washed away by the sea, Europe is the less, as well as if a promontory were, as well as if a manor of thy friend's or of thine own were. Any man's death diminishes me because I am involved in mankind, and therefore never send to know for whom the bell tolls; it tolls for thee. —JOHN DONNE

QUOTATION WITH ELLIPSES

No man is an island . . . every man is a piece of the continent, a part of the main. . . . Any man's death diminishes me because I am involved in mankind. —JOHN DONNE

Note 1: Three spaced periods are sometimes used to signal a pause or a deliberately unfinished statement, especially in dialogue:

Love, like other emotions, has causes . . . and consequences.
—LAWRENCE CASLER

"You watch your step," Wilson said, "and Mrs. Rolt . . . "
"What on earth has Mrs. Rolt got to do with it?"
—GRAHAM GREENE

Note 2: Spaced periods covering a whole line mark the omission of a full paragraph or more in a prose quotation or the omission of a full line or more in a poetry quotation.

All I can say is—I saw it!
. . . .
Impossible! Only—I saw it!
—from "Natural Magic" by ROBERT BROWNING

The Question Mark

17b
Use the question mark after direct (but not indirect) questions.

Who started the riot?

Did he ask *who started the riot*? [The sentence as a whole is a direct question despite the indirect question at the end.]

Did you hear him say, "What right have you to ask about the riot?" [Double direct question followed by a single question mark]

Declarative sentences may contain direct questions:

"Who started the riot?" he asked. [No comma follows the question mark.]

He asked, "Who started the riot?" [No period follows the question mark.]

He told me—did I hear him correctly?—that he started the riot. [Interpolated question]

A declarative or an imperative sentence may be converted into a question:

He started the riot?
Start the riot?

Question marks may be used between the parts of a series:

Did he plan the riot? employ assistants? give the signal to begin? [Question marks cause full stops and emphasize each part. Compare "Did he plan the riot, employ assistants, and give the signal to begin?"]

Note: A question mark within parentheses is used to express the writer's uncertainty as to the correctness of the preceding word, figure, or date:

Chaucer was born in 1340(?) and died in 1400.

Caution: Do not use a comma or a period after a question mark.

"What is an acronym?" asked Marjorie.
Marjorie asked, "What is an acronym?"

The Exclamation Point

17c

Use the exclamation point after an emphatic inter-jection and after a phrase, clause, or sentence to express a high degree of surprise, incredulity, or other strong emotion.

Wow! What a desperation pass!
"Man! We've been conned!" he said.
Act now! Get involved!

Caution 1: Avoid overuse of the exclamation point. Use a comma after mild interjections, and end mildly exclamatory sentences and mild imperatives with a period. See also **17a(1)**.

Oh, don't get involved.
How quiet the lake was.

Caution 2: Do not use a comma or a period after an exclamation point.

"Get off the road!" he yelled.
He yelled, "Get off the road!"

■ **Exercise 1** Illustrate the chief uses of the period, the question mark, and the exclamation point by composing and correctly punctuating brief sentences that meet the descriptions given in the items below.

EXAMPLE
a declarative sentence containing a quoted direct question
"What does fennel taste like?" she asked.

1. a direct question
2. a mild imperative
3. a declarative sentence containing a quoted exclamation
4. a declarative sentence containing an indirect question
5. a declarative sentence containing an interpolated question

The Colon

17d

Use the colon as a formal introducer to call attention to what follows and as a mark of separation in scriptural and time references and in certain titles. Avoid needless colons.

(1) The colon may direct attention to an explanation or summary, an appositive, a series, or a quotation.

> For in her heart of hearts, Isabelle-Marie was like her brother: a creature of innate purity. —MARIE-CLAIRE BLAIS

> Three times he drags me over to the bulletin board to show me his team's enviable record: five straight league titles.
> —HAROLD BRODKEY

> So this was her kingdom: an octagonal house, a roomful of books, and a bear. —MARIAN ENGEL

> Ruth-Anne waits for Dorothy in the cloakroom. She delivers the highest accolade a listener can receive: "I'm sorry I didn't invite you, Dorothy. I didn't know you half as well then as I do now." —SYLVIA FRASER

The colon may separate two main clauses or sentences when the second explains or amplifies the first:

> The scientific value of even the most recent contributions to this literature, however, is seriously qualified: The sole witness to the dream is the dreamer himself.
> —SCIENTIFIC AMERICAN

151

The American conceives of fishing as more than a sport: it is his personal contest against nature. —JOHN STEINBECK

Note: After the colon, quoted sentences regularly begin with a capital, but other sentences (as the preceding examples show) may begin with either a capital letter or a lower-case letter.

(2) Use the colon between figures in scriptural and time references and between titles and subtitles.

The text of the sermon was Matthew 6:10.
At 2:15 A.M. the phone rang.
I had just read *On Being Funny: Woody Allen and Comedy* by Eric Lax.

Note: The colon is also used after the salutation of a business letter and in bibliographical data: see **33b(4)** and **34a(3)**.

(3) Avoid needless colons.

When there is no formal introduction or summarizing word, the colon is usually a needless interruption of the sentence:

NEEDLESS In one day we had: rain, hail, and snow.
BETTER   In one day we had rain, hail, and snow.

NEEDLESS Enrolment was limited in courses such as: Futur-
          istic Fiction and Soap Operas.
BETTER   Enrolment was limited in courses such as Futur-
          istic Fiction and Soap Operas.

■ **Exercise 2** Punctuate the following sentences by adding colons. Put a checkmark after any sentence that needs no change.

1. At 1230 A.M. he was still repeating his favourite quotation "TV is the opiate of the people."
2. The downtown streets are narrow, rough, and junky.
3. Even people in rural areas were not safe many criminals had left the cities and the suburbs.

4. Dr. Morris recommended three magazines *Books in Canada,* the *Malahat Review,* and the *Dalhousie Review.*
5. All their thoughts were centred on liberation.

The Dash

17e

Use the dash to set off a sudden break in thought, an interruption in dialogue, an introductory series, and a parenthetical element for emphasis or clarity.

On the typewriter, the dash is indicated by two hyphens without spacing before, between, or after. In handwriting, the dash is an unbroken line about the length of two or three hyphens.

(1) Use the dash to mark a sudden break in thought or an abrupt change in tone.

A hypocrite is a person who—but who isn't? —DON MARQUIS

And we gathered together all the spades and buckets and towels, empty hampers and bottles, umbrellas and fishfrails, bats and balls and knitting, and went—oh, listen, Dad!—to the Fair in the dusk on the bald seaside field.

—DYLAN THOMAS

These men and women are up for election in November—if they live until then. —STOKELY CARMICHAEL

(2) Use the dash to indicate an unfinished or interrupted statement and faltering speech in dialogue.

"Of course," I come back at her quickly. "I'm well aware of that. I only meant—"
"You must have dozed," she says. —MARGARET LAURENCE

"Would—would you mind telling me—" he said to the guide, much deflated, "what was so stupid about that?"

—KURT VONNEGUT, JR.

(3) Use the dash between an introductory series and the main part of the sentence that explains or amplifies the series.

She was fair-haired, discreet, wanly solicitous— already an old maid.   —ALICE MUNRO

Marble-topped tables, two Singer sewing machines, a big vase of pampas grass— everything was rich and grand.
—CARSON McCULLERS

(4) Use the dash to set off a parenthetical element for emphasis or (if it contains commas) for clarity.

It had been for Nancy— unreservedly loving one day, withdrawn and sullen the next— to pronounce.
—MORDECAI RICHLER

His mother and the lady— whom Moses, had he been pressed, would have identified as Mrs. Pyopyo— hovered about the bed, their attitudes intent.   —ADELE WISEMAN

Isn't it strange how people— not people in universities, like you and me, but just people— keep forgetting that 'crisis' is Greek for 'judgement'.   —ROBERTSON DAVIES

Caution: Use the dash carefully in formal writing. Do not use dashes as awkward substitutes for commas, semicolons, or end marks.

Parentheses

17f

Use parentheses to set off parenthetical, supplementary, or illustrative matter and to enclose figures or letters when used for enumeration within a sentence.

The *Bentely* spent the entire night at it and arrived at Gravely Bay (Port Colbourne on Lake Erie) the following morning.   —EDITH FOWKE

She caters mainly to people who have had (or thought they needed) psychotherapy and who live (or dream of living) in an opulent, sophisticated world. —ROBERT FULFORD

When confronted with ambiguities we are not certain as to how we should interpret (1) single words or phrases, (2) the sense of a sentence, (3) the emphases or accents desired by the writer or speaker, or (4) the significance of a statement. —LIONEL RUBY

Each entry will be judged on the basis of (a) its artistic value, (b) its technical competence, and (c) its originality.

Note: In sentences such as the following, the commas and periods are placed after the closing parenthesis, not before the opening parenthesis.

> According to Herbert J. Muller (1905–1967), instability is one of the conditions of life. [No comma before the first parenthesis]
> Bliss Perry taught at Princeton (although he was there for only seven years).

If a whole sentence beginning with a capital is in parentheses, the period or other end mark is placed just before the closing parenthesis.

> Chance entered into things when a North York controller died. (Controllers are elected borough-wide.) —THE FINANCIAL POST

> Whatever else may be happening, Madame Colette is never *really* unaware, never *really* confused, never *really* afraid. (She can get mighty irritated sometimes.) —STEPHEN KOCH

Punctuation of Parenthetical Matter

Dashes, parentheses, commas—all are used to set off parenthetical matter. Dashes set off parenthetical elements sharply and therefore tend to emphasize them:

> Man's mind is indeed— as Luther said— a factory busy with making idols. —HARVEY COX [See 17e(4).]

Parentheses tend to minimize the importance of the elements they enclose:

> Man's mind is indeed (as Luther said) a factory busy with making idols. [See 17f.]

Commas are the mildest, most commonly used separators and tend to leave the elements they enclose more closely connected with the sentence:

> Man's mind is indeed, as Luther said, a factory busy with making idols. [See 12d.]

Brackets

17g

Use brackets to set off editorial corrections or explanations in quoted matter and, when necessary, to replace parentheses within parentheses.

> Deems Taylor has written: "Not for a single moment did he [Richard Wagner] compromise with what he believed with what he dreamed."
>
> The *Home Herald* printed the mayor's letter, which was an appeal to his "dear fiends [*sic*] and fellow citizens." [A bracketed *sic*—meaning "thus"—tells the reader that the error appears in the original.]
>
> Perhaps Marshall McLuhan's book should be required reading for prospective teachers (*City as Classroom* [Agincourt: The Book Society of Canada Limited, 1977]).

The Slash

17h

Use the slash when needed to indicate options.

> Recent experiments in playing down the importance of grades—including the pass / fail idea—are being scuttled.
> —U.S. NEWS & WORLD REPORT

Equally rare is a first-rate adventure story designed for those who enjoy a smartly told tale that isn't steeped in blood and / or sex. —JUDITH CRIST

We are taught by ubiquitous custom to smile, "How was your Christmas (Easter / Hanukkah / Vacation)?" in the knowledge that no other answer is possible except "Wonderful (Great / Just fine / Good)."

—EDMOND G. ADDEO AND ROBERT E. BURGER

Note: The slash indicates the end of a line of poetry that is run in with the text: see **16a(2)**. The slash is also used to set off phonemic transcriptions (symbols for sounds) in regular writing.

In *ten percent* the /n / may accommodate itself to the following /p /, so that *ten* comes out *tem*.

—DWIGHT BOLINGER

■ **Exercise 3** Correctly punctuate each of the following sentences by supplying commas, dashes, parentheses, brackets, or the slash. Be prepared to explain the reason for all marks you add, especially those you choose for setting off parenthetical matter.

1. Gordon Gibbs or is it his twin brother? plays left tackle.
2. Joseph who is Gordon's brother is a guard on the second string.
3. "Dearest" he began, but his voice broke; he could say no more.
4. This organization needs more of everything more money, brains, initiative.
5. Some of my courses for example, French and biology demand a great deal of work outside the classroom.
6. A penalty clipping cost the Steers fifteen yards.
7. This ridiculous sentence appeared in the school paper: "Because of a personal fool *sic* the Cougars failed to cross the goal line during the last seconds of the game."
8. The word *zipper* once a trademark like Polaroid is now a common noun.

9. Rugged hills, rich valleys, beautiful lakes these things impress the tourist in Connecticut.

10. Some innovations for example the pass fail system did not contribute to grade inflation.

■ **Exercise 4** Punctuate the following sentences (selected and adapted from *Saturday Night*) by supplying appropriate end marks, commas, colons, dashes, and parentheses. Do not use unnecessary punctuation. Be prepared to explain the reason for each mark you add, especially when you have a choice of correct marks (for example, commas, dashes, or parentheses).

1. "People are beginning to discover" said a programme coordinator at the Consumers' Association of Canada "that the old wartime slogan 'Use it up Wear it out Make it do Or do without' is making sense all over again

2. "That's more appropriate" Thomas says when I do it right

3. Nathan Cohen was the only critic who disliked it He found it a "distressingly mediocre amusement"

4. We don't have to ask ourselves "What am I doing" or "Why am I doing it" or the most agonizing question of them all "What will I do if"

5. "If we will only be natural and stop going about in this eternal defensive fear of being ourselves" wrote Frank Underhill in 1951 "we shall discover that we are very like the Americans both in our good qualities and in our bad qualities"

6. He will sacrifice a friendship for an epigram yet he can be hurt and hurt deeply

7. He views Canada's agony with a ruthless not to say triumphant calm even disaster has its charms when you've predicted it

8. The four artists interviewed here are typical of most though by no means all American intellectuals who have come here

SPELLING AND DICTION

Spelling
and Hyphenation

18

Spell every word according to established usage as shown by a good dictionary. Hyphenate words in accordance with current usage.

Spelling

As you write, you use conventional combinations of letters to represent certain spoken sounds. Although pronunciation can serve as a guide to correct spelling, it can also be misleading: the written forms of many words (like *listen, whole*) do not reflect their exact pronunciation; some words that sound alike (*blew, blue*) have different spellings, different meanings; some spellings represent a number of different sounds (like *ough* in *rough, though, through*); and some sounds have various spellings (such as /sh/ in *ocean, ration, tissue*).

In spite of irregularities, there is consistency within the framework of our spelling system. For example, observe the relationship of the long vowel sound to the unpronounced final *e*, and of the short vowel sound to the double consonant.

Long vowel sounds	*Short vowel sounds*
hope, hoped, hoping	hop, hopped, hopping
shine, shined, shining	shin, shinned, shinning
plane, planed, planing	plan, planned, planning
later, filed, write	latter, filled, written

In the following words "soft" *c*, representing /s/, and "soft" *g*, representing /j/, are followed by *e* or *i*. Before letters other than *e* or *i*, the *c* and *g* are "hard" and stand for /k/ and /g/ respectively:

/s/	/k/	/j/	/g/
decide	decade	angel	angle
innocent	significant	changeable	navigable
parcel	particle	margin	bargain
participate	decorate	sergeant	elegant

Notice in the following examples the relationship between *t* and *c*:

absent	absence
accurate	accuracy
different	difference
existent	existence
important	importance
present	presence
prophet	prophecy
significant	significance

Adding a suffix like *-ity, -ation,* or *-ic* can change pronunciation in such a way that the correct spelling of the base word becomes apparent:

moral	morality
similar	similarity
damn	damnation
definite	definition
geography	geographic
symbol	symbolic
dictator	dictatorial
grammar	grammatical

Spelling, of course, is a highly individual problem. You as an individual can improve your spelling by referring frequently to a dictionary and by studying this section, giving special attention to the words you misspell.

18a

Do not allow pronunciation (whether incorrect or correct) to cause you to misspell words by omitting, adding, or transposing letters.

Mispronunciation often leads to the misspelling of such words as those listed below. To avoid difficulties resulting from mispronunciation, pronounce problem words aloud several times, clearly and distinctly, in accordance with the pronunciation shown by a dictionary. Be careful not to omit, add, or transpose any letter or syllable.

athletic	pertain
everything	prescription
disastrous	probable
drowned	recognize
hungry	relevant
library	represent
lightning	umbrella
mischievous	

A word that is difficult to spell may have two correct pronunciations. Of these, one may be a better guide to spelling. For example, the person who correctly leaves out the first /n/ when saying *government* or the first /r/ when saying *surprise* may be more likely to omit the *n* or *r* when writing these words than one who, again correctly, pronounces these sounds.

Each word in the following list has more than one correct pronunciation. If you tend to misspell any of these words because of the way you say them, then depend on your vision and memory to learn their correct spellings.

arctic	literature
boundary	memory
comparable	perhaps
February	sophomore
generally	temperature
hundred	veteran
interest	where
laboratory	

Note: Do not carelessly transpose letters in the following words:

children	prejudice	tragedy
doesn't	relevant	

■ **Exercise 1** All the words below are spelled correctly. Circle those letters that you think may, in time, become totally "silent" or unpronounced. If because of your pronunciation you tend to misspell a word in the list, single it out for special study.

1. quantity
2. candidate
3. studying
4. liberal
5. desperate
6. incidentally
7. misery
8. mathematics
9. identity
10. chocolate

■ **Exercise 2** Make an individual spelling list of words that you tend to misspell (perhaps words like *picture, strength,* or *euthanasia*) because of the way you pronounce them.

18b

Distinguish between words of similar sound and spelling; use the spelling required by the meaning.

Words such as *heroin* and *heroine* or *sole* and *soul* sound alike but have vastly different meanings. Always be sure to choose the right word for your context.

Words Frequently Confused

Following is a list of words that are frequently confused in writing. You may find it helpful to study the list in units of ten word groups at a time, using your dictionary to check the meaning of words not thoroughly familiar to you. Add any words you tend to misspell to your individual spelling list

[I] accent, ascent, assent
accept, except
advice, advise
affect, effect
all ready, already
all together, altogether
allusive, elusive, illusive
altar, alter
bare, bear
born, borne

[II] canvas, canvass
capital, Capitol
choose, chose
cite, sight, site
coarse, course
complement, compliment
conscience, conscious
consul, council, counsel
decent, descent, dissent
desert, dessert

[III] device, devise
dominant, dominate
dyeing, dying
elicit, illicit
fair, fare
formally, formerly
forth, fourth
hear, here
holey, holy, wholly
instance, instants

[IV] its, it's
know, no
later, latter
lead, led
loose, lose
maybe, may be
moral, morale
of, off
passed, past
peace, piece

[V] personal, personnel
plain, plane
pore, pour, poor
precede, proceed
presence, presents
principal, principle
prophecy, prophesy
quiet, quit, quite
right, rite, -wright, write
sense, since

[VI] shone, shown
stationary, stationery
than, then
their, there, they're
to, too, two
weak, week
weather, whether
were, where
who's, whose
your, you're

18c
Distinguish between the prefix and the root. Apply the rules for spelling in adding suffixes.

The root is the base to which the prefix or the suffix is added.

PREFIXES

(1) Add the prefix to the root without doubling or dropping letters.

disappear	**dis**satisfied
unusual	**un**necessary

SUFFIXES

(2) Drop final *e* before a suffix beginning with a vowel but not before a suffix beginning with a consonant.

com*e* ing → coming	care ful → careful
fam*e* ous → famous	entire ly → entirely
valu*e* able → valuable	safe ty → safety

Exceptions: *argument, awful, duly, truly.* Before suffixes beginning with *a* or *o*, the final *e* is retained after "soft" *c* or *g*: *noticeable, courageous.*

(3) If a one-syllable word—or a word accented on the last syllable—ends with a single consonant preceded by a single vowel, double the consonant before adding a suffix beginning with a vowel. Otherwise do not double the consonant.

WORDS HAVING ONLY ONE SYLLABLE:

sad →	sa**dd**er	sa**dd**est	sa**dd**en
bat →	ba**tt**ed	ba**tt**ing	ba**tt**er
drop →	dro**pp**ed	dro**pp**ing	dro**pp**er
plan →	pla**nn**ed	pla**nn**ing	pla**nn**er

COMPARE ba**it**ing, dr**oo**ping, pla**nt**ing

165

WORDS ACCENTED ON THE LAST SYLLABLE:

admit′	→	admitted	admitting	admittance
forget′	→	forgotten	forgetting	forgettable
occur′	→	occurred	occurring	occurrence
refer′	→	referred	referring	BUT ref′erence

COMPARE

| ben′efit | → | benefited | benefiting | |
| dif′fer | → | differed | differing | difference |

(4) Except before -*ing*, final *y* is usually changed to *i*.

happy + ness → happiness   funny + er → funnier
study + es → studies   hurry + ed → hurried
BUT study ing → studying   hurry ing → hurrying

Note: Verbs ending in *y* preceded by a vowel do not change the *y* to form the third person singular of the present tense or the past participle: *array, arrays, arrayed.* Exceptions: *lay, laid; pay, paid; say, said.*

■**Exercise 3** Add the designated prefixes and suffixes in the following items.

1. big + est
2. prefer + ence
3. profit + ed
4. definite + ly
5. un + noticed
6. mis + state + ment
7. im + moral + ity
8. length + en + ing
9. care + less + ly
10. lone + ly + ness

18d

Apply the rules for spelling to avoid confusion of *ei* and *ie*.

When the sound is /ē/, write *ie* (except after *c*, in which case write *ei*).

				(After *c*)	
chief	grief	pierce	wield	ceiling	deceive
field	niece	relief	yield	conceit	perceive

When the sound is other than /ē/, usually write *ei*.

deign	feign	height	neighbour	sleigh	vein
eight	foreign	heir	reign	stein	weigh

Exceptions: *fiery, financier, seize, species, weird.*

■ **Exercise 4** Write out the following words, filling out the blanks with *ei* or *ie*.

1. pr____st
2. dec____t
3. conc____ve
4. fr____ght
5. s____ve

6. p____ce
7. f____nd
8. bes____ge
9. r____gned
10. th____f

18e

As a rule, form the plural of nouns by adding *s* or *es* to the singular.

(1) Form the plural of most nouns by adding *s* to the singular:

boy	→	boys	desk	→	desks	typist	→	typists
safe	→	safes	cupful	→	cupfuls	radio	→	radios

sister-in-law → sisters-in-law [Chief word pluralized]

Note: To form the plural of some nouns ending in *f* or *fe*, change the ending to *ve* before adding the *s*:

shelf → shelves
life → lives
yourself → yourselves

(2) Add *es* to singular nouns ending in *s, ch, sh,* or *x*.

loss	→	losses	porch	→	porches
bush	→	bushes	hoax	→	hoaxes

[Note that each plural above makes an extra syllable.]

167

(3) Add *es* to singular nouns ending in *y* preceded by a consonant, after changing the *y* to *i*.

city → cities
a copy → two copies
comedy → comedies
a reply → the replies

Although *es* is often added to a singular noun ending in *o* preceded by a consonant, usage varies:

embargoes   potatoes   tomatoes   heroes   [-*es* only]
jumbos   pueblos   hypos   old pros   [-*s* only]
mosquitoes   OR   mosquitos
ghettos   OR   ghettoes

For other plurals which are formed irregularly, consult your dictionary.

Note: Add *'s* or *s* alone to form the plurals of letters, abbreviations, figures, symbols, and words used as words: see **15c**.

■ **Exercise 5**   Supply plural forms (including any optional spelling) for the following words, applying **18e**. (If a word is not covered by the rule, use your dictionary.)

1. cliff	6. theory	11. woman	16. industry
2. leaf	7. carafe	12. bath	17. business
3. zero	8. church	13. valley	18. fantasy
4. altar	9. belief	14. height	19. crisis
5. child	10. domino	15. bus	20. wife

A List of Words Frequently Misspelled

Like the words discussed in Section **18b**, the following list may be studied in groups of ten or twenty at a time. Blank spaces are provided at the end of the list for the addition of other words which you may wish to master (possibly those from your special field of interest) or which your instructor may recommend.

1. a lot of
2. acceptable
3. accidentally
4. accommodate
5. accuracy
6. across
7. actually
8. adapt
9. adequately
10. admission

11. adolescent
12. against
13. all right
14. always
15. amateur
16. among
17. amount
18. analyze
19. annually
20. anticipated

21. apparent
22. appearance
23. appropriate
24. article
25. assassination
26. attacked
27. attendance
28. audience
29. author
30. awkward

31. bargain
32. battery
33. beautiful
34. beginning
35. beneficial
36. breath
37. breathe
38. brilliant
39. bureaucracy
40. calendar

41. carefully
42. category
43. character
44. clothes
45. committee
46. compare
47. competition
48. completely
49. condemned
50. controlled

51. controversial
52. convenient
53. couldn't
54. courtesy
55. criticized
56. curiosity
57. dealt
58. decide
59. definitely
60. description

61. develop
62. dining room
63. disappoint
64. discussion
65. disease
66. division
67. during
68. efficient
69. eighth
70. eligible

71. embarrassed
72. environment
73. equipment
74. especially
75. exaggerate
76. excellent
77. expense
78. experience
79. explanation
80. familiar

81. fascinate
82. fascist
83. favourite
84. finally
85. financially
86. forty
87. fulfil
88. governor
89. guaranteed
90. happened

91. height
92. humorous
93. illogical
94. imaginary
95. immediately
96. independent
97. indispensable
98. influence
99. inoculate
100. intelligent

121. nuclear
122. nuisance
123. occasional
124. omission
125. opportunity
126. oppressed
127. optimistic
128. paid
129. parallel
130. paroled

151. psychology
152. pumpkin
153. questionnaire
154. received
155. recommend
156. rehearsal
157. religious
158. repetition
159. representative
160. roommate

101. interruption
102. invariably
103. irresistible
104. jewellery
105. knowledge
106. leisurely
107. length
108. licence
109. luxury
110. magnificent

131. particularly
132. pastime
133. peculiar
134. performance
135. permanent
136. permissible
137. pleasant
138. poison
139. politician
140. pollute

161. sacrifice
162. sandwich
163. satellite
164. scarcity
165. schedule
166. secretary
167. separate
168. sincerely
169. ski, skiing
170. souvenir

111. manoeuvre
112. marriage
113. meant
114. minutes
115. missile
116. mortgage
117. mysterious
118. necessary
119. nickel
120. ninety

141. possession
142. possibly
143. prepare
144. privilege
145. probably
146. procedure
147. proceed
148. professor
149. pronunciation
150. propaganda

171. speak
172. speech
173. statistics
174. straight
175. strategy
176. strength
177. strictly
178. stubbornness
179. suburban
180. succeed

181. summarized	191. tyranny	201. _____
182. swimming	192. unanimous	202. _____
183. technique	193. undoubtedly	203. _____
184. tendency	194. until	204. _____
185. themselves	195. used to	205. _____
186. therefore	196. useful	206. _____
187. thought	197. usually	207. _____
188. together	198. vacuum	208. _____
189. truly	199. visibility	209. _____
190. twelfth	200. vitamin	210. _____

Note: Some words have more than one correct spelling: *judgment/judgement; fulfill/fulfil*. In Canada, British and American spelling often coexist, although British forms are preferred for some words (*travelled* instead of *traveled*) and American forms for others (*criticize* instead of *criticise*). Where choices exist, use the same form within a single piece of writing. See the *Gage Canadian Dictionary* for Canadian spelling preferences.

Hyphenation

18f

Hyphenate words chiefly to express the idea of a unit and to avoid ambiguity. For the division of words at the end of a line, see 8b(9).

Words forming a compound may be written separately, written as one word, or connected by hyphens. For example, three modern dictionaries all have the same listings of these compounds:

> hair stylist   hairsplitter   hair-raiser

Another modern dictionary, however, lists *hairstylist*, not *hair stylist*. Compounding is in such a state of flux that authorities do not always agree.

Writers may coin their own compounds, using hyphenated structures to express ideas:

> The ethic of the Chamber of Commerce, do-it-yourself my-way-is-as-good-as-yours, who-are-you-anyway-to-prefer-brains-to-what-I-have, is artlessly turned into a hippie slogan. —J. BRONOWSKI

(1) Use the hyphen to join two or more words serving as a single adjective before a noun.

the bluish green sea   chocolate covered peanuts
peace loving natives   his know it all glance
the twenty two year old laboratory technician
> [Note the singular form of the noun *year* after the numeral in the hyphenated modifier.]

Notice that in the examples below the modifiers after the noun are not hyphenated:

> The sea was bluish green.
> The peanuts, which were chocolate covered, tasted stale.
> The laboratory technician was twenty-two years old.
> [Numbers like *twenty-two* are hyphenated wherever they appear in a sentence.]

The hyphen is also omitted after an adverb ending in -*ly* in phrases such as the following:

> a hopelessly lost cause
> a frequently used example

Note: "Suspension" hyphens may be used in such series as the following:

> two , three , and four hour classes

(2) Use the hyphen with compound numbers from twenty-one to ninety-nine and with fractions.

twenty two, forty five, ninety eight
one half, two thirds, nine tenths

Note: Some writers omit the hyphen in fractions used as nouns.

> *Two thirds* of the voters endorsed the amendment.
> [*Two thirds* is the subject, not an adjective. Compare
> "A *two thirds* vote is needed."]

(3) Use the hyphen to avoid ambiguity or an awkward combination of letters or syllables between prefix and root or suffix and root.

> His *re creation* of the setting was perfect. [BUT Fishing is
> good *recreation.*]
> Her father owns a small animal hospital. [Compare "Her
> father owns a small animal hospital."]
> semi independent, shell like [BUT semifluid, childlike]

(4) The hyphen is generally used with prefixes like *ex-* ("former"), *self-, all-,* and *great-;* between a prefix and a proper name; and with the suffix *-elect.*

> ex judge, self made, all purpose, great aunt, pro French,
> mayor elect

■ **Exercise 6** Convert the following word groups according to the pattern of the examples.

EXAMPLES

| an initiation lasting two months | *a two-month initiation* |
| ideas that shake the world | *world-shaking ideas* |

1. an apartment with six rooms
2. examinations that exhaust the mind
3. fingers stained with nicotine
4. a voter who is eighteen years old
5. shoppers who are budget minded
6. tents costing a hundred dollars
7. peace talks that last all night
8. a program that trains teachers
9. a hitchhiker who was waving a flag
10. ponds covered with lilies

Good Use— Glossary

19

Use a good dictionary to help you select the words that express your ideas exactly.

You can find valuable information about words by referring to a good dictionary, such as one of the following:

The American Heritage Dictionary
The Concise Oxford Dictionary
Gage Canadian Dictionary
The Random House Dictionary
Webster's New Collegiate Dictionary
Webster's New World Dictionary

Occasionally you may need to refer to an unabridged or special dictionary: see the two lists on page 357.

19a
Use a good dictionary intelligently.

Intelligent use of a dictionary requires some understanding of its plan and of the special abbreviations given in the introductory matter. Knowing how the dictionary arranges and presents material will enable you to interpret much of the information provided in its entries.

Below are two sample dictionary entries.[1] First, note the various definitions of *empty* as an adjective, as a transitive verb, as an intransitive verb, as a noun, and as part of an idiomatic phrase (with *of*). Next, observe the examples of usage. Finally, note the various other kinds of information (labelled in colour) that the dictionary provides.

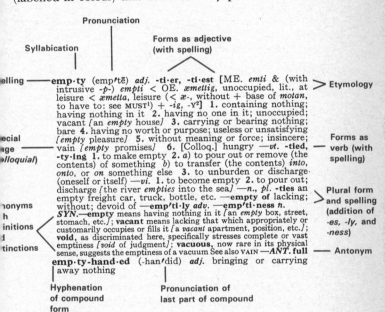

Pronunciation

Forms as adjective (with spelling)

Syllabication

elling —— **emp·ty** (emp′tē) *adj.* **-ti·er, -ti·est** [ME. *emti* & (with intrusive *-p-*) *empti* < OE. *æmettig*, unoccupied, lit., at leisure < *æmetta*, leisure (< *æ-*, without + base of *motan*, to have to: see MUST[1]) + *-ig, -Y*[2]] **1.** containing nothing; having nothing in it **2.** having no one in it; unoccupied; vacant *[an empty house]* **3.** carrying or bearing nothing; bare **4.** having no worth or purpose; useless or unsatisfying *[empty pleasure]* **5.** without meaning or force; insincere; vain *[empty promises]* **6.** [Colloq.] hungry —*vt.* **-tied, -ty·ing 1.** to make empty **2.** *a)* to pour out or remove (the contents) of something *b)* to transfer (the contents) *into, onto,* or *on* something else **3.** to unburden or discharge (oneself or itself) —*vi.* **1.** to become empty **2.** to pour out; discharge *[the river empties into the sea]* —*n., pl.* **-ties** an empty freight car, truck, bottle, etc. —**empty of** lacking; without; devoid of —**emp′ti·ly** *adv.* —**emp′ti·ness** *n.* **SYN.**—**empty** means having nothing in it *[an empty box, street, stomach, etc.]*; **vacant** means lacking that which appropriately or customarily occupies or fills it *[a vacant apartment, position, etc.]*; **void,** as discriminated here, specifically stresses complete or vast emptiness *[void of judgment]*; **vacuous,** now rare in its physical sense, suggests the emptiness of a vacuum See also VAIN —**ANT. full** **emp·ty-hand·ed** (-han′did) *adj.* bringing or carrying away nothing

> Etymology

Forms as verb (with spelling)

Plural form and spelling (addition of *-es, -ly,* and *-ness*)

Antonym

ecial
age
olloquial)

nonyms
h
initions
d
tinctions

Hyphenation of compound form

Pronunciation of last part of compound

(1) Spelling, syllabication, and pronunciation As a writer, use a good dictionary not only to check spelling but also to find where words may be divided at the end of a line: see **8b(9)**. As a speaker, check the pronunciation of unfamiliar words in your dictionary. Keys to the

---

[1] With permission. From *Webster's New World Dictionary,* Second College Edition. Copyright © 1976 by William Collins + World Publishing Co., Inc.

sound symbols are at the bottom of each two-page
spread as well as in the introductory matter at the front
of the dictionary. A primary stress mark (′) normally
follows the syllable that is most heavily accented. Secondary stress marks follow lightly accented syllables.

■ **Exercise 1**   With the aid of your dictionary, write out the
following words using sound symbols and stress marks to indicate the correct pronunciation (or a correct one if options are
given).

(1) harass,   (2) incongruous,   (3) performance,   (4) *Zeitgeist,*
(5) pica,   (6) interest,   (7) egalitarian,   (8) surveillance,
(9) halogen, (10) oceanography.

(2) Parts of speech and inflected forms   Your dictionary
provides labels indicating the possible uses of words in
sentences—for instance, *adj.* (adjective), *adv.* (adverb),
v.t. (verb, transitive). It also lists ways that given nouns,
verbs, and modifiers change form to indicate number,
tense, or comparison or to serve as another part of
speech (for example, under *repress, v.t.,* may appear
repressible, adj.).

■ **Exercise 2**   With the aid of your dictionary, classify each of
the following words as a verb (transitive or intransitive), a noun,
an adjective, an adverb, a preposition, or a conjunction. Give the
principal parts of each verb, the plural (or plurals) of each noun,
and the comparative and superlative of each adjective and adverb. (Note that some words are used as two or more parts of
speech.)

(1) permit, (2) lonely, (3) sweet-talk, (4) tattoo, (5) subtle,
(6) for, (7) late, (8) bring, (9) crisis, (10) fine.

(3) Definitions and examples of usage   Observe how
your dictionary arranges the definitions of a word:
whether the most common meaning is given first or
whether the definitions are listed in historical order.

Notice also that an illustration of the usage of a word often clarifies a definition.

■ **Exercise 3** Study the definitions of any five of the following pairs of words, paying special attention to any examples of usage in your dictionary; then write sentences to illustrate the shades of difference in meaning.

1. rot—putrefy
2. sensual—sensuous
3. viable—practicable
4. yukking—guffawing
5. mercy—clemency
6. charisma—charm
7. infamous—notorious
8. free—liberate
9. jaded—a jade
10. necrophile—vampire

(4) Synonyms and antonyms Lists and discussions of synonyms in dictionaries often help to clarify the meaning of closely related words. By studying the connotations and denotations of words with similar meanings, you will find that you are able to choose your words more exactly and to convey more subtle shades of meaning. Lists of antonyms can help you to find a word that is the direct opposite of another in meaning. (For more complete lists of synonyms, antonyms, related and contrasted words, and idiomatic phrases, refer to a special dictionary such as *Roget's Thesaurus* [London: Longman, 1962].)

■ **Exercise 4** With the aid of your dictionary or thesaurus, list two synonyms and one antonym for each of the following words: (1) hatred, (2) pleasure, (3) false, (4) oppose, (5) stingy.

(5) Origin: development of the language In most dictionaries the origin of the word—also called its *derivation* or *etymology*—is shown in square brackets. For example, after *expel* might be this information: "[< L *expellere* < *ex-* out + *pellere* to drive, thrust]." This means that *expel* is derived from (<) the Latin (L) word *expellere*, which is made up of *ex-*, meaning "out," and the combining form *pellere*, meaning "to drive or thrust." Breaking up a word, when possible, into prefix (and also suffix, if any) and combining form, as in the case of *expel*, will often help to get at the basic meaning of a word.

	Prefix		Combining form		Suffix	
dependent	*de-* down	+	*pendere* to hang	+	*-ent* one who	
intercede	*inter-* between	+	*cedere* to pass			
preference	*pre-* before	+	*ferre* to carry	+	*-ence* state of	
transmit	*trans-* across	+	*mittere* to send			

The bracketed information given by a good dictionary is especially rich in meaning when considered in relation to the historical development of our language. English is one of the Indo-European (IE)[2] languages, a group of languages apparently derived from a common source. Within this group of languages, many of the more familiar words are remarkably alike. Our word *mother,* for example, is *mater* in Latin (L), *meter* in Greek (Gk.), and *matar* in ancient Persian and in the Sanskrit (Skt.) of India. Words in different languages that apparently descend from a common parent language are called *cognates.* The large number of cognates and the many correspondences in sound and structure in most of the languages of Europe and some languages of Asia indicate that they are derived from the common language that linguists call Indo-European, which it is believed was spoken in parts of Europe about five thousand years ago. By the opening of the Christian era the speakers of this language had spread over most of Europe and as far

---

[2] The parenthetical abbreviations for languages here and on the next few pages are those commonly used in bracketed derivations in dictionaries.

east as India, and the original Indo-European had developed into eight or nine language families. Of these, the chief ones that influenced English were the Hellenic (Greek) group on the eastern Mediterranean, the Italic (Latin) on the central and western Mediterranean, and the Germanic in northwestern Europe. English is descended from the Germanic.

Two thousand years ago the Hellenic, the Italic, and the Germanic branches of Indo-European each comprised a more or less unified language group. After the fall of the Roman Empire in the fifth century, the several Latin-speaking divisions developed independently into the modern Romance languages, chief of which are Italian, French, and Spanish. Long before the fall of Rome the Germanic group was breaking up into three families: (1) East Germanic, represented by the Goths, who were to play a large part in the history of the last century of the Roman Empire before losing themselves in its ruins; (2) North Germanic, or Old Norse (ON), from which we have modern Danish (Dan.) and Swedish (Sw.), Norwegian (Norw.) and Icelandic (Icel.); and (3) West Germanic, the direct ancestor of English, Dutch (Du.), and German (Ger.).

The English language may be said to have begun about the middle of the fifth century, when the West Germanic Angles, Saxons, and Jutes began the conquest of what is now England and either absorbed or drove out the Celtic-speaking inhabitants. (Celtic—from which Scots Gaelic, Irish Gaelic, Welsh, and other languages later developed—is another member of the Indo-European family.) The next six or seven hundred years are known as the Old English (OE) or Anglo-Saxon (AS) period of the English language. The fifty or sixty thousand words then in the language were chiefly Anglo-Saxon, with a small mixture of Old Norse words as a result of the Danish (Viking) conquests of England beginning in the eighth century. But the Old Norse words were so much like the Anglo-Saxon that they cannot always be distinguished.

The transitional period from Old English to Modern English—about 1100 to 1500—is known as Middle English (ME). The Norman Conquest began in 1066. The Normans, or "Northmen," had settled in northern France during the Viking invasions and had adopted Old French (OF) in place of their native Old Norse. Then, crossing over to England by the thousands, they made French the language of the king's court in London and of the ruling classes—both French and English—throughout the land, while the masses continued to speak English. Only toward the end of the fifteenth century did English become once more the common language of all classes. But the language that emerged at that time had lost most of its Anglo-Saxon inflections and had taken on thousands of French words (derived originally from Latin). Nonetheless, it was still basically English, not French, in its structure.

The marked and steady development of the English language (until it was partly stabilized by printing, which was introduced in London in 1476) is suggested by the following passages, two from Old English and two from Middle English.

Hē ǣrst gescēop   eorðan bearnum
He first created   *for earth's children*

heofon tō hrōfe,   hālig scippend.
heaven as a roof,   *holy creator.*

> From the "Hymn of Cædmon"
> (middle of the Old English period)

Ēalā, hū lēas and hū unwrest is þysses middan-eardes wēla.
Alas! how false and how unstable is this midworld's weal!

Sē þe wæs ǣrur rīce cyng and maniges landes hlāford,
He that was before powerful king and of many lands lord,

hē næfde þā ealles landes būton seofon fōt mæl.
he had not then of all land but seven foot space.

From the *Anglo-Saxon Chronicle*, A.D. 1087
(end of the Old English period)

A knight ther was, and that a worthy man,
That fro the tyme that he first bigan
To ryden out, he loved chivalrye,
Trouthe and honour, fredom and curteisye.

From Chaucer's Prologue to the
Canterbury Tales, about 1385

Thenne within two yeres king Uther felle seke of a grete
maladye. And in the meane whyle hys enemyes usurped
upon hym, and dyd a grete bat"ta"ylle upon his men, and slewe
many of his peple.

From Sir Thomas Malory's *Morte d'Arthur*,
printed 1485

A striking feature of Modern English (that is, English
since 1500) is its immense vocabulary. As already noted,
Old English used some fifty or sixty thousand words, very
largely native Anglo-Saxon; Middle English used perhaps a hundred thousand words, many taken through the
French from Latin and others taken directly from Latin;
and unabridged dictionaries today list over four times as
many. To make up this tremendous word hoard, we have
borrowed most heavily from Latin, but we have drawn
some words from almost every known language. English
writers of the sixteenth century were especially eager to
interlace their works with words from Latin authors.
And, as the English pushed out to colonize and to trade
in many parts of the globe, they brought home new
words as well as goods. Modern science and technology
have drawn heavily from the Greek. As a result of all
this borrowing, English has become the richest, most
cosmopolitan of all languages.

In the process of enlarging our vocabulary we have lost most of our original Anglo-Saxon words. But those that are left make up the most familiar, most useful part of our vocabulary. Practically all our simple verbs, our articles, conjunctions, prepositions, and pronouns are native Anglo-Saxon; and so are many of our familiar nouns, adjectives, and adverbs. Every speaker and writer uses these native words over and over, much more frequently than the borrowed words. Indeed, if every word is counted every time it is used, the percentage of native words runs very high—usually between 70 and 90 per cent. Milton's percentage was 81, Tennyson's 88, Shakespeare's about 90, and that of the King James Bible about 94. English has been enriched by its extensive borrowings without losing its individuality; it is still fundamentally the *English* language.

■ **Exercise 5**   With the aid of your dictionary, give the etymology of each of the following words:

1. laser
2. Teflon
3. ecology
4. OK
5. helicopter
6. bacitracin
7. geriatrics
8. chauvinism
9. sputnik
10. polyester

(6) Special usage labels   Dictionaries ordinarily carry no usage labels for the bulk of English words. Unlabelled, or general, words range from the very learned words appropriate in the most formal situations to the simple words used every day in both formal and informal situations.

Most dictionaries, however, provide a variety of special usage labels for words or for particular definitions of words. These labels indicate varieties of usage that differ from the general. Below is a sampling of labelled definitions, each one from two or more college dictionaries.

unalienable	*Archaic, Obsolete*	inalienable
lift	*Informal, Colloquial*	plagiarize
nowheres	*Nonstandard, Dialect, Colloquial*	not anywhere, nowhere
stink	*Slang*	to be of low quality

As the examples above indicate, the classification of words is often difficult and controversial because our language is constantly changing. Good writers try to choose the words, whatever their labels, that exactly fit the audience and the occasion, informal or formal.

■ **Exercise 6** Classify the following words and phrases according to the usage labels in your dictionary. If a word has no special usage label, classify it as *General.*

1. tote
2. tote bag
3. whopper
4. twit
5. unto
6. mugger
7. pogey
8. irregardless
9. tickle
10. live it up

19b

Avoid informal words in formal writing.

Words or expressions labelled *Informal* or *Colloquial* in college dictionaries are standard English and are used by speakers and writers every day. These words are thus appropriate in informal writing, especially in dialogue. But informal words or expressions are usually inappropriate in formal expository compositions. In formal writing, use instead the general English vocabulary, the unlabelled words in your dictionary.

INFORMAL   In class the teacher gave a definition of *polyunsaturated,* but I didn't **get it.**

GENERAL   In class the teacher gave a definition of *polyunsaturated,* but I didn't **understand it.**

As a rule, contractions are avoided in formal writing. Contracted forms like *won't, there's,* or *she'd* are normally written out: *will not, there is* or *there has, she would* or *she had.*

■ **Exercise 7**   Make a list of ten words that you would consider informal in your writing. Then check your dictionary to see how or if each definition you have in mind is labelled.

19c

Use slang and jargon only when appropriate to the audience.

Slang words, including certain coinages and figures of speech, are variously considered as breezy, racy, extremely informal, nonstandard, facetious, taboo, offbeat—and vigorous. On occasion, slang can be used effectively, even in formal writing. Below is an example of the effective use of the word *spiels,* still labelled by dictionaries as *Slang:*

> Here comes election year. Here come the hopefuls, the conventions, the candidates, the spiels, the postures, the press releases, and the TV performances. Here comes the year of the hoopla.   —JOHN CIARDI

A few years ago the word *hoopla* was also generally considered as slang, but now dictionaries disagree: one classifies this word *Standard* (unlabelled); another, *Colloquial (Informal);* still another, *Slang.* Like *hoopla,* words such as *spiel, uptight* (or *up-tight* or *up tight*), *paddy wagon, raunchy,* and *party pooper* have a particularly vivid quality; they soon may join former slang words such as *sham* and *mob* as part of the general English vocabulary.

But much slang is trite, tasteless, and inexact. For instance, when used to describe almost anything approved of, *neat* becomes inexact, flat.

Like some slang words, trade language or professional jargon is confusing and sometimes meaningless outside the special field in which it originated. One type of confusing jargon is sometimes found in bureaucratic writing.

> JARGON All personnel functioning in the capacity of clerks will indicate that they have had opportunity to take due cognizance of this notice by transmitting signed acknowledgment of receipt of same.
>
> GENERAL All clerks will acknowledge in writing the receipt of this notice.

Words that are considered jargon in general usage may have precise—and unique—meanings in specialized technical, business, or professional fields, and therefore serve a necessary function.

Caution: As you avoid the use of ineffective slang in your writing, remember that many of the most vivid short words in our language are general, standard words. Certain long words can be as inexact and as drab as trite slang.

■ **Exercise 8** Replace the italicized words in the following sentences with more exact words or specific phrases.

1. The Grand Canyon is really *neat*.
2. Lately the weather has been *lousy* on weekends.
3. Her coiffure certainly looked *groovy*.
4. The coffee at that *joint* is *crummy*.

19d

Use regional words only when appropriate to the audience.

Regional, or *dialectal,* words (also called *localisms* or *provincialisms*) should normally be avoided in speaking and writing outside the region where they are current. Speakers and writers may, however, safely use regional words known to the audience they are addressing.

REGIONAL   Monty was *fixing to* feed his steak to the *critter.*
GENERAL   Monty was *about to* feed his steak to the *dog.* [OR *animal* OR *creature*]

19e
Avoid nonstandard words and usages.

Words and expressions labelled by dictionaries as *Nonstandard* or *Illiterate* should be avoided in most writing and speaking. Many common illiteracies are not listed in college dictionaries.

NONSTANDARD   *They's* no use asking them.
STANDARD   *There's* no use asking them.

19f
Avoid archaic and obsolete words.

All dictionaries list words (and meanings for words) that have long since passed out of general use. Such words as *ort* (fragment of food) and *yestreen* (last evening) are still found in dictionaries because these words, once the standard vocabulary of great authors, occur in our older literature and must be defined for the modern reader.

A number of modern "mistakes in grammar" are in reality obsolete or archaic words still in use, such as *worser* (for *worse*) or *holp* (for *helped*).

OBSOLETE   You want to know where Wishbone Corner is? Well, this is *hit!*
STANDARD   You want to know where Wishbone Corner is? Well, this is *it!*

19g
Use technical words only when appropriate to the audience.

When you are writing for the general reader, avoid all unnecessary technical language. Since the ideal of good writing is to make one's thought clear to as many people as possible, the careful writer will not describe an apple tree as a *Malus pumila* or a high fever as *hyperpyrexia*. (Of course, technical language, with its greater precision, is highly desirable when one is addressing an audience that can understand it, as when a physician addresses a group of physicians.)

19h
Avoid overwriting, an ornate or flowery style. Do not needlessly combine distracting sounds.

Overwriting, as well as the combination of distracting sounds, calls attention to words rather than to ideas. Such writing is generally fuzzy and repetitious, or carelessly indifferent to the importance of sound and its relationship to meaning.

ORNATE	Since the halcyon days of my early youth I have always anticipated with eagerness and pleasure the exciting vistas of distant climes and mysterious horizons.
BETTER	Since childhood I have looked forward to seeing the world.
AWKWARD	The use of catalytic converters is just one contribution to the solution of the problem of air pollution.
BETTER	The use of catalytic converters is just one way to help solve the problem of air pollution.

Equally unpleasing to the average reader is the overuse o
alliteration (repetition of the same consonant sound), as ir
"Some people *sh*un the *seash*ore."

■ **Exercise 9** Rewrite the following sentences, using simple
formal, straightforward English.[3]

1. It is obvious from the difference in elevation with relation tc
   the short depth of the property that the contour is such as tc
   preclude any reasonable developmental potential for active
   recreation.

2. Verbal contact with Mr. Blank regarding the attached noti
   fication of promotion has elicited the attached representa
   tion intimating that he prefers to decline the assignment

3. Voucherable expenditures necessary to provide adequate
   dental treatment required as adjunct to medical treatmen
   being rendered a pay patient in in-patient status may be
   incurred as required at the expense of the Public Health
   Service.

4. I hereby give and convey to you, all and singular, my estate
   and interests, right, title, claim and advantages of and ir
   said orange, together with all rind, juice, pulp and pits, anc
   all rights and advantages therein.

5. I prefer an abbreviated phraseology, distinguished for it:
   lucidity.

6. Realization has grown that the curriculum or the experi
   ences of learners change and improve only as those who are
   most directly involved examine their goals, improve thei
   understandings and increase their skill in performing the
   tasks necessary to reach newly defined goals.

---

[3] From *Power of Words* by Stuart Chase. Reprinted by permission c
Harcourt Brace Jovanovich, Inc., and Ann Watkins, Inc.

Glossary of Usage

19i
Consult the following glossary to determine the standing of a word or phrase and its appropriateness to your purpose.

The entries in the following glossary are authoritative only to the extent that they describe current usage. They do not duplicate the descriptions in any one dictionary, but justification for each usage label can usually be found in at least two of the leading dictionaries.

For a discussion of the special usage labels used in dictionaries, see **19a(6)**. The following labels appear most frequently in this glossary:

General
> Words in the standard English vocabulary, listed in dictionaries without special usage labels and appropriate in both formal and informal writing and speaking (for example, *acquaintance, associate, friend*).

Informal
> Words or expressions labelled *Informal* or *Colloquial* in dictionaries—words widely used by educated as well as uneducated writers and speakers but not appropriate in a formal context (for example, *buddy, pal*). See also **19b**

Standard
> All general and informal words or expressions (for example, *acquaintance, associate, buddy, friend, pal*).

Nonstandard
> Words or expressions labelled in dictionaries as *Archaic, Illiterate, Nonstandard, Obsolete, Slang,* or *Substandard*—words not considered a part of the standard English vocabulary (for example, *sidekick*). See also **19c, e,** and **f**.

Of course, the following glossary can include only a few of the words likely to cause difficulty. If the word you are looking for is not included, or if you need more information about any word in the list, consult a good college dictionary.

a, an Use *a* before a consonant sound, *an* before a vowel sound.

> *a* heavy load, *a* nap, *a* uniform, *a* one-man show
> *an* honest boy, *an* ape, *an* umpire, *an* only child

accept, except The verb *accept* means "to receive." As a preposition, *except* means "other than or but."

> All the boys *accept* John as their leader.
> All the boys *except* John are leaders.

accidentally, incidentally When using these adverbs, remember that *-ly* is added to the adjective forms *accidental* and *incidental*, not to the noun forms *accident* and *incident*.

> NONSTANDARD   Mr. Kent *accidently* overheard the report.
> STANDARD   Mr. Kent *accidentally* overheard the report.

advice, advise Pronounced and spelled differently, *advice* is a noun, *advise* a verb.

> Patients should follow their doctors' *advice*.
> Patients should do what their doctors *advise*.

affect, effect *Affect* is usually a verb meaning "to influence." The verb *effect* means "to bring about, to achieve"; the noun *effect* means "the result."

> The reforms *affected* many citizens.
> The citizens *effected* a few reforms.
> She said that wars *affect* the economy.
> She stressed the *effect* of wars on the economy.

aggravate Informally *aggravate* means "to provoke or exasperate, to arouse to anger." In general usage it means "to make worse" or "to intensify."

> INFORMAL   Undisciplined children *aggravate* baby sitters.
> GENERAL   Lack of water *aggravated* the suffering.

ain't   A nonstandard contraction avoided by most writers, unless used for humorous effect.

alibi   Used informally as a noun meaning "excuse" or as a verb meaning "to make an excuse." Inappropriate in general writing except in a legal context.

> INFORMAL   He gave his usual *alibi*.   Don't *alibi*.
> GENERAL   He gave his usual *excuse*.   Don't *make excuses*.

all right, alright   *Alright* is still a questionable spelling of *all right*.

allusion, illusion   Do not confuse *allusion*, "an indirect reference," with *illusion*, "an unreal image or false impression."

> Timothy made an *allusion* to the Trojans.
> The Trojan Horse was no optical *illusion*.

almost, most   *Most* is used informally as a substitute for *almost*.

> INFORMAL   *Most* all referees strive to be fair.
> GENERAL   *Almost* all referees strive to be fair.

a lot   Sometimes misspelled as *alot*.

already, all ready   *Already* means "before or by the time specified." *All ready* means "completely prepared."

> The theatre was *already* full by seven o'clock.
> The cast was *all ready* for the curtain call.

altogether, all together   *Altogether* means "wholly, thoroughly." *All together* means "in a group."

> That type of rule is *altogether* unnecessary.
> They were *all together* in the lobby.

A.M., P.M. (OR **a.m., p.m.**)   Use only with figures.

> The auction begins at 8:30 A.M. and ends at 4:00 P.M. [*Compare* "The auction begins at *half-past eight in the morning* and ends at *four o'clock in the afternoon*."]

among, between   *Among* always implies more than two, a group; *between* literally implies only two. *Between*, however, is now often used for three or more items when each is regarded individually.

What honour was there *among* the forty thieves?

What is the difference *between* a thief and a robber?

The difference *between* the three girls was so slight that they might have been triplets.

amount, number   *Amount* refers to things in bulk or mass; *number* refers to the countable.

A large *amount* of rice is consumed annually.

A large *number* of disgruntled workers barred the entrance.

an, a   See **a, an**.

and etc.   See **etc.**

anyone, any one   *Anyone* means "any person at all." *Any one* refers to a specific person or thing in a group. Similar forms are *everyone, every one; someone, some one*.

Anyone can wax a floor.

Any one of those men can wax a floor.

anyways, anywheres   Dialectal or colloquial for *anyway, anywhere*.

as   In your formal writing avoid using *as* instead of *that* or *whether*. Do not use *as* as a substitute for *because, for, since, which, while,* or *who*.

INFORMAL   I do not know *as* I should go.

GENERAL   I do not know *whether* I should go.

AMBIGUOUS   *As* it was snowing, we played cards.

CLEAR   *While* it was snowing, we played cards.

OR   *Because* it was snowing, we played cards.

See also **like, as, as if**.

at   Although *from* after *where* is standard, *at* after *where* is not standard.

NONSTANDARD   Where did the Brownings live at?

STANDARD   Where did the Brownings live?

awhile, a while   Distinguish between the adverb *awhile* and the article and noun *a while*.

Rest *awhile* before you leave.

Rest for *a while* before you leave.

be sure and Formal English requires *be sure to* in such sentences as "*Be sure to* consult a lawyer."

because See **reason . . . because**.

being as, being that Nonstandard for *since, because*.

beside, besides When meaning "except," *beside* and *besides* are interchangeable prepositions. Distinguish, however, between *beside* meaning "by the side of" and *besides* meaning "in addition to."

> I sat *beside* the window.
> Herbert has income *besides* his salary.

between, among See **among, between**.

bug Informal for *germ* or *defect;* slang for *annoy*.

> INFORMAL   The new car had a few *bugs*.
> GENERAL   The new car had a few *defects*.
> SLANG   Tailgating *bugs* me.
> GENERAL   Tailgating *annoys* me.

burst, bursted, bust, busted *Burst* is the standard verb form. *Bursted* is not a standard past form. *Bust* and *busted* are still considered slang.

but what Informal for *that* in negative expressions.

> INFORMAL   Brad has no doubt *but what* the Lions will win.
> GENERAL   Brad has no doubt *that* the Lions will win.

can't hardly A double negative in implication. Use *can hardly*.

case, line Often used in wordy expressions.

> WORDY   In the case of Jones there were good intentions.
> CONCISE   Jones had good intentions.
> WORDY   Buy something in the line of fruit.
> CONCISE   Buy some fruit.

complementary, complimentary Do not confuse *complementary*, "completing" or "supplying needs," with *complimentary*, "expressing praise" or "given free."

> His talents and hers are *complementary*.
> He made several *complimentary* remarks.

considerable Used generally as an adjective, informally as a noun. Nonstandard as an adverb.

NONSTANDARD　Prices have dropped considerable.

INFORMAL　　*Considerable* has been donated to the civic fund.

GENERAL　　A *considerable* amount has been donated to the civic fund.

contact Frequently overused for more exact words or phrases such as *ask, consult, inform, query, talk with, telephone, write to.*

could of Nonstandard for *could have.*

deal Used informally to mean "business transaction." Frequently overworked in place of more exact words such as *sale, agreement, plan, secret agreement.*

different from In formal usage the preferred preposition after *different* is *from.* But the more informal *different than* is accepted by many writers if the expression is followed by a clause.

The Stoic philosophy is *different from* the Epicurean.
The outcome is *different from* what I expected.　OR　The outcome is *different than* I expected.

differ from, differ with *Differ from* means "to stand apart because of unlikeness." *Differ with* means "to disagree."

done Standard as an adjective and as the past participle of the verb *do.* Nonstandard as an adverb and as a substitute for *did.*

NONSTANDARD　The bread is done sold.

STANDARD　　　The bread is *already* sold.　OR
　　　　　　　The bread is *done.*

NONSTANDARD　Do the police know who done it?

STANDARD　　　Do they know who *did* it?　OR
　　　　　　　Who *has done* it?

don't A contraction of *do not* rather than of *does not.*

NONSTANDARD　He don't smoke. (He do not smoke.)

STANDARD　　　He *doesn't* smoke. (He *does not* smoke.)

STANDARD　　　They *don't* smoke. (They *do not* smoke.)

each and every Redundant.

effect, affect   See **affect, effect.**

either, neither   Used to refer to one or the other of two. As subjects, both words are regularly singular.

> Let's serve *either* a salad *or* a dessert.
> *Neither* of the paintings *is* finished.

eminent, imminent, immanent   *Eminent* means "distinguished." *Imminent* means "about to happen, threatening" *Immanent* means "indwelling" or "invading all creation"

> She is an *eminent* scientist.
> Bankruptcy seemed *imminent*.
> We discussed Hardy's concept of the *Immanent* Will.

enthuse, enthused   *Enthuse* is informal as a verb meaning "to show enthusiasm." *Enthused* is informal for *enthusiastic*.

> INFORMAL   We were all *enthused* about the new club.
> GENERAL   We were all *enthusiastic* about the new club.

etc.   An abbreviation of the Latin *et* (meaning "and") *cetera* (meaning "other things"). Use *etc.* sparingly. Do not place *and* before *etc.*, for then the *and* becomes redundant.

everyone, every one   See **anyone, any one.**

except, accept   See **accept, except.**

expect   Informal when used for *suppose* or *think*.

> INFORMAL   I *expect* James voted yesterday.
> GENERAL   I *suppose* James voted yesterday.

farther, further   These words are often used interchangeably to express geographic distance, although some writers prefer *farther*. *Further* is used to express additional time, degree, or quantity.

> Winnipeg is *farther* south than Edmonton.
> Will there be *further* improvements in city government?

fewer, less   Informally used interchangeably. Formally, *fewer* refers to number, to the countable; *less* refers to value, degree, or amount.

> Women now spend *fewer* hours in the kitchen.
> Women now spend *less* time in the kitchen.

former Refers to the first named of two. If three or more item are named, use *first* and *last* instead of *former* or *latter*.

> The Folger and the Huntington are two famous libraries; the *former* is in Washington, D.C., and the latter is in Sa Marino, California.

get The verb *to get* is one of the most versatile words in standard English. It is common in such standard idioms as *get along with* (someone), *get the better of* (someone), *get at* (information), *get o* (a horse), or *get over* (an illness). But avoid slang or very informal usages of *get* or *got*.

> INFORMAL Their reactionary attitudes really *get* me.
> GENERAL Their reactionary attitudes *baffle* me.

good Nearly always used as an adjective. Generally considere informal when used as an adverb.

> INFORMAL Mrs. Nevins sings *good*.
> GENERAL She sings *well*.

guys Informal for *men, women, boys, girls*.

had of, had ought Nonstandard for *had, ought*.

half a, a half, a half a Use *half a* or *a half* (perhaps mor formal), but avoid the redundant *a half a*.

> REDUNDANT He worked a half a day.
> GENERAL He worked *half a* day.
> GENERAL He worked *a half* day.

hanged, hung Informally, *hanged* and *hung* are often use interchangeably. Formal usage prefers *hanged* in referring t executions and *hung* in referring to objects.

> The cattle thieves were *hanged*.
> Children's art was *hung* on the south wall.

hardly, scarcely Such negatives as *can't hardly* and *don scarcely* are still nonstandard.

> NONSTANDARD I couldn't hardly quit then.
> STANDARD I *could hardly* quit then.

have, of See **of, have.**

himself See **myself** (**himself**, etc.).

hisself Nonstandard for *himself*.

illusion, allusion See **allusion, illusion**.

imminent, immanent See **eminent, imminent, immanent**.

imply, infer The writer or speaker *implies;* the reader or listener *infers*. *Imply* means "to suggest without stating"; *infer* means "to reach a conclusion based on evidence." Often used interchangeably in informal English.

> His statement *implies* that he will resign.
> From his statement I *infer* that he will resign.

in, into *In* generally indicates "location within." Although *in* may be used for *into*, formal usage prefers *into* to indicate "motion or direction to a point within."

> GENERAL   A man came *in* the library to call the police.
> PREFERRED   A man came *into* the library to call the police.

Compare the meaning of these sentences:

> We flew *in* another jet.
> We flew *into* another jet.

incidentally, accidentally See **accidentally, incidentally**.

incredible, incredulous *Incredible* means "too extraordinary to be believed." *Incredulous* means "inclined not to believe."

> The four-year-old told *incredible* stories.
> The *incredulous* audience grew restless.

infer, imply See **imply, infer**.

inferior than Nonstandard. Use *inferior to* or *worse than*.

in regards to Nonstandard for *in regard to* or *as regards*.

inside of, outside of The *of* is often unnecessary. *Inside of* is informal for *within*. *Outside of* is informal for *except, besides*.

> INFORMAL   The job will be finished *inside of* ten days.
> GENERAL   The job will be finished *within* ten days.
> INFORMAL   He has no hobbies *outside of* golf.
> GENERAL   He has no hobbies *except* golf.

irregardless   Nonstandard for *regardless*.

is when, is where   Do not use *when* and *where* after *is* in giving definitions.

> AWKWARD   Steamrolling is when opposition is suppressed.
> BETTER   Steamrolling is the suppression of opposition.
> AWKWARD   "Future shock" is where extremely rapid change causes mental disturbance.
> BETTER   "Future shock" is mental disturbance caused by extremely rapid change.

its, it's   *Its* is a possessive pronoun. *It's* is a contraction of *it is* or *it has*.

kind, sort   Singular forms, which may be modified by *that* or *this*. Formally, use *those* or *these* to modify only plural forms.

> INFORMAL   Mr. Pratt prefers *these kind* to *those kind*.
> GENERAL   Mr. Pratt prefers *this kind* to *those kinds*.

kind of a   Omit the *a* in your formal writing.

later, latter   *Later*, referring to time, is the comparative form of *late*. *Latter* refers to the last named of two. If more than two items are named, use *last* instead of *latter*.

lay, lie   Do not confuse these verbs: see **7a(2)**.

learn, teach   *Learn* means "to acquire knowledge"; *teach* · "to impart knowledge."

> Professor Evans *taught* Earl only one we͏ͅˑ
> how to study during that time.

leave, let   Do not use *leave* for *let*. Leav͏ˌ
from"; *let* means "to permit." But "Leave (OR ˌ
standard idiom.

> NONSTANDARD   I will not leave you go today
> STANDARD   I will not *let* you go today.

less, fewer   See **fewer, less**.

let's us   Redundant for *let's*, which is a contraction

lie, lay   Do not confuse these verbs: see **7a(2)**.

like, as, as if   In general usage, *like* functions as a preposition; *as* and *as if* (or *as though*) function as conjunctions. Although widely used in conversation and in public speaking, *like* as a conjunction is still controversial in a formal context.

GENERAL	He drives *like* me. [Prepositional function]
CONTROVERSIAL	He drives *like* I do. [Conjunction]
GENERAL	He drives *as* a considerate person should. [Conjunction]
CONTROVERSIAL	He drives *like* he was angry. [Conjunction]
GENERAL	He drives *as if* he were angry. [Conjunction]

In such elliptical constructions as the following, however, the conjunction *like* is appropriate, even in a formal context.

> A child is drawn to indulgent grandparents *like* a moth to lights.

likely, liable   Informally, *liable* is sometimes substituted for *likely*. Formally, *likely* means "probable" or "to be expected"; *liable* means "susceptible to something unpleasant" or "legally responsible."

INFORMAL	My favourite program is *liable* to win an award.
GENERAL	My favourite program is *likely* to win an award.
GENERAL	John is *liable* to cut his foot with the power saw.

line, case   See **case, line**.

lose, loose, loosen   Do not confuse. *Lose* means "to cease having." The adjective *loose* means "free, not fastened." The verb *loosen* (or *loose*) means "to free from restraint."

> I was warned not to *lose* the keys.
> All *loose* bolts should be tightened.
> They forgot to *loosen* the growing puppy's collar.

may be, maybe   Distinguish between the verb form *may be* and the adverb *maybe,* meaning "perhaps."

> April *may be* the best time for a vacation.
> *Maybe* the family will take a vacation in April.

mighty Informally used for *very, exceedingly.* The general meaning of *mighty* is "powerful, strong."

> INFORMAL   The Wards are *mighty* good neighbours.
> GENERAL   The Wards are *very* good neighbours.
> GENERAL   In Rhodes stood the *mighty* statue of Colossus.

moral, morale The noun *moral* means "lesson, maxim"; the adjective *moral* means "pertaining to right conduct" or "ethical." *Morale,* a noun, means "a cheerful, confident state of mind."

> What is the *moral* of Thurber's fable?
> Has the *morale* of the team improved?

most, almost See **almost, most**.

myself (himself, etc.) Properly an intensive or reflexive pronoun: "I *myself* will go; I must see for *myself.*" In general, *myself* is not a proper substitute for *I* or *me;* but it is informally substituted for *I* after comparisons with *than* or *as* and for *me* when used as the second member of a compound object.

> INFORMAL   Everyone worked as well as *myself.*
> GENERAL   Everyone worked as well as *I.*
> INFORMAL   He encouraged my brother and *myself.*
> GENERAL   He encouraged my brother and *me.*

neither, either See **either, neither**.

nohow, nowheres Nonstandard for *not at all, nowhere.*

not . . . no A nonstandard construction when the two negatives have a negative meaning.

> NONSTANDARD   They do not keep no records.
> STANDARD   They do not keep records.   [OR any records]
> STANDARD   They keep no records.

number, amount See **amount, number**.

of, have The preposition *of* is nonstandard when substituted in writing for the verb form *have.*

> NONSTANDARD   Mary could of (would of, may of, might of, must of, ought to of) done that last week.
> STANDARD   Mary could *have* (would *have,* may *have,* might *have,* must *have,* ought to *have*) done that last week.

off of   Omit the *of* in your formal writing.

OK, O.K., okay   All three are accepted as standard forms expressing general approval. A more specific word, however, usually replaces *OK* in a formal context.

outside of, inside of   See **inside of, outside of**.

plenty   Informal when used as an adverb meaning "very."

INFORMAL   The chemistry test was *plenty* hard.
GENERAL   The chemistry test was *very* hard.

plus   *Plus*, as a preposition, means "increased by"; the word is also used as an informal substitution for *and* between main clauses (see **12a**).

INFORMAL   Barbara is taking five courses, *plus* she has to work three hours a day.
GENERAL   Barbara is taking five courses, *and* she has to work three hours a day.

P.M., A.M.   See **A.M., P.M.**

practical, practicable   *Practical* means "useful, sensible" or "not theoretical." *Practicable* means "feasible, capable of being put into practice."

The sponsors are *practical*, and their plans are *practicable*.

principal, principle   Distinguish between *principal*, an adjective or noun meaning "chief" or "chief official," and the noun *principle*, meaning "fundamental truth."

A *principal* factor in the decision was the belief in the *principle* that might does not make right.

raise, rise   See **rise, raise**.

rap   Informal when used as a verb meaning "to talk or chat." Slang when used as a noun meaning "punishment or blame" in such phrases as *take the rap* or *beat the rap*.

INFORMAL   We sat around the campfire and *rapped* for a while.
GENERAL   We sat around the campfire and *talked* for a while.

real   Informal when used as an adverb meaning "very, extremely."

INFORMAL   The victorious team was *real* tired.
GENERAL   The victorious team was *extremely* tired.

reason . . . because   Informal redundancy. Use *that* instead of *because* or recast the sentence.

INFORMAL   The *reason* he missed his class was *because* he overslept.

GENERAL   The *reason* he missed his class was *that* he overslept.

OR

He missed his class *because* he overslept.

reckon   Informal for *guess, think.*

respectfully, respectively   *Respectfully* means "in a manner showing respect." *Respectively* means "each in the order given."

Tom rose *respectfully* when the rabbi entered.
Mary, George, and Edna were born in 1952, 1956, and 1958, *respectively.*

rise, raise   Do not confuse. *Rise* (*rose, risen*), an intransitive verb, means "to move upward." *Raise* (*raised, raised*), a transitive verb, means "to cause to move upward, to place erect."

Franklin *rises* promptly at seven.
Franklin *raises* his hand often in English class.

says, said   Not interchangeable. *Says* is present tense; *said,* past.

NONSTANDARD   Allen dashed into the cafeteria and says, "Helen won the essay contest."

STANDARD   Allen dashed into the cafeteria and *said,* "Helen won the essay contest."

scarcely   See **hardly, scarcely.**

sit, set   Do not confuse these verbs: see **7a(2).**

someone, some one   See **anyone, any one.**

somewheres   Nonstandard for *somewhere.*

sort, kind   See **kind, sort.**

sort of a   Omit the *a* in your formal writing.

stationary, stationery   *Stationary* means "in a fixed position"; *stationery* means "writing paper and envelopes."

such that When *such* is completed by a result clause, it should be followed by *that*.

The rain was *such that* we had to stop on the freeway.

supposed to See **used to, supposed to**.

sure Informal for *surely* or *certainly*.

INFORMAL   The sunrise *sure* was beautiful.
GENERAL   The sunrise *surely* was beautiful.

sure and See **be sure and**.

teach, learn See **learn, teach**.

than, then *Than* and *then* are not interchangeable. Do not confuse the conjunction *than* with the adverb or adverbial conjunction *then*, which relates to time.

Nylon wears better *than* rayon.
First it snowed; *then* it sleeted.

their, there, they're Do not confuse. *Their* is a possessive pronoun; *there* is an adverb or an expletive; *they're* is a contraction of *they are*.

There is no explanation for *their* refusal.
They're installing a traffic light *there*.

theirself, theirselves Nonstandard for *themselves*.

these kind, these sort, those kind, those sort See **kind, sort**.

this here, that there, these here, them there Nonstandard expressions. Use *this, that, these, those*.

to, too, two Distinguish the preposition *to* from the adverb *too* and the numeral *two*.

If it isn't *too* cold, I will take my *two* poodles *to* the park.

try and Informal for *try to*.

used to, supposed to Be sure to add the *-d* to *use* and *suppose* when writing these expressions.

Horses *used to* be indispensable.
James was *supposed to* be in charge.

used to could Nonstandard or humorous for *used to be able*.

wait on Used generally to mean "to attend, to serve." Used informally to mean "to wait for."

INFORMAL At the station, Doris *waited on* her sister a full hour.
GENERAL At the station, Doris *waited for* her sister a full hour.
GENERAL She *waited on* her invalid father for years.

want in, out, down, up, off, through Informal or regional for *want to come* or *want to get in, out, down, up, off, through*.

want that Nonstandard when a *that* clause is the object of *want*.

NONSTANDARD I want that he should have a chance.
STANDARD I *want* him to have a chance.
STANDARD I *want that*.

ways Informal for *way* when referring to distance.

INFORMAL It's a long *ways* to Inuvik.
GENERAL It's a long *way* to Inuvik.

where Informal for *that*.

INFORMAL I saw in the newspaper *where* the strike had been settled.
GENERAL I saw in the newspaper *that* the strike had been settled.

which, who Use *who* or *that* instead of *which* to refer to persons.

while Do not overuse as a substitute for *and* or *but*. The conjunction *while* usually refers to time.

who, which See **which, who.**

worst way *In the worst way* is informal for *very much*.

INFORMAL Mrs. Simmons wanted a colour TV *in the worst way*.
GENERAL Mrs. Simmons wanted a colour TV *very much*.

would of Nonstandard for *would have*.

you was Nonstandard for *you were*.

Exactness

20

Select words that are exact, idiomatic, and fresh.

Especially when writing, you should strive to choose words that express your ideas exactly, precise words that convey the emotional suggestions you intend. Words that are effective in an informal composition may be inappropriate in a formal one: see **19b**. On certain occasions, slang or non-standard or archaic words can have power, persuasive force; on other occasions, these words can be weak, out of place: see **19c**, **19e**, and **19f**. Regional diction that is desirable in a given geographical area may be humorous or confusing elsewhere: see **19d**. Similarly, technical words that make sense to a special group of listeners or readers may be wholly unintelligible to those outside the group: see **19g**. The choice of the right word will depend on your purpose, your point of view, and your reader.

If you can make effective use of the words you already know, you need not have a huge vocabulary. In fact, as shown by the following example, professional writers often choose short, familiar words.

> The ball was loose, rolling free near the line of scrimmage. I raced for the fumble, bent over, scooped up the ball on the dead run, and turned downfield. With a sudden burst of speed, I bolted past the line and past the linebackers. Only

two defensive backs stood between me and the goal line. One came up fast, and I gave him a hip feint, stuck out my left arm in a classic straight-arm, caught him on the helmet, and shoved him to the ground. The final defender moved toward me, and I cut to the sidelines, swung sharply back to the middle for three steps, braked again, and reversed my direction once more. The defender tripped over his own feet in confusion. I trotted into the end zone, having covered seventy-eight yards on my touchdown run, happily flipped the football into the stands, turned and loped casually toward the sidelines. Then I woke up.   —JERRY KRAMER[1]

Of course, as you gain experience in writing, you will become increasingly aware of the need to add to your vocabulary. When you discover a valuable new word, make it your own by mastering its spelling, its meaning, and its exact use.

20a
Select the exact word needed to express your idea.

(1) Select the word that precisely denotes what you have in mind.

WRONG A loud radio does not *detract* me when I am reading a good novel. [*Detract* means "to subtract a part of" or "to remove something desirable."]

RIGHT A loud radio does not *distract* me when I am reading a good novel. [*Distract* means "to draw the attention away."]

INEXACT Arnold was willing to pay the bill, *and* his billfold was empty. [*And* adds or continues.]

EXACT Arnold was willing to pay the bill, *but* his billfold was empty. [*But* contrasts.]

---

[1]From *Farewell to Football* by Jerry Kramer. Published by Bantam Books, Inc., 1969. Copyright © 1969 by Jerry Kramer and Dick Schaap. Reprinted with permission of Thomas Y. Crowell Co., Inc.

INEXACT	A registration official *brainwashed* the freshmen for forty-five minutes. [*To brainwash* is "to alter personal convictions, beliefs, and attitudes by means of intensive, coercive indoctrination."]
EXACT	A registration official *briefed* the freshmen for forty-five minutes. [*To brief* is "to prepare in advance by instructing or advising."]

■ **Exercise 1** With the aid of your dictionary, give the exact meaning of each italicized word in the quotations below. (Italics have been added.)

1. The moon has become our *cosmic* Paris.
—WERNHER VON BRAUN

   Malcolm did not invent the new *cosmology*—black power, black is beautiful, think black—or the mystique of Africanism. —PETER SCHRAG

2. The capacity for rage, spite and aggression is part of our endowment as *human beings*. —KENNETH KENISTON

   Man, all down his history, has defended his uniqueness like a point of honor. —RUTH BENEDICT

3. Travel is no cure for melancholia; space-ships and time machines are no *escape* from the human condition.
—ARTHUR KOESTLER

   Well, Columbus was probably regarded as an *escapist* when he set forth for the New World. —ARTHUR C. CLARKE

4. Once, a full high school education was the best achievement of a minority; today, it is the *barest minimum* for decent employment or self-respect. —ERIC SEVAREID

   Study and planning are an *absolute prerequisite* for any kind of intelligent action. —EDWARD BROOKE

5. We had a *permissive* father. He *permitted* us to work.
—SAM LEVENSON

■ **Exercise 2** Prepare for a class discussion of diction. After the first quotation below are several series of words that the author might have used but did not select. Note the differences in meaning when an italicized word is substituted for the related word at the head of each series. Be prepared to supply your own alternatives for each of the words that follow the other four quotations.

1. Creeping gloom hits us all. The symptoms are usually the same: not wanting to get out of bed to start the day, failing to smile at ironies, failing to laugh at oneself.

—CHRISTOPHER BUCKLEY

a. gloom: *sadness, depression, dismals* (hit), *melancholy*
b. hits: *strikes, assaults, infects, zaps*
c. usually: *often, frequently, consistently, as a rule*
d. failing: *too blue, unable, neglecting, too far gone*

2. Our plane rocked in a rain squall, bobbed about, then slipped into a patch of sun.   —THEODORE H. WHITE
a. rocked   b. bobbed   c. slipped   d. patch

3. She stood on the riverbank quite still, conscious that every motion made a foreign sound, even her hands rubbing in her pockets for warmth.   —MARIAN ENGEL
a. still   b. conscious   c. foreign   d. warmth

4. How is it that the same work can create stress or distress?

—HANS SELYE

a. stress   b. distress

5. Believing the program to be true, people drove into the country to escape; others barricaded themselves in their cellars, prepared to die fighting.   —AUSTIN REPATH
a. escape   b. barricaded   c. prepared   d. die

(2) Select the word with the connotation, as well as the denotation, appropriate to the idea you wish to express.

The denotation of a word is what the word actually signifies. According to the dictionary, the word *hair* denotes "one of the fine, threadlike structures that grow from the skin of most mammals." The connotation of a word is what the word suggests or implies. *Hair,* for instance, may connote beauty, fertility, nudity, strength, uncleanliness, temptation, rebellion, or primitivism.

The connotation of a word includes the emotions or associations that surround it. For instance, *taxi, tin lizzie, limousine, dune buggy, station wagon, dump truck, hot rod*—all denote much the same thing. But to various readers, and in various contexts, each word may have a special connotation. *Taxi* may suggest a city rush hour; *tin lizzie*, a historical museum; *limousine*, an airport; *dune buggy*, a seaside vacation; *station wagon*, children and dogs; *dump truck*, highway construction; *hot rod*, noise and racing. Similarly, *hatchback, bus, clunker, bookmobile, moving van, ambulance, squad car*—all denote a means of transportation, but each word carries a variety of connotations.

A word may be right in one situation, wrong in another. *Female parent*, for instance, is a proper expression in a biology laboratory, but it would be very inappropriate to say "John wept because of the death of his female human parent." *Female human parent* used in this sense is literally correct, but the connotation is wrong. The more appropriate word, *mother*, conveys not only the meaning denoted by *female human parent* but also the reason why John wept. The first expression simply implies a biological relationship; the second includes emotional suggestions.

■ **Exercise 3** Give one denotation and one connotation for each of the following words.

1. red
2. system
3. astrology
4. Chicago
5. conservative
6. law
7. dog
8. tennis shoes
9. technology
10. Saudi Arabia

■ **Exercise 4** Be prepared to discuss the words below that because of their connotative value serve to intensify the authors' meanings.

1. The country seemed to be dozing in an easy chair, belching intermittently to prove it was not quite asleep.

—JACK NEWFIELD

2. Does not a mountain unintentionally evoke in us a sense of wonder? otters along a stream a sense of mirth? night in the woods a sense of fear? Do not rain falling and mists rising up suggest the love binding heaven and earth?
   —JOHN CAGE

3. To the rest of the family, thrashing furiously and uselessly in various snarled dilemmas, she must often have appeared to live in a state of perpetual grace, but I'm certain she didn't think of it that way either. —MARGARET LAURENCE

4. People tumble down for a brunch at nine o'clock, telling stories about all-night parties, of singing to a guitar in the Saskatchewan Suite, of being stuck in overloaded elevators and having a fabulous time. —SATURDAY NIGHT

(3) Select the specific and concrete word rather than the general and abstract.

A *general* word is all-inclusive, indefinite, sweeping in scope. A *specific* word is precise, definite, limited in scope.

General	Specific	More Specific
food	dessert	apple pie
prose	fiction	short stories
people	Canadians	the Smiths

An *abstract* word deals with concepts, with ideas, with what cannot be touched, heard, or seen. A *concrete* word has to do with particular objects, with the practical, with what can be touched, heard, or seen.

ABSTRACT WORDS   democracy, loyal, evil, hate, charity
CONCRETE WORDS   mosquito, spotted, crunch, wedding

All writers must sometimes use abstract words and must occasionally resort to generalizations, as in the following sentence:

Only mankind can generate signals of communication of infinite variety; only mankind can speak with the use of symbols and therefore recall the past and suppose the future. —WILLIAM JOVANOVICH

In a case like this, abstractions and generalizations are vital to the communication of ideas and theories. To be effective, however, the use of these words must be based upon clearly understood and well-thought-out ideas.

Experienced writers may have little difficulty handling general and abstract words. Many inexperienced writers, however, tend to use too many such words, leaving their writing drab and lifeless due to the lack of specific, concrete words. As you select words to fit your context, be as specific as you can. For example, instead of the word *bad*, consider using a more precise adjective (or adjectival) in phrases such as the following:

bad planks: rotten, warped, scorched, knotty, termite-eaten
bad children: rowdy, rude, ungrateful, selfish, perverse
bad meat: tough, tainted, overcooked, contaminated

To test whether or not a word is specific, ask one or more of these questions: Exactly who does the word describe? Exactly what? Precisely when? Exactly where? Precisely how? As you study the examples below, notice what a difference specific, concrete words can make in the expression of an idea. Notice, too, how specific details can be used to expand or develop ideas.

DULL   He never liked the weakness and lack of purpose of modern organized religion.

SPECIFIC   One point which remained constant was his dislike of liberalized Protestantism. He disliked its air of compromise, its soft rounded edges, its failure to face the full implications of evil.—GEORGE H. FORD

DULL   The discontented people debated the matter and finally found a suitable leader in William Lyon Mackenzie.

SPECIFIC   The malcontents argued on the platforms and in the end they found a leader to their hearts in William Lyon Mackenzie, a Scot, arrived in 1820, editing the *Colonial Advocate*, as honest as daylight, and as uncompromising as the Westminster Catechism.   —STEPHEN LEACOCK

DULL   I remember my pleasure at discovering new things about language.

SPECIFIC   I remember my real joy at discovering for the first time how language worked, at discovering, for example, that the central line of Joseph Conrad's *Heart of Darkness* was in parentheses.

—JOAN DIDION

DULL   Eventually, dogs that are not claimed are done away with and then used in various ways.

SPECIFIC   Eventually, dogs that are not claimed are humanely killed (more than 6,000 dogs a year are too many for continuous boarding) and rendered into animal proteins for hog food supplement or low-phosphate grease for soap.   —ALAN M. BECK

■ **Exercise 5**   Expand the following ideas by using specific, concrete words.

EXAMPLES

When the Liberals call an election this spring the odds will be against them.
When the Grits come calling with their ballot boxes this spring, they'll be walking into the machine guns.

—MACLEAN'S

The hero must be a character with flaws but he must also have virtues.
Traditionally the hero must have a tragic flaw or two; he may be a man destroyed by his own pride, like Oedipus, or by his own indecisiveness, like Hamlet, but he must also have great virtues. Above all he must be central, significant.

—MARGARET ATWOOD

1. In pawn shops there are frequently items of interest to collectors.
2. The crowded midway was a miniature battlefield.
3. A mechanical genius, my roommate can repair almost anything.
4. To many Torontonians, Ontario is Canada.
5. Many slang words and expressions are related to drugs and drug users.

■ **Exercise 6** Study the italicized words below, first with the aid of a dictionary and then in the context of the sentences. Substitute a synonym for each italicized word and compare its effectiveness with that of the original.

1. It would be *sentimentality* to think that our society can be changed easily and without pain. —ROBERT PENN WARREN

2. What is disappearing is the *song* of the land.
—DONALD JACKSON

3. He *wandered back* in a heartbroken *daze,* his sensitive face *eloquent* with grief. —JOSEPH HELLER

4. Her moral indignation was always *on the boil.*
—ALDOUS HUXLEY

5. Her beauty was *paralyzing*—beyond all words, all experience, all dream. —CONRAD AIKEN

■ **Exercise 7** Replace the general words and phrases in italics with specific ones.

1. A police state *has certain characteristics.*
2. *A lot of people* are threatened by *pollution* and by *ripoffs.*
3. *My relatives* gave me *two gifts.*
4. Every Monday he has *the same thing* in his lunch box.
5. Our history professor suggested that we subscribe to *some magazines.*
6. Backpacking has *numerous advantages.*
7. The winning touchdown *was the result of luck.*
8. My father looked at my grade in science and said *what I least expected to hear.*
9. *Various aspects of the television show* were criticized *in the newspaper.*
10. *Cities* have their *problems.*

(4) Use appropriate figurative language to create an imaginative or emotional impression.

A figure of speech is a word or words used in an imaginative rather than in a literal sense. The two chief figures of speech are the *simile* and the *metaphor.* A *simile* is an explicit comparison between two things of a different kind or quality, usually introduced by *like* or *as*. A *metaphor* is an implied comparison of dissimilar things. In a metaphor, word of comparison, such as *like* and *as*, are not used.

SIMILES

The trench was *like a tunnel with a black heavy layer o smoke as its roof.* —TIMOTHY FINDLEY

Canadians have taken to ballet *as happily as the Russian have taken to hockey.* —MALCOLM ROSS

METAPHORS

The sun was *a distant blowtorch.* —DON BAILEY

Language is not *a tough plant that always grows toward the sun, regardless of weeds and trampling feet.*

—DOUGLAS BUSH

We are *born princes* and the civilizing process *turns us into frogs.* —ERIC BERNE

Similes and metaphors are especially valuable when they are concrete and tend to point up essential relationships that cannot otherwise be communicated. (For faulty metaphors see **23c**.) Sometimes writers extend a metaphor beyond a sentence:

Some women have managed to shape up and ship out into the mainstream of life, handling the currents and the rapids and the quiet pools with a gracious, confident ease. Others are trapped in one eddy after another, going nowhere at all, hung up in swirling pockets of confusion. Everyone gets sidetracked once in a while, and requires a rescue operation. That's the way life is. But some have been caught in an eddy or on a piece of dead wood for so long that they have forgotten that life was meant to be lived in the mainstream.

—GLADYS HUNT[2]

---

[2]From *Ms. Means Myself* by Gladys Hunt. Copyright © 1972 by Gladys M. Hunt and printed by Zondervan Publishing House and is used by permission.

Two other frequently used figures of speech are *hyperbole* and *personification*. *Hyperbole* is deliberate overstatement or fanciful exaggeration. *Personification* is the attribution to the nonhuman (objects, animals, ideas) of characteristics possessed only by the human.

HYPERBOLE
I, for one, don't expect till I die to be so good a man as I am at this minute, for just now I'm *fifty thousand feet high—a tower with all the trumpets shouting.* —G. K. CHESTERTON

PERSONIFICATION
Time talks. It speaks more plainly than words. . . . *It can shout* the truth where words lie. —EDWARD T. HALL

■ **Exercise 8** Complete each of the following sentences by using a simile, a metaphor, hyperbole, or personification. Use vivid and effective figures of speech.

EXAMPLES
It was a voice like *a stream of crystal water fighting to reach the sea.* —AUSTIN CLARKE

The utopia of Karl Marx, like all utopias before or since, was *an image in a rearview mirror.* —MARSHALL McLUHAN

1. Sightseers flocked around the commune like _____ .
2. A revolutionary idea in the 1970s, like a revolutionary idea in any age, is _____ .
3. The mosquitoes in the Yukon _____ .
4. The worst blizzard in living memory slashed through Manitoba _____ .
5. Death in a hovel or in a penthouse is _____ .
6. Like _____ , the class sat speechless.
7. The lecture was as _____ .
8. Her eyes looked like _____ .
9. Surging forward, the rioters _____ .
10. The opinions of politicians with vested interests are as predictable as _____ .
11. She was as self-confident as _____ .
12. The alarm sounded like _____ .

20b

Select words that are idiomatic.

An idiomatic expression—such as *many a man, Sunday week,* or *hang fire*—means something beyond the simple combination of the definitions of its individual words. An idiom may be metaphorical: *He gets under my skin.* Such expressions cannot be meaningfully translated word for word into another language. Used every day, they are at the very heart of the English language.

Be careful to use idiomatic English, not unidiomatic approximations. *Many a man* is idiomatic; *many the man* is not. Ordinarily, native speakers use idiomatic English naturally and effectively, but once in a while they may have difficulty choosing idiomatic prepositions.

UNIDIOMATIC	comply to, superior than, buy off of
IDIOMATIC	comply *with,* superior *to,* buy *from*

When you are in doubt about what preposition to use after a given word, look up that word in the dictionary. For instance, *agree* may be followed by *with, to,* or *about.* The choice depends on the context: *agree with us, agree to that, agree about plans.*

■ **Exercise 9** Using your dictionary, classify the following expressions as idiomatic or unidiomatic. Revise any expressions that are unidiomatic. Classify idiomatic expressions according to the usage labels in your dictionary, using *General* as the classification for unlabelled expressions.

EXAMPLES
similar with   *Unidiomatic—similar to*
to let on   *Idiomatic, Informal*

1. oblivious about
2. to go at
3. to dress down
4. capable to
5. distaste for
6. to compare against
7. to break with
8. prior than
9. to drop in
10. to plug for

20c

Select fresh expressions instead of trite, worn-out ones.

Such trite expressions as *to the bitter end, get it all together,* and *every inch a gentleman* were once striking and effective. Excessive use, however, has drained them of their original force and made them clichés. Euphemisms such as *laid to rest* (for *buried*) and *stretches the truth* (for *lies* or *exaggerates*) are not only trite but wordy. Such comparisons as *sticks out like a sore thumb* and *as plain as day* are also hackneyed expressions.

Good writers do not use trite, well-known phrases when simple, straightforward language and original expressions would be more effective. Compare the effectiveness of the following sentences.

> TRITE   *It goes without saying* that it is time we stopped regarding Indians as *something out of the past* with no relevance to America *in this day and age.*
>
> BETTER   Clearly, it is time we stopped regarding Indians as living museum pieces with no relevance to America today.   —PETER FARB

To avoid trite phrases you must be aware of current usage, for catch phrases and slogans age quickly. Pat political phrases, such as *pulse of public opinion, grassroots support,* and *viable options,* are notoriously short-lived. Similarly, expressions drawn from commercial advertising quickly become hackneyed. Owners of damaged freight might advertise that they "sell it like it is," or managers of high-rise apartments might use such slogans as "Your chance to live it up" or "Think tall." But slogans that are effective in advertising often become so familiar that they lose their force.

Nearly every writer uses clichés from time to time because they are so much a part of the language, especially of spoken English, and do contribute to the clear expression of ideas in written English.

> We feel free when we escape—even if it be but *from the frying pan into the fire.* —ERIC HOFFER

It is not unusual for a professional writer to give a new twist to an old saying.

> He is every other inch a gentleman. —REBECCA WEST
>
> If a thing is worth doing, it is worth doing badly.
> —G. K. CHESTERTON
>
> Into each life a little sun must fall. —L. E. SISSMAN

Many writers use familiar lines from literature or the Bible and quote proverbs.

> Our lives are empty of belief. They are *lives of quiet desperation.* —ARTHUR M. SCHLESINGER, JR.
> [Compare Thoreau's *Walden:* "The mass of men lead lives of quiet desperation."]
>
> Slowly but steadily, in the following years, a new vision began gradually to replace the dream of political power—a powerful movement, the rise of another ideal to guide the unguided, another *pillar of fire by night* after a clouded day.
> —W. E. B. DU BOIS [Compare Exodus 13:21: "And the Lord went before them . . . by night in a pillar of fire, to give them light."]

Good writers, however, do not rely heavily on the phraseology of others; they choose their own words to communicate their own ideas.

■ **Exercise 10** Substitute one carefully chosen word for each trite expression below.

EXAMPLES
stick to your guns   *persevere*
the very picture of health   *robust*

1. white as a sheet
2. a crying shame
3. busy as a bee
4. too cute for words
5. really down to earth
6. smart as a whip

7. over and done with
8. at the crack of dawn

9. few and far between
10. follow in the footsteps of

Exercise 11 Write short sentences with ten hackneyed expressions that you often use; then rewrite each expression in exact, straightforward words of your own that fit the context of your sentence.

Exercise 12 Choose five of the ten items below as the basis for five original sentences. Use language that is exact, idiomatic, and fresh.

EXAMPLES
the condition of her hair
Her hair, which she wore in two braids around her head, was the same colour as her skin, pallid. —SHIRLEY FAESSLER

OR
Her dark hair was gathered up in a coil like a crown on her head. —D. H. LAWRENCE

OR
She had been fussing with her hair, couldn't get it right; the brittle broken-off dyed yellow ends were curling the wrong way, breaking off on the brush, standing out from her head as if she were some strange aborigine preparing herself for the puberty rites. —JEAN RIKHOFF

1. the look on his face
2. her response to fear
3. the way she walks
4. the condition of the streets
5. spring in the air

6. the noises of the city
7. the appearance of the room
8. the scene of the accident
9. the final minutes of play
10. the approaching storm

Exercise 13 Following are two descriptions, one of bounty, the other of terror. Read each selection carefully in preparation for a class discussion of the authors' choice of words, their use of concrete, specific language, and their use of figurative language.

219

[1]The days were short, and often sombre, but we kept a good fire going in the house, we ate pumpkin pie, we sorted walnut and corn. [2]We also set tomatoes to ripen on the window sills and on certain days the whole house was permeated with the odour of pickles cooking over a gentle fire in large pans. [3]The saw could be heard singing in the yard; its two-toned song, first clear, then deeper and heavier as it bit into the wood, seemed to me to promise us joyfully, "I'm cutting you fine logs, fine logs, for the whole winter." [4]All this time the house, like a ship ready to weigh anchor or a city about to undergo a siege, was being filled with provisions—sauerkraut, maple syrup from Quebec, red apples from British Columbia, plums from Ontario. [5]Soon also we began to receive from our uncles in the country fat geese and turkeys, dozens of chickens, hams and salt bacon, cases of fresh eggs and farm butter. [6]To help ourselves we only had to go into our summer kitchen, now transformed into a storehouse, where the frost preserved our stock. [7]Such were the joys of autumn, based upon abundance and a feeling of security that think I appreciated even then. —GABRIELLE ROY[3]

[1]They say, too, that nature did its best to co-operate. [2]A wind came up from somewhere, bending trees, shaking the house. [3]You could hear the screech of giant trunks grinding against each other. [4]You could hear the squeal of nails wrenched in the lumbered walls and the cedar roof above you. [5]The water in the strait was churned up into waves that smashed against the cliff and leapt upwards high enough to spray the windows and toss driftwood logs like sticks across the yard. [6]A door flew open in the wind, crashed against the wall, and was forced shut again by someone whose face was streaming with rain and salt water and strips of kelp. [7]Sticks and bits of limbs went flying across the floor. [8]Dead pine needles clotted like hairballs in the corner. [9]Keneally's voice rose above the tumult to include it.

[10]He would be transformed, Keneally said, his voice suddenly heavy with importance. [11]He would be transformed from flesh into spirit this night. [12]He would, in fact, be dead. [13]The organ

[3]From *The Road Past Altamount* by Gabrielle Roy reprinted by permission of The Canadian Publishers, McClelland and Stewart Limited, Toronto.

music spiralled upward into a final impossible note that lay across the sudden silence like a clear metallic lid, though frightened Kathleen's feet kept pumping madly still and her forehead pressed against the elaborately carved wood of the instrument like a cyclist against the wind. [14]Logs crashed on the verandah; men whimpered; bladders weakened; a light in the ceiling dimmed.   —JACK HODGINS[4]

Exercise 14 Choose the word inside parentheses that best suits the context of each item below.

1. Driving east to Regina the wind is blowing, a heavy gusting wind that (scoops, lifts) topsoil off the farmland.

—AL PURDY

2. The creeks were (foaming, rushing) as brown as vat-run lager.   —DENNIS T. PATRICK SEARS

3. A poem is an Alka-Seltzer tablet: orthodoxies begin to (fizz, complain) when one is dropped into their midst.

—IRVING LAYTON

4. Every evening at the rush hour the subway (unveils, disgorges) its millions.   —JACQUES BARZUN

5. There was a roaring in my ears like the rushing of (music, rivers).   —STEPHEN VINCENT BENÉT

Wordiness

21

Avoid wordiness. Repeat words only when needed for emphasis or clarity.

The best way to eliminate wordiness in compositions is to write and rewrite. As you proofread and revise, delete unneeded words but keep or add exact ones. In this way, you can use fewer words and yet say more.

WORDY FIRST DRAFT

In the early part of the month of August
there was a really mean hurricane with very
high winds that was moving threateningly
toward Port Arthur.

FIRST REVISION

In ~~the~~ early ~~part of the month of~~ August
~~there was~~ a really mean hurricane with very
high winds ~~that~~ was moving threateningly
toward Port Arthur.

SECOND REVISION

In early August a ~~really mean~~ *vicious* hurricane with
~~very high~~ *150-kilometre-per-hour* winds was ~~moving threateningly~~ *threatening*
~~toward~~ Port Arthur.

FINAL DRAFT

In early August a vicious hurricane with

150—kilometre—per—hour winds was threatening Port

Arthur.

21a

Make every word count; omit words or phrases that add nothing to the meaning.

Notice below that the words in brackets contribute nothing to the meaning. Avoid such wordiness in your own writing.

[important OR basic] essentials, in [the city of] Calgary
cooperated [together], as a [usual] rule, [true] facts
yellow [in colour], small [in size], eleven [in number]

Bureaucratic jargon is often extremely wordy. See the example on page 185.

■ **Exercise 1**   Substitute one word for each item below.

EXAMPLES
on account of the fact that   *because*
persons who travel in outer space   *astronauts*

1. at the present time
2. persons who run for political office

3. at whatever time OR every time that
4. students who are in their first year at university
5. spoke in a very low and hard-to-hear voice

■ **Exercise 2** Without changing the meaning of the followin
sentences, strike out all unnecessary words. Put a checkma
after any sentence that needs no revision.

1. In the year 1976, Uncle Vance was close to the point
   bankruptcy.
2. The editorial gave reasons why the Chinese citizens in Ea:
   Asia cannot leave their home towns that they live in unles
   they have a permit from the government giving them pe
   mission to leave town.
3. The award-winning English playwright made ruthless mu
   der and flagrant blackmail the absurd hobbies of his heroes
4. One reason why Canadians are well informed is because
   the fact that books of all sorts on a great variety of subjec
   are available to them as inexpensive paperbacks.
5. The backlash that followed as a result of the Supreme Cou
   ruling was stronger than I myself had expected that it woul
   be.

21b

**If necessary, restructure the sentence to avoid wordi
ness.**

Notice in the following examples how changes in sentenc
structure reduce two sentences with a total of sixteen word:
to briefer sentences containing ten, nine, eight, and finally
five words. Also observe differences in emphasis.

> There was a mist that hung like a veil. It obscured the top o:
> the mountain.
> The mist hung like a veil and obscured the mountaintop
> The mist, hanging like a veil, obscured the mountaintop
> The mist, like a veil, obscured the mountaintop.
> The mist veiled the mountaintop.

Depending on the context, any one of these sentences may meet the special needs of the writer. By studying these examples, you can learn methods of restructuring your sentences to eliminate undesirable wordiness.

■ **Exercise 3** Restructure the following sentences to reduce the number of words.

1. There is one opera singer who works with mentally retarded children. He teaches them songs and games.
2. When the Indians made tools, they used flint and bones.
3. Ken McCoy strutted into the room, and as he did so he tripped over a briefcase.
4. A deep blue grass covered the lawn. It looked like a carpet.
5. Being in junior high school was like being in a circus having three rings.

■ **Exercise 4** Noting differences in emphasis, restructure the sentences below, following the patterns of the examples.

EXAMPLE
Value is conferred by scarcity.
Scarcity confers value. ——OSBORN SEGERBERG, JR.

1. Thieves are encouraged by brownouts.
2. The court's decision was ignored by the strikers.

EXAMPLE
Until recently, gold was the backbone of the international monetary system. So was the dollar.
Until recently, gold and the dollar were the backbone of the international monetary system. ——PETER T. WHITE

3. In fact, Peter is realistic. So is Sarah.
4. Of course, law-abiding citizens will use dart guns for self-defence. So will crooks.

EXAMPLE
The eyes of Annabel were brimming again. They were responding to his sympathy.
Annabel's eyes were brimming again, responding to his sympathy. ——MURIEL SPARK

225

5. The hands of the referee were waving again. They were indicating another costly penalty.
6. The daughter of the professor was attending graduate school. She was planning to become a geologist.

EXAMPLE

He was starey-eyed and almost incoherent. He indicated that he subsisted in the woods on berries, nuts, fish, birds and frogs.

Starey-eyed, almost incoherent, he indicated that he subsisted in the woods on berries, nuts, fish, birds and frogs.
—STUART TRUEMAN

7. He was tense and apparently apprehensive. He flinched each time the telephone rang.
8. The young doctor was crisp and a bit shy. He seemed to be clinically detached from personalities.

EXAMPLE

Not only do we want you standing up straight, but we want you looking respectable.
We want you standing up straight, looking respectable.
—SINCLAIR ROSS

9. Not only were taxes spiralling upward, but prices were sky-rocketing.
10. Not only were my grades improving, but my interests were expanding.

21c

Avoid careless or needless repetition of words and ideas.

Unless you are repeating intentionally for emphasis or for clarity and smoothness of transition, be careful in your writing not to use the same word twice or to make the same statement twice in slightly different words.

CARELESS   Their solution to the problem of overpopulation at first sounded like an outlandish solution.

CONCISE	Their solution to the problem of overpopulation at first sounded outlandish.
NEEDLESS	In 1976 the Canadiens beat the Flyers; in 1977 the Canadiens beat the Bruins.
CONCISE	In 1976 the Canadiens beat the Flyers; in 1977, the Bruins. [Omission of *the Canadiens beat* is indicated by use of a comma.]
NEEDLESS	Julia delights in giving parties; entertaining guests is a real pleasure for her.
CONCISE	Julia delights in giving parties.

Use a pronoun instead of needlessly repeating a noun. As long as the reference remains clear, several pronouns in succession, even in successive sentences, may refer to the same antecedent noun. In the following paragraph, for example, the italicized pronouns refer clearly to the noun *Robert*, which is not once repeated. See also **31b(2)**.

Twenty feet away, Robert sat on his haunches watching them. *His* pistol hung down from *his* fingers between *his* knees. *He* still wore *his* uniform with its torn lapels and burned sleeves. In the firelight, *his* eyes were very bright. *His* lips were slightly parted. *He* could not breathe through *his* nose. It was broken. *His* face and the backs of *his* hands were streaked with clay and sweat. *His* hair hung down across *his* forehead. *He* was absolutely still. *He* had wandered now for over a week.   —TIMOTHY FINDLEY[1]

■ **Exercise 5** Revise the following sentences to eliminate wordiness and useless repetition.

1. In the last act of the play there is the explanation of the title of the play.
2. Statistics show that in the decade from 1950 to 1960, enrolments at universities doubled; in 1960 there were twice as many students as in 1950.

---

[1] From *The Wars* by Timothy Findley, © 1977. Used by permission of Clarke, Irwin & Company Limited.

3. *Fantabulous* is a blend of the words *fantastic* and *fabulous; galumph* is a blend of *gallop* and *triumph.*

4. The National Gallery of Art, which is in Washington, D.C., and which houses the Mellon, Kress, and Widener collections, is one of the largest marble structures in the entire world.

5. The radio announcer repeatedly kept saying, ''Buy Peterson's Perfect Prawns,'' over and over and over again.

6. There were fifty people in the hospital ward who were among those who received great benefit from the new drug.

7. I had an advantage over the other contestants because of the fact that I had just looked up the word myself in a dictionary.

8. In this day and time, it is difficult today to find in the field of science a chemist who shows as much promise for the future as Joseph Blake shows.

9. He found the problem of discovering the legal status of the refugees an almost insoluble problem.

10. In order that immigrants may apply to become citizens of Canada they must make out an application stating their intention to become citizens.

Omission of Necessary Words

22

Do not omit a word or phrase necessary to the meaning of the sentence. (See also 26b.)

In many instances a word or a phrase is optional; a writer may use it or omit it without changing the meaning of the sentence. In the following example, optional words are in brackets:

> It seems [that] the security force on [the] campus over-reacted.

In other instances a word like *that* or *the* is necessary or desirable for clarity:

> I know *that* the security force on *the* other campus over-reacted.

The omission of words in a comparison may distort meaning:

> INCOMPLETE   Snow here is as scarce as Miami.
> COMPLETE   Snow here is as scarce as *it is in* Miami.

If you omit necessary words in your compositions, your mind may be racing ahead of your pen, or your writing may reflect omissions in your spoken English.

The analyst talked about the tax dollar goes. [The writer
 thought "talked about where" but did not write *where*.]
You better be there on time! [When speaking, the writer
 omits *had* before *better*.]

To avoid omitting necessary words, proofread your compositions carefully and study 22a–c.

22a

**Do not omit a necessary article, pronoun, conjunc-
tion, or preposition.**

(1) Omitted article or pronoun

INCOMPLETE   Feelings of inferiority are at bottom of person's
                jealousy.
COMPLETE   Feelings of inferiority are at *the* bottom of *a*
                person's jealousy.

INCOMPLETE   Beth knows a woman had a lawyer like that
COMPLETE   Beth knows a woman *who* had a lawyer like
                that.

When it is necessary to indicate plural number, repeat a
pronoun or an article before the second part of a compound

My mother and father were there. [Clearly two persons—
 repetition of *my* before *father* not necessary]
A friend and *a* helper stood nearby. [Two persons clearly
 indicated by repetition of *a*]

(2) Omitted conjunction or preposition

CONFUSING   Fran noticed the passenger who was sleeping
               soundly had dropped his wallet in the aisle
               [The reader may be momentarily confused by
               "noticed the passenger."]
BETTER   Fran noticed *that* the passenger who was sleep-
               ing soundly had dropped his wallet in the aisle

INCOMPLETE	Such comments neither contribute nor detract from his reputation.
COMPLETE	Such comments neither contribute *to* nor detract from his reputation.
	[When two verbs requiring different prepositions are used together, do not omit the first preposition. See also **20b**.]
INFORMAL	I had never seen that type movie before.
GENERAL	I had never seen that type *of* movie before.

■ **Exercise 1** Fill in the blanks below with appropriate articles, pronouns, conjunctions, or prepositions.

1. _____ good are not always rewarded; _____ evil often prosper. Life is not _____ morality play.
   —MICHAEL NOVAK

2. The battle left him untouched: it was the peace _____ undid him. —VIRGINIA WOOLF

3. Quarrelling means trying to show _____ the other man is in the wrong. —C. S. LEWIS

4. You can see _____ pride she takes in being _____ lowliest of _____ low. —PAULINE KAEL

5. To me, there are two kinds of liberals: the type _____ fellow _____ would take off his coat in a snowstorm and put it around my shoulders, and the type _____ fellow _____ would caution me to wear a coat against the snow. —JAMES ALAN McPHERSON

22b

Avoid awkward omission of verbs and auxiliaries.

AWKWARD	Preston has never and cannot be wholly honest with himself.
BETTER	Preston has never *been* and cannot be wholly honest with himself.

INCOMPLETE   Since I been in college, some of my values have changed.

COMPLETE   Since I *have* been in college, some of my values have changed.

Usage is divided regarding the inclusion or the omission of verbs in such sentences as the following:

> The Lions are overwhelming; the event is unavoidable.
> —E. B. WHITE [Plural *are* is used with *Lions,* and singular *is* with *event.*]

> The sounds were angry, the manner violent.
> —A. E. VAN VOGT [Plural *were* is used with *sounds,* but singular *was* after *manner* is omitted.]

22c

Do not omit words needed to complete comparisons.

INCOMPLETE   Ed's income is less than his wife.

COMPLETE   Ed's income is less than *that of* his wife.
OR
Ed's income is less than his wife*'s.*

CONFUSING   Bruce likes me more than Ann.

BETTER   Bruce likes me more than *he likes* Ann.
OR
Bruce likes me more than Ann *does.*

INCOMPLETE   Harry is as old, if not older than, Paul.

COMPLETE   Harry is as old *as,* if not older than, Paul.
OR
Harry is as old *as* Paul, if not older.

In a comparison such as the following, the word *other* may indicate a difference in meaning:

> Fuller runs faster than any player on the team. [Fuller is apparently not on the team. (In context, however, this may be an informal sentence meaning that Fuller is the fastest of the players on the team.)]

232

Fuller runs faster than any *other* player on the team.   [*Other* clearly indicates that Fuller is on the team.]

Some writers still prefer to avoid such intensives as *so, such,* and *too* when used without a completing phrase or clause:

Albert Einstein was thought to have so little promise at graduation *that no school or university bothered to offer him a job.*   —MITCHELL WILSON

Many a man is praised for his reserve and so-called shyness when he is simply too proud *to risk making a fool of himself.*   —J. B. PRIESTLEY

■ **Exercise 2** Supply the words that have been omitted from the following sentences. Put a checkmark after any sentence that needs no revision.

1. In our province the winter is as bad as Quebec.
2. The mystery of the stolen jewels reminds me of mysteries like Sherlock Holmes.
3. His wife and mother were standing beside him.
4. Mr. Carter paid me more than Jim.
5. Nick announced the winner of the debate had not yet been voted on.
6. If Jack goes into a profession which he is not trained, he will fail.
7. The lawyer had to prove whatever the witness said was false.
8. I been on scholastic probation before, and I better spend more time in the library this term.
9. Many cases it is true justice does not prevail.
10. Peggy always has and always will live in Saskatchewan.

EFFECTIVE SENTENCES

Unity and Logical Thinking

Unity, coherence, emphasis, variety—these are fundamental qualities of effective prose. Unity and coherence in sentences help to make ideas logical and clear. Emphasis makes them forceful. Variety lends interest.

23

Write unified, logical sentences.

A sentence is unified when all its parts contribute to making one clear idea or impression. The parts of an ideal sentence form a perfect whole, so that a clause, a phrase, or even a word cannot be changed without disturbing the clarity of the thought or the focus of the impression. A study of this section should help you to write unified, logical sentences, sentences that are not cluttered with obscurities, irrelevancies, or excessive details.

23a
Bring into a sentence only related thoughts; use two or more sentences for thoughts not closely related.

Make sure that the ideas in each sentence are related and that the relationship is immediately clear to the reader. Use two or more sentences to develop ideas that are too loosely linked to belong in one sentence.

UNRELATED   The ancient name for Paris, a city which has an annual rainfall of over twenty inches, was Lutetia.

BETTER   Paris has an annual rainfall of over twenty inches. The ancient name of the city was Lutetia. [The unrelated ideas are put into separate sentences, possibly in different parts of the composition.]

UNRELATED   Yesterday Ted sprained his ankle, and he could not find his chemistry notes anywhere.

RELATED   Accident-prone all day yesterday, Ted not only sprained his ankle but also lost his chemistry notes. [The relationship of the two ideas is made clear by the addition of the opening phrase.]

■ **Exercise 1** All the sentences below contain ideas that are apparently unrelated. Adding words when necessary, rewrite each of the sentences to indicate clearly a relationship between ideas. If you cannot establish a close relationship, put the ideas in separate sentences.

1. Although the visiting professor has different and refreshing views, I played badminton on September 20.
2. I hate strong windstorms, and pecans pelted my bedroom roof all night.
3. The fence and barn need repairs, and why are property taxes so high?
4. There are many types of bores at social gatherings, but personally I prefer a quiet evening at home.
5. A telephone lineman who works during heavy storms can prove a hero, and cowards can be found in any walk of life.
6. Jones was advised to hire a tutor in French immediately, but the long hours of work at a service station kept his grades low.
7. Macbeth was not the only man to succumb to ambition, and Professor Stetson, for example, likes to draw parallels between modern men and literary characters.

8. Brad sent his sister a dozen red roses, and she sang on a fifteen-minute program on CKFM radio.
9. The food in the cafeteria has been the subject of many jokes, and most university students do not look underfed.
10. Birds migrate to the warmer countries in the fall and in summer get food by eating worms and insects that are pests to the farmer.

23b

Do not allow excessive detail (including excessive subordination) to obscure the central thought of the sentence or awkwardly separate the sentence base. See also **24c** and **25a(5)**.

Bring into a sentence only pertinent details. Omit tedious minutiae and irrelevant side remarks.

EXCESSIVE DETAIL   In 1867, Sir John A. Macdonald, who was born in Glascow in 1815, the third child of Hugh Macdonald, a native of Sutherlandshire, and who had worked in a law office in Kingston, then a very small but thriving town, from the age of fifteen, six years before he volunteered for military service during the 1837 rebellion, became the first Premier of the Dominion of Canada.

BETTER   In 1867, Sir John A. Macdonald, a one-time legal clerk, became the first Premier of the Dominion of Canada.

AWKWARD SEPARATION   Our vet, who specializes in dermatology, which has to do with skin diseases, has, because he has successfully treated the skin disorders of countless animals, an excellent reputation.

BETTER   Because our vet has successfully treated the skin diseases of countless animals, he has an excellent reputation as a dermatologist.

As you strive to eliminate irrelevant details, remember that length alone does not make a sentence ineffective. Good writers can compose very long sentences, sometimes of paragraph length, without loss of unity. Parallel structure, balance, rhythm, careful punctuation, and well-placed connectives can bind a sentence into a perfect unit. Notice how many specific details John Steinbeck presents in the long second sentence below as he develops the key idea of the first sentence:

> Every summer morning about nine o'clock a stout and benign-looking lady came down the stairs from her flat to the pavement carrying the great outdoors in her arms. She set out a canvas deck chair, and over it mounted a beach umbrella—one of the kind which has a little cocktail table around it—and then, smiling happily, this benign and robust woman rolled out a little lawn made of green raffia in front of her chair, set out two pots of red geraniums and an artificial palm, brought a little cabinet with cold drinks—Coca-Cola, Pepsi-Cola—in a small icebox; she laid her folded copy of the *Daily News* on the table, arranged her equipment, and sank back into the chair—and she was in the country.
>
> —JOHN STEINBECK[1]

■ **Exercise 2** Recast the following sentences to eliminate excessive subordination or detail.

1. During the first period last Monday in room 206 of the English building, we students enjoyed discussing the implications of language in various advertisements.
2. The fan that Joan bought for her brother, who frets about any temperature that exceeds twenty degrees Celsius and insists that he can't stand the heat, arrived today.
3. When I was only four, living in a house built during the colonial period, little of which remains today, I often walked alone the two miles between my house and the lake.
4. Four cars of various designs and makes piled up on the freeway, which cost the province over $2 million.
5. In a white suit and in a straight chair, the alderman advocated drastic reforms, occasionally taking time out for a sip of water.

[1] From *America and Americans* by John Steinbeck. Copyright © 1966 by John Steinbeck. All rights reserved. Reprinted by permission of Viking Penguin Inc.

6. The dilapidated boat, seaworthy ten years ago but badly in need of repairs now, moved out into the bay.

7. Flames from the gas heater that was given to us three years ago by friends who were moving to Alberta licked at the chintz curtains.

8. After finishing breakfast, which consisted of oatmeal, toast, and coffee, Sigrid called the tree surgeon, a cheerful man approximately fifty years old.

9. At last I returned the book that I had used for the report which I made Tuesday to the library.

10. A course in business methods helps undergraduates to get jobs and in addition helps them to find out whether they are fitted for business and thus to avoid postponing the crucial test, as so many do, until it is too late.

23c
Avoid mixed or illogical constructions.

(1) Do not mix metaphors by changing rapidly from one to another. See also 20a(4).

MIXED   Playing with fire can get a person into deep water.
BETTER   Playing with fire can result in burned fingers.

MIXED   Her plans to paint the town red were nipped in the bud.

BETTER   Her plans to paint the town red were thwarted. OR Her plans for a gala evening were nipped in the bud.

(2) Do not mix constructions. Complete each construction logically.

MIXED   When Howard plays the hypochondriac taxes his wife's patience. [Adverb clause + predicate.]
CLEAR   When Howard plays the hypochondriac, *he* taxes his wife's patience. [Adverb clause, main clause.]
CLEAR   Howard's playing the hypochondriac taxes his wife's patience. [Subject + predicate.]

ILLOGICAL An example of discrimination is a cafe owner, especially after he has refused to serve foreigners. [It is the refusal, not the cafe owner, that is an example of discrimination.]

LOGICAL An example of discrimination is a cafe owner's refusal to serve foreigners.

In defining words, careful writers tell *what* a thing is, not when it is or where it is.

AWKWARD A sonnet is when a poem has fourteen lines.

BETTER A sonnet is a poem of fourteen lines.

AWKWARD Banishing a person is where he is driven out of his country.

BETTER Banishing a person is driving him out of his country.

(3) Make each part of the sentence agree logically with the other parts.

Often a sentence is flawed by a confusion of singular and plural words.

CONFUSED Hundreds who attended the convention drove their own car.

BETTER Hundreds who attended the convention drove their own cars.

■ **Exercise 3** Revise the following sentences to eliminate mixed or illogical constructions.

1. For Don, money does grow on trees, and it also goes down the drain quickly.
2. Because his feet are not the same size explains the difficulty he has finding shoes that fit.
3. Friction is when one surface rubs against another.
4. Several of the delegates brought their wife with them.
5. One example of a ripoff would be a butcher, because he could weigh his heavy thumb with the steak.
6. Like a bat guided by radar, Alexander never skated on thin ice.

7. To be discreet is where a person carefully avoids saying or doing something tactless.
8. Does anyone here know why George resigned or where did he find a better job?
9. Tourists are not permitted to bring their camera indoors.
10. When a child needs glasses causes him to make mistakes in reading and writing.

23d
Base your writing on sound logic.

Be sure that your sentences are well thought out and contain no slips or weaknesses of logic. The following principles of sound thinking may help you to avoid the most common errors.

(1) Be sure your generalizations are sufficiently supported.

FAULTY None of the children in my family drink coffee; children do not like coffee. [The writer leaps to the conclusion without offering a sufficient number of examples.]

FAULTY When an automobile accident occurs in the city, the police are never on hand. [To make this assertion truthfully, the writer would have to know about every automobile accident in the city. By avoiding such words as *never* and *always,* using instead such qualifiers as *sometimes* or *often,* one can generalize more safely.]

(2) Be sure your evidence is objective and relevant to your assertion.

FAULTY Henry is an honest person; he will be successful in anything he tries. [Henry's honesty cannot possibly guarantee his success at every task. The writer's inference does not follow from the evidence.]

FAULTY That merchant is allegedly a thief and a liar; his arguments against a sales tax are worthless. [The merchant might steal and lie and yet have excellent views on economic matters such as a sales tax. The evidence is not relevant to the assertion.]

Note: Try not to confuse fact and opinion. To support your opinions, choose your facts carefully.

FACT Within forty-eight hours eleven persons were killed in plane crashes.

OPINION It is no longer safe to travel by air.

FACT Postal workers, miners, nurses, and teachers were among the nation's strikers during the 1970s.

OPINION By 1988 the nation will be a police state.

■ **Exercise 4** Prepare for a class discussion of the faulty logic in the sentences below.

1. Everyone goes to Florida in the winter.
2. Breaking a mirror brings seven years of bad luck.
3. Do not elect my opponent; his parents were not born in Canada.
4. Young people today do not obey their parents.
5. Jacqueline will be a good club president because all the members like her.
6. The other car was at fault, for the driver was a teenager.
7. All Germans like opera; I have never met a German who did not.
8. Gertrude has a migraine headache because she ate popcorn last night and got that phone call.
9. These razor blades give the smoothest shave; all the baseball players use them.
10. After that oil spill, the fish I caught tasted greasy. The report from the marine lab is wrong. Those fish are contaminated!

■ **Exercise 5** Choose any one of the following statements and support or refute it in a paragraph of approximately one hundred words. As you write, be careful to bring only related ideas and

243

pertinent details into each sentence. Avoid mixed or obscure constructions, and present logical, convincing evidence in support of your point of view.

1. The media can create fear in others without feeling it themselves.   —ROBERT FULFORD

2. You can command any response—you can even command people to die—but you cannot command love.

   —ERIC BERNE

3. The notion that advertising can somehow "manipulate" people into buying products which they should not buy is both arrogant and naive.   —MARTIN MAYER

4. If one wishes to have a career outside Canada one has to be known outside. No one will come and get you here even if you have the most marvellous talent in the world.

   —MONIQUE MERCURE

Subordination

24

Use subordination to relate ideas concisely and effectively; use coordination only to give ideas equal emphasis.

One of the marks of a mature writing style is the ability to connect and relate ideas effectively, either by coordination or by subordination. Coordination gives equal grammatical emphasis to two or more ideas. See also **12a** and **14a**. Subordination is the use of dependent elements to give grammatical focus to a main clause or a sentence base.

> COORDINATION   A baseball player can't hide mistakes or clumsiness; he stands alone and naked.
> —MARSHAL SMELSER
> [The semicolon separates two main clauses. The conjunction *or* coordinates two nouns; the conjunction *and,* two modifiers.]

> SUBORDINATION   Unless we *apply* the concepts of space and time to the impressions we receive, **the world is unintelligible,** just a kaleidoscopic jumble of colors and patterns and noises and smells and pain and tastes without meaning.
> —ROBERT M. PIRSIG
> [All the sentence elements not in boldface type are subordinate to the main clause, "the world is unintelligible."]

As this example shows, grammatically subordinate structures may contain very important ideas.

Inexperienced writers tend to use too much coordination—too many short simple sentences or stringy compound ones. To express relationships between ideas, do not overwork coordinating connectives like *so* or *and* or conjunctive adverbs like *then* or *however*. Use relative pronouns (*who, which, that*) appropriately as subordinators. Also use subordinating conjunctions to indicate such relationships as cause (*because, since*), concession (*although, though*), time (*after, as, before, since, when, whenever, while, until*), place (*where, wherever*), condition (*if, unless*), and comparison (*as if*). Notice the differences in emphasis in the following sentences:

> **Clem had finished the pre-employment course,** *and* **he was ready for an on-the-job experience.**
>
> **Clem,** *who* **had finished the pre-employment course, was ready for an on-the-job experience.**
>
> *Because* **Clem had finished the pre-employment course, he was ready for an on-the-job experience.**

24a

Use subordination to combine a related series of short sentences into longer, more effective units.

When combining a series of related sentences, first choose one complete idea for your sentence base; then use subordinate structures (such as modifiers, parenthetical elements, and appositives) to relate the ideas in the other simple sentences to the base.

> CHOPPY   Two days passed. Then helicopters headed for the mountaintop. The blizzard had stranded several climbers.
>
> BETTER   After two days, helicopters headed for the mountaintop because the blizzard had stranded several climbers.

CHOPPY   Douglas was waiting for the bus. He wrote a quick
         note. It was to Nora. She is his former employer.
BETTER   Waiting for the bus, Douglas wrote a quick note to
         Nora, his former employer.

■ **Exercise 1**   Combine the following short sentences into
longer sentences by using effective subordination as well as
coordination. (If you wish, keep one short sentence for emphasis:
see **29h**.)

[1] I wrote a short paper on the ideas of Thomas Carlyle. [2] I was
especially interested in his analysis of the great man. [3] I was
also interested in his treatment of the divinity of heroes. [4] It is
hard to relate his views to current thought. [5] There is a basic
difference between his time and ours. [6] His ideas fit the mood of
the Victorian era. [7] Then men agreed on certain values. [8] And
their heroes could be measured by those principles. [9] Today,
values are fluctuating. [10] We have our heroes—and antiheroes.

24b

**Do not string main clauses together with *and, so,* or
but when ideas should be subordinated. Use coordination only to give ideas equal emphasis.** See also **30c**.

AWKWARD   Burns won, and it was a landslide vote, but he
               had rigged the election.
BETTER   Burns, who had rigged the election, won by a
               landslide vote.
COORDINATION   The offer was tempting, but I did not accept
               it.   [Equal grammatical stress on the offer
               and the refusal]
SUBORDINATION Although the offer was tempting, I did not
               accept it.   [Stress on the refusal]
               OR
               Although I did not accept it, the offer was
               tempting.   [Stress on the offer]

247

■ **Exercise 2** To improve sentence unity, revise the following sentences by using effective subordination and, when needed, coordination.

1. First she selected a lancet and sterilized it, and then she gave the patient a local anesthetic and lanced the infected flesh.
2. Yesterday I was taking a shower, so I did not hear the telephone ring, but I got the message in time to go to the party.
3. Two ambulances tore by, and an oncoming bus crowded a truckload of labourers off the road, but nobody got hurt.
4. Jean Henri Dunant was a citizen of Switzerland, and he felt sorry for Austrian soldiers wounded in the Napoleonic Wars; therefore, he started an organization, and it was later named the Red Cross.
5. The administrators stressed career education, and not only did they require back-to-basics courses, but they also kept students informed about job opportunities.

24c

Avoid excessive or overlapping subordination. See also **23b**.

AWKWARD	I have never before known a man like Ernie, my friend who is always ready to help anybody who is in trouble that involves finances.
BETTER	I have never before known a man like my friend Ernie, who is always ready to help anybody in financial trouble.
AWKWARD	These were the voters who were concerned about unemployment that kept rising, who were worried about the dollar, which was diminishing in value.
BETTER	These were the voters concerned about rising unemployment and the diminishing value of the dollar.

■ **Exercise 3** Prepare to contribute to a class discussion of the subordination of ideas in the following paragraph.

¹ Very few people anywhere in the world were prepared for the first transplant of the human heart. ² Even in the surgical profession, where the literature included many documented reports of successful transplantation of hearts in dogs by Dr. Norman Shumway and Richard Lower at Stanford University Medical School, there was little serious acceptance of Shumway's published prediction that the time for a human experiment was near. ³ Consequently, when news came from South Africa on December 3, 1967, that Dr. Christiaan Barnard had taken the heart of a young woman killed in a road accident and put it into a middle-aged grocer whose own heart was failing, the popular reaction everywhere was as to a miracle. —JOHN LEAR[1]

---

[1]From John Lear's review of *One Life* by Christiaan Barnard and Curtis Bill Pepper, *Saturday Review*, May 23, 1970. Copyright 1970 Saturday Review, Inc. Reprinted by permission.

Coherence:
Misplaced Parts,
Dangling Modifiers

25

Avoid needless separation of related parts of the sentence. Avoid dangling modifiers.

Since the meaning of most English sentences depends largely on word order, the position of the parts of a sentence is especially important to clear communication.

MISPLACED   According to Sybil, the gypsies believe that anyone who eats honey and garlic every day will live a long time *in England.*

BETTER   According to Sybil, *the gypsies in England* believe that anyone who eats honey and garlic every day will live a long time.

DANGLING   *When discussing creativity,* a person's ability to finish a pun is stressed by John E. Gibson.

BETTER   *When discussing creativity, John E. Gibson* stresses a person's ability to finish a pun.

The parts of a sentence should be placed to convey the precise emphasis or meaning desired. Note how the meaning of the following sentences changes according to the position of the modifiers:

Rex *just* died, with his boots on.
Rex died, with *just* his boots on.

The man *who drowned* had tried to help the child.
The man had tried to help the child *who drowned*.

Normally the modifier should be placed as near the word modified as idiomatic English will permit.

Misplaced Parts

25a

Avoid needless separation of related parts of the sentence.

(1) In standard written English, modifiers such as *almost, only, just, even, hardly, nearly,* and *merely* are regularly placed immediately before the words they modify.

In speech such modifiers are often put before the verb.

SPOKEN The hut only costs $450. [OR costs *only* $450]
WRITTEN The hut costs *only* $450.

SPOKEN Stacey will not even write us a postcard. [OR write us *even* a postcard]
WRITTEN Stacey will not write us *even* a postcard.

■ **Exercise 1** Revise the following sentences, placing the modifiers in correct relation to the words they modify.

1. The bomb of the terrorists only killed one student.
2. Bruce polished his silver dollars almost until they looked like new.
3. The transistor nearly cost fifty dollars.
4. He even works during his vacation.
5. Some contemporary poets hardly show any interest in making their poems intelligible.

(2) The position of a modifying prepositional phrase should clearly indicate what the phrase modifies.

A prepositional phrase used as an adjective nearly always comes immediately after the word modified.

> MISPLACED   A garish poster attracts the visitor's eye *on the east wall.*
>
> BETTER   A garish poster *on the east wall* attracts the visitor's eye.

Adverb phrases may be placed near the word modified or at the beginning or end of a sentence. Sometimes, however, the usual placement can be awkward or unclear.

> MISPLACED   One student said that such singing was not music but a throat ailment *in class.*
>
> BETTER   *In class* one student *said* that such singing was not music but a throat ailment.   OR   One student *said in class* that such singing was not music but a throat ailment.

■ **Exercise 2**   Revise the following sentences to correct undesirable separation of related parts.

1. Newspapers carried the story of the satellite's fall in every part of the country.
2. Candy bakes date muffins just for her friends with pecans in them.
3. At the picnic Gertrude served sundaes to hungry guests in paper cups.
4. The professor made it clear why plagiarism is wrong on Monday.

(3) Adjective clauses should be placed near the words they modify.

> MISPLACED   We bought gasoline in the States at a small country store *which cost $3.12.*
>
> BETTER   At a small country store in the States, we bought gasoline *which cost $3.12.*

252

(4) Avoid "squinting" constructions—modifiers that may refer to either a preceding or a following word.

SQUINTING   Eating out *often* pacifies her.
BETTER   Eating out *can often pacify* her.
           OR
           It pacifies her *to eat out often*.

(5) Avoid the awkward separation of the sentence base and the awkward splitting of an infinitive.

AWKWARD   I *had* in spite of my not living in a neighbourhood as fine as Jane's *pride*. [Awkward separation of a verb from its object]
BETTER   In spite of my not living in a neighbourhood as *fine as Jane's,* I had pride.
AWKWARD   Hawkins is the man *to,* whether you are a Liberal, Conservative, or New Democrat, *vote for.* [Awkward splitting of an infinitive]
BETTER   Whether you are a Liberal, Conservative, or New Democrat, Hawkins is the man *to vote for.*

Note: Many times, though, splitting an infinitive is not only natural but also desirable.

For her to *never* complain seems unreal.
I wished to *properly* understand meditating.

■ **Exercise 3** Revise the following sentences to eliminate squinting modifiers or needless separation of related sentence parts.

1. An official warned the hunter not to carry a rifle in a car that was loaded.
2. Selby said in the evening he would go.
3. Marvin wanted to, even during the 6:15 P.M. sports news, finish our game of checkers.
4. Harriet promised when she was on her way home to stop at the library.
5. The car was advertised in last night's paper which is only two years old and is in excellent condition.

Dangling Modifiers

25b
Avoid dangling modifiers.

Although any misplaced word, phrase, or clause can be said to dangle when it hangs loosely within a sentence, the term *dangling* is applied primarily to incoherent verbal phrases and elliptical adverb clauses. A dangling modifier does not refer clearly and logically to another word or phrase in the sentence.

To correct a dangling modifier, rearrange the words in the sentence to make the modifier clearly refer to the right word, or add words to make the meaning clear and logical.

(1) Avoid dangling participial phrases.

DANGLING   *Discouraged by low grades,* dropping out made sense.

REVISED   *Because I was discouraged by low grades,* dropping out made sense.   OR

Discouraged by low grades, I thought dropping out made sense.

The second revision above follows this pattern:

PARTICIPIAL PHRASE, SUBJECT—PREDICATE.

In the following sentence, the participial phrase is an appended rather than an introductory element.

DANGLING   The evening passed very pleasantly, *playing backgammon and swapping jokes.*

REVISED   *They* passed the evening very pleasantly, *playing backgammon and swapping jokes.*

In the revision above, the participial phrase refers to the subject, as the pattern on the following page illustrates:

> SUBJECT—PREDICATE, PARTICIPIAL PHRASE.

(2) Avoid dangling phrases containing gerunds or infinitives.

DANGLING *Instead of watching the "Late Show," a novel was read.*

REVISED *Instead of watching the "Late Show," Nancy read a novel.*

DANGLING *Not able to swim that far, a lifeguard came to my rescue.*

REVISED *I was not able to swim that far, so a lifeguard came to my rescue.*
OR
Because I was not able to swim that far, a lifeguard came to my rescue.

(3) Avoid dangling elliptical adverb clauses.

Elliptical clauses have words that are implied rather than stated.

DANGLING *When confronted with these facts, not one word was said.*

REVISED *When confronted with these facts, nobody said a word.*
OR
When they were confronted with these facts, not one word was said.

DANGLING *Although only a small boy, my father expected me to do a man's work.*

REVISED *Although I was only a small boy, my father expected me to do a man's work.*

Note 1: Absolute constructions do not dangle:

RIGHT *This being the case, we had no choice.*

RIGHT Macbeth stood there, *his hands dripping blood.*

Verbal phrases such as the following (often called *sentence modifiers* because they qualify a whole clause or the rest of the sentence) are not classified as dangling modifiers but are considered standard usage.

> *To judge from reports,* all must be going well.
> His health is fairly good, *considering his age.*

Note 2: Current usage accepts the following structures. Notice that the italicized modifiers are used with this basic pattern: *it + be +* adjective *+* infinitive phrase.

> *Living out in the suburbs,* it is easy to assume that ours is, indeed, an affluent society.   —MICHAEL HARRINGTON
> [Compare "If you are living out in the suburbs, it is easy for you to assume. . . ."]

> *When demonstrating,* it is good to carry a placard stating one's position.   —WOODY ALLEN
> [Compare "When one is demonstrating, it is good for one to carry. . . ."]

■ **Exercise 4** Revise the following sentences to eliminate dangling modifiers. Put a checkmark after any sentence that needs no revision.

1. While wondering about this phenomenon, the sun sank from view.
2. By standing and repeating the pledge, the meeting came to an end.
3. Once made, you must execute the decision promptly.
4. Prepare to make an incision in the abdomen as soon as completely anesthetized.
5. After sitting there awhile, it began to snow, and we went indoors.
6. Darkness having come, we stopped for the night.
7. Having taken his seat, we began to question the witness.
8. Ready to pitch camp, the windstorm hit.
9. The convicts did not yield, thinking they could attract the support of the press.
10. Burned to the ground, the Welches had to build a new house.

Exercise 5 Combine the two sentences in each item below into a single sentence. Use an appropriately placed verbal phrase or elliptical clause as an introductory parenthetical element.

EXAMPLES

We were in a hurry to leave Quebec City. The dented fender was not noticed.

Being in a hurry to leave Quebec City, we did not notice the dented fender.

A person may sometimes be confused. At such times he ought to ask questions.

When confused, a person ought to ask questions.

1. The statue has a broken arm and nose. I think it is an interesting antique.
2. James sometimes worried about the world situation. At such times joining CUSO seemed to him a good idea.
3. I read the first three questions on the test. The test covered materials that I had not studied.
4. Larry was only twelve years old. His teachers noticed his inventive abilities.
5. I turned on the flashers and lifted the hood. A speeding motorist, I thought, might slow down, see my predicament, and offer me a ride.

257

Parallelism

26

Use parallel structure as an aid to coherence.

Parallel (grammatically equal) sentence elements regularly appear in lists, series, and compound structures. Connectives like *and, or, but, yet* link and relate balanced sentence elements. Faulty parallelism disrupts the balance.

AWKWARD   What do the super-rich know about disease, those who are hungry, and poverty?

PARALLEL   What do the super-rich know about *disease, hunger,* and *poverty?* [Nouns in series]

PARALLEL   What do the super-rich know about those who are *sick, hungry,* and *poor?* [Adjectives in series]

Remember to use parallel elements to express parallel ideas. Do not coordinate ideas that should be subordinated; see Section 24.

26a

For parallel structure, balance nouns with nouns, prepositional phrases with prepositional phrases, main clauses with main clauses, and so on.

As you study the parallel words, phrases, clauses, and sentences that follow, notice that repetition can be used to emphasize the balanced structure and that one item in a series may be expanded without disturbing the total effect of the parallelism.

(1) Parallel words and phrases

People begin to feel || *faceless*
     and || *insignificant.* —S. L. HALLECK

|| *Opportunity for purposeful activity,*
|| *opportunity for self-realization,*
|| *opportunity for work and rest and love and play—*
this is what men think of as liberty today.
—CLINTON ROSSITER

The two most powerful words in the world today are
not || *guns and money,*
but || *wheat and oil.* —FREDRIC BIRMINGHAM

She had || *no time to be human,*
      || *no time to be happy.* —SEAN O'FAOLAIN

(2) Parallel clauses

      || *What we say*
and || *what we do*
somehow seem out of joint. —NORMAN COUSINS

|| Women can smoke Marlboros,
    yet || no man dares smoke Eve;
|| women wear pantsuits,
    yet || no American male wears a dress.
—WARREN FARRELL

(3) Parallel sentences

|| *The danger of the past was that men became slaves.*
|| *The danger of the future is that men may become robots.*
—ERICH FROMM

259

■**Exercise 1**   Underline the parallel structures in the following sentences.

1. We are all sick, all lonely, all in need of love.

—JEAN VANIER

2. Montreal has something of American luxury, the sagacity of London, the briskness of New York, the gaiety of Europe.

—V. S. PRITCHETT

3. Tufts of hair sprouted from his ears, from his nose; his jowls were grey with afternoon beard, and his handshake almost furry.   —TRUMAN CAPOTE

4. Broadly speaking, human beings may be divided into three classes: those who are toiled to death, those who are worried to death, and those who are bored to death.

—WINSTON CHURCHILL

5. I hold no brief for private enterprise. But I have unshakeable faith in individual enterprise.   —C. L. BURTON

26b

To make the parallel clear, repeat a preposition, an article, the sign of the infinitive, or the introductory word of a long phrase or clause.

The reward rests not ‖*in* the task
but ‖*in* the pay.   —JOHN K. GALBRAITH

Life is ‖*a* mystery
and ‖*an* adventure
which he shares with all living things.

—JOSEPH WOOD KRUTCH

It is easier ‖*to love humanity as a whole*
than ‖*to love one's neighbor.*   —ERIC HOFFER

We say ‖*that* civilization cannot survive an atomic war,
‖*that* there can be no victory and no victors,
‖*that* nuclear weapons can annihilate all life on this
‖planet.   —ADLAI E. STEVENSON

■ **Exercise 2** Insert words needed to bring out the parallel structure in the following sentences.

1. They would lie on the battlefield without medical attention for an hour or day.
2. Two things I intend to do: to try and succeed.
3. I told him politely that I could not go and I had reasons.
4. I finally realized that one can learn much more by studying than worrying.
5. On the safari Eva took photographs of a tiger and elephant.

26c

Correlatives (*both . . . and; either . . . or; neither . . . nor; not only . . . but also; whether . . . or*) usually connect parallel structures.

AWKWARD	We judge our friends both by what they say and actions.
PARALLEL	We judge our friends both ‖ *by their words* and ‖ *by their actions.*
PARALLEL	We judge our friends both ‖ *by what they say* and ‖ *by how they act.*
AWKWARD	Not only the booing, but the team also resents the announcer's obvious partiality.
PARALLEL	The team resents not only ‖ *the booing* but also ‖ *the announcer's obvious partiality.*
OR	Not only does the team resent the booing, but it also resents the announcer's obvious partiality. [The *also* may be omitted.]
AWKWARD	Whether drunk or when he was sober, he liked to pick a fight.
PARALLEL	Whether ‖ *drunk* or ‖ *sober,* he liked to pick a fight.

261

26d

Be sure that a *who, whom,* or *which* clause precedes *and who, and whom,* or *and which.*

AWKWARD Mary Dumont is a woman with an open mind and who is seeking office. [A *who* clause does not precede the *and who.*]

PARALLEL Mary Dumont is a woman ‖ *who has an open mind*
                   and ‖ *who is seeking office.*

■ **Exercise 3** Revise the following sentences by using parallel structure to express parallel ideas. Put a checkmark after any sentence that needs no revision.

1. Shirley likes to play tennis and watching basketball.
2. Our personalities are shaped by both heredity and what type of environment we have.
3. Someone has said that North Americans cannot enjoy life without a TV set, an automobile, and a summer cottage.
4. My friend told me that the trip would be delayed but to be ready to start on Friday.
5. William is a man with the best intentions and who has the highest principles.
6. A seal watches carefully the way his fellows act and how they obey their trainer.
7. He was quiet and in a serious mood after the talk.
8. The secretary must attend all meetings, call the roll, and keep the minutes.
9. People fall naturally into two classes: the workers and those who like to depend on others.
10. Neither the dull 1950s nor what the rebels tried to do in the 1960s affected my young life.

■ **Exercise 4** First study the parallelism in the sentences below. Then use one of the sentences as a structural model for a sentence of your own.

1. In the ghetto everybody gets a piece of the action: those who are Jews and those who are Christians; those who are white and those who are black; those who run the numbers

and those who operate the churches; those—black and white—who own tenements and those—black and white—who own businesses.   —BAYARD RUSTIN

[Note that semicolons sharply divide the long, compound items in the series and contribute to clarity.]

2. Finally to laugh, to chatter, to smile and know the warmth of responding smiles, to feel somebody's arm on one's shoulder, to put one's arm through another's in walking along, to have allies, supporters, to be wanted, sought, joined gratefully, left regretfully, to be liked, to be loved: with such a rich experience suddenly proffered, why should earlier solitude be a barrier?   —SALLY CARRIGHAR

[Note that the colon here is used (instead of the dash) to call attention to the question that follows.]

Shifts

27

Avoid needless shifts in grammatical structures, in tone or style, and in viewpoint.

Abrupt, unnecessary shifts—for example, from past to present, from singular to plural, from formal diction to slang, from one perspective to another—tend to obscure a writer's meaning and thus to cause needless difficulty in reading.

27a

Avoid needless shifts in tense, mood, and voice. See also Section 7.

SHIFT   During their talk Harvey *complained* about the idiocy of overkill while his father *discusses* the dangers of overlive. [Shift from past to present tense]

BETTER   During their talk Harvey *complained* about the idiocy of overkill while his father *discussed* the dangers of overlive. [Both verbs in the past tense]

SHIFT   If I *were* rich and if my father *was* still alive, my life would be different. [Shift from subjunctive to indicative mood]

BETTER   If I *were* rich and if my father *were* still alive, my life would be different. [Verbs in the subjunctive mood]

SHIFT   The old widower finally *had to enter* a nursing home, but it *was* not *liked* by him. [The voice shifts from active to passive.]

BETTER   The old widower finally *had to enter* a nursing home, but he *did* not *like* it. [Both verbs are active.]

When the literary present is used (see page 62), as in summarizing plots of novels and plays, care should be taken to avoid slipping from the present tense into the past tense.

Romeo and Juliet fall in love at first sight, marry secretly, and die (NOT *died*) together in the tomb within the same hour.

27b

Avoid needless shifts in person and in number. See also 6b.

SHIFT   A *person* has to expect criticism when *we* succeed. [Shift in person]

BETTER   A person has to expect criticism when *he* [OR *he or she* OR *he/she*] succeeds.
OR
One has to expect criticism when *one* succeeds.

SHIFT   Every *student* in favour of the legalization of marijuana *was* asked to sign *their names* on a master ditto sheet. [Shift in number]

BETTER   All *students* in favour of the legalization of marijuana *were* asked to sign *their names* on a master ditto sheet.

■ **Exercise 1**   Correct all needless shifts in tense, mood, voice, person, and number in the following sentences.

1. After his easy victory, Kurt strutted over to me and asks a smart-aleck question.
2. Jennings recommended that property taxes be raised and spend wisely for the poor.

3. Marvin added meat to the frozen pizza, and then it was baked fifteen minutes by him.
4. Every bystander was suspect, so they were hauled away for questioning.
5. I was told that billions of germs live on one's skin and that you should bathe often.

27c

Avoid needless shifts from indirect to direct dis course. See also 26a.

SHIFT   The Gordons wonder *how the thief got the car key* and *why didn't he or she steal the tapes?* [Shift from indirect to direct discourse—a mixture of indirect and direct questions]

BETTER   The Gordons wonder *how the thief got the car key* and *why he or she didn't steal the tapes.* [Two indirect questions]

OR

The Gordons asked, *"How did the thief get the car keys? Why didn't they steal the tapes?"* [The shift in number from *thief* to *they* is typical of conversational English.]

SHIFT   The secretary said *that he was sick* and *would please read the minutes.* [Shift from indirect to direct discourse]

BETTER   The secretary said *that he was sick* and *asked me to read the minutes.* [Indirect discourse]

27d

Avoid needless shifts in tone or style throughout the sentence (as well as throughout the larger elements of the composition).

INAPPROPRIATE   Journalists who contend that the inefficiency of our courts will lead to the total elimination of the jury system are *a bunch of kooks*. [A shift from formal to colloquial style. Replace *a bunch of kooks* with a phrase such as *a group of eccentrics*.]

INAPPROPRIATE After distributing the grass seed evenly over the lawn, rake the ground at least twice and then *gently bedew it with fine spray*. [The italicized expression is too "poetic" in a sentence with a prosaic purpose. Substitute something like *water it lightly*.]

27e

Avoid needless shifts in perspective or viewpoint throughout the sentence (as well as throughout the larger elements of the composition).

FAULTY PERSPECTIVE From the top of the CN Tower, the city looked like an oversize beehive, and the workers buzzed around busily in their office cells. [The perspective shifts from the tower to the interior of the city's buildings.]

CONSISTENT PERSPECTIVE From the top of the CN Tower, the city looked like an oversize beehive, and it was easy to imagine the workers buzzing around busily in their office cells.

■**Exercise 2** Correct all needless shifts in the following sentences. Put a checkmark after any sentence that needs no revision.

1. A woman stepped forward, grabs the mugger's belt, snatches the purses, and got lost in the crowd.
2. A vacation is enjoyed by all because it refreshes the mind and the body.
3. Aunt Leila spent her summers in Nova Scotia but flew to Florida for the winters.
4. Jim wondered whether Jack had left and did he say when he would return?
5. Every cook has their own recipes for making chili.

6. The underwater scene was dark and mysterious; the branches of the willows lining the shores dipped gracefully into the water.
7. The darkness of the auditorium, the monotony of the ballet, and the strains of music drifting sleepily from the orchestra aroused in me a great desire to sack out.

■ **Exercise 3** Revise the following paragraph to eliminate all needless shifts. If necessary, expand the paragraph.

¹ He was a shrewd businessman, or so it had always seemed to me. ² He has innocent-looking eyes, which are in a baby face, and swaggered when he walks. ³ When questioned about his recent windfall, he up and says, ''I'm lucky enough to have the right contacts.'' ⁴ Not one name was mentioned by him; moreover, his reluctance to discuss his business transactions was evident. ⁵ Take these comments for what they are worth; they may help one in your dealings with this big shot.

■ **Exercise 4** Prepare for a class discussion on the consistency of tone, style, and perspective—as well as on any shifts in grammatical structures within the sentence—in paragraphs 28 and 34, Section **31** (or any other paragraphs selected by your instructor).

Reference of Pronouns

28

Make a pronoun refer unmistakably to its antecedent. See also **6b**.

Each italicized pronoun below clearly refers to its antecedent, a single word or a word group:

> Languages are not invented; *they* grow with our need for expression. —SUSANNE K. LANGER

> There is no country in the world *whose* population is stationary. —KENNETH BOULDING

> Thus, being busy is more than merely a national passion; *it* is a national excuse. —NORMAN COUSINS

A pronoun may clearly refer to a whole clause:

> Some people think that the fall of man had something to do with sex, but *that*'s a mistake. —C. S. LEWIS [Compare "*To think this* is a mistake."]

As you proofread your compositions, check to see that the meaning of each pronoun is immediately obvious. If there is any chance of confusion, repeat the antecedent, use a synonym for it, or recast your sentence.

28a

Avoid an ambiguous reference.

A pronoun, of course, may clearly refer to two or more antecedents: "*Jack* and *Jill* met *their* Waterloo." Ambiguous reference, however, causes the reader to be unsure of the meaning of a pronoun because it could refer to one antecedent or to another.

AMBIGUOUS Lisa wrote to Jennifer every day when she was in the hospital.

CLEAR When Lisa was in the hospital, she wrote to Jennifer every day. OR
Every day that Jennifer was in the hospital Lisa wrote to her.

AMBIGUOUS After listening to Ray's proposal and to Sam's objections, I liked his ideas better.

CLEAR I agreed with Sam after listening to his objections to Ray's proposal.

28b

Avoid a remote or an obscure reference.

Do not run the risk of your reader's momentarily losing track of the antecedent of a pronoun because you have placed the pronoun too far from its antecedent. Also avoid an obscure reference to an antecedent in the possessive case.

REMOTE A student found herself the unanimously elected president of a group of enthusiastic reformers, mostly townspeople, *who* was not a joiner of organizations. [*Who* is too far removed from the antecedent *student*. See also **25a(3)**]

BETTER A *student who* was not a joiner of organizations found herself the unanimously elected president of a group of enthusiastic reformers, mostly townspeople.

OBSCURE When Johnson's club was organized, *he* asked
Goldsmith to become a member. [Reference to
antecedent in the possessive case]

BETTER When *Johnson* organized his club, *he* asked Goldsmith to become a member.

Note: As a rule, writers avoid using a pronoun like *it, this,* or
he to refer to the title of a composition or to a word in the
title.

Title: Death with Dignity

AWKWARD FIRST SENTENCE How can this ever be?
BETTER How can death ever be dignified?

■ **Exercise 1** Revise each sentence below to eliminate ambiguous, remote, or obscure pronoun reference.

1. The misunderstanding between the Kemps and the Dixons
did not end until they invited them over for a swim in their
new pool.

2. On the dashboard the various buttons and knobs seldom
cause confusion on the part of the driver that are clearly
labelled.

3. After Martin's advertising campaign was launched, he had
more business than he could handle.

4. The lake covers a large area. Near the shore, water lilies
grow in profusion, spreading out their green leaves and
sending up white blossoms on slender stems. It is well
stocked with fish.

5. Elaine waved to Mrs. Edwards as she was coming down the
ramp.

28c

Use broad reference only with discretion.

Pronouns such as *it, this, that, which,* and *such* may refer to a
specific word or phrase or to the general idea of a whole
clause, sentence, or paragraph:

SPECIFIC REFERENCE His nose was absolutely covered with warts of different sizes; it looked like a sponge, or some other kind of marine growth. —DAN JACOBSEN [*It* refers to *nose.*]

BROAD REFERENCE This was One World now—and he owned a Volkswagen and a Japanese camera to prove it.
—ARNOLD M. AUERBACH [*It* refers to *This was One World now.*]

When used carelessly, however, broad reference can interfere with clear communication. To ensure clarity, inexperienced writers may be advised to make each of their pronouns refer to a specific word.

(1) Avoid reference to the general idea of a preceding clause or sentence unless the meaning is clear.

VAGUE The story referred to James, but Henry misapplied it to himself. This is true in real life. [*This* has no antecedent.]

CLEAR The story referred to James, but Henry misapplied it to himself. Similar mistakes occur in real life.

(2) As a rule, do not refer to a word or an idea not expressed but merely implied.

VAGUE He wanted his teachers to think he was above average, as he could have been if he had used it to advantage. [*It* has no expressed antecedent.]

CLEAR He wanted his teachers to think he was above average, as he could have been if he had used his ability to advantage.

(3) Avoid awkward use of the indefinite *you* or *it*.

AWKWARD When one cannot swim, you fear deep, stormy waters. [See also **27b.**]

BETTER The person who cannot swim fears deep, stormy waters.

AWKWARD In the book *it* says that many mushrooms are edible.

BETTER The book says that many mushrooms are edible.

Note: In some contexts, the use of the impersonal, or indefinite, *you* is both natural and acceptable. Notice in the example below that *you* is equivalent in meaning to "people in general" or "the reader." (See also page 344.)

> The study of dreams has become a significant and respectable scientific exploration, one that can directly benefit *you.*
> —PATRICIA GARFIELD

Some writers, however, prefer not to use *you* in a formal context.

28d

Avoid the awkward placement of the pronoun *it* near the expletive *it*.

AWKWARD Although it would be unwise for me to buy the new model now, it is a beautiful machine. [The first *it* is an expletive; the second *it* is a pronoun referring to *model.*]

BETTER Although it would be unwise for me to buy one now, the new model is a beautiful machine. OR For me to buy the new model would be unwise now, but it is a beautiful machine.

■ **Exercise 2** Revise the following sentences as necessary to correct faults in reference. Put a checkmark after any sentence that needs no revision.

1. At the Chinese restaurant, the Meltons had a hard time eating with chopsticks, but that is their favourite food.
2. The car apparently needed gaskets; it leaked all over the garage floor.
3. Copiers and other fine modern office machines enable business executives to accomplish more work because their assistants can manage them easily and quickly.

4. In the book it states that Mrs. Garrett can see through her fingertips.
5. Our language is rich in connectives that express fine distinctions of meaning.
6. I did not even buy a season ticket, which was very disloyal to my school.
7. Mary told Ann that she had to read *Ecotactics*.
8. When building roads the Romans tried to detour around valleys as much as possible for fear that flood waters might cover them and make them useless.
9. The extra fees surprised many freshmen that seemed unreasonably high.
10. In Frank's suitcase he packs only wash-and-wear clothes.

Emphasis

29

Select words and arrange the parts of the sentence, as well as sentences in paragraphs, to give emphasis to important ideas. See also Section **32**, especially **32e**.

Since ideas vary in importance, expression of them should vary in emphasis. Short, factual statements and routine description or narration cannot always be varied for emphasis without doing violence to the natural word order of the English language. For example, it would be absurd for a sportswriter to describe a football play by saying, "Short was the pass that Randy caught, and across the goal line raced he." But in most types of writing, word order may be changed to achieve emphasis without losing naturalness of expression.

You may emphasize ideas through the use of concrete words, especially verbs and nouns (see Section **20**); through economy of language (see Section **21**); and through subordination (see Section **24**). You may also gain emphasis—

a by placing important words at the beginning or end of the sentence;
b by changing loose sentences into periodic sentences;
c by arranging ideas in the order of climax;

d by using the active voice instead of the passive voice;
e by repeating important words;
f by occasionally inverting the word order of a sentence;
g by using balanced sentence construction;
h by abruptly changing sentence length.

29a

Gain emphasis by placing important words at the beginning or end of the sentence—especially at the end.

UNEMPHATIC Total deafness is worse than total blindness, however, in many ways. [Parenthetical elements in an important position weaken the sentence.]

EMPHATIC Total deafness, however, is in many ways worse than total blindness.

UNEMPHATIC There was an underground blast that rocked the whole area. [Unemphatic words begin the sentence.]

EMPHATIC An underground blast rocked the whole area.

Since semicolons, sometimes called weak periods, are strong punctuation marks, words placed before and after a semicolon have an important position.

Always start with Socrates; aim high.
—WERNER J. DANNHAUSER

Note: Introductory transitional expressions, of course, do not ordinarily weaken a sentence beginning.

Above all, the spirit of science is the spirit of progress.
—HERMANN J. MULLER

And appended specific details, such as the two words after the dash in the following sentence, are often emphatic:

There they found and filmed men leaping and laughing amidst the terrified animals, clubbing them on their rumps as often as on their skulls, sticking the seals with knives in the necks, bellies, backs—even flippers. —GEORGE REIGER

■ **Exercise 1** Prepare for a class discussion of emphasis in the following paragraph, giving special attention to the choice of words at the beginning and end of each sentence.

[1]Into the numb days of November, dulling to greyness under the leaden bowl of the heavens, the blizzard tore. [2]One day hung wan, the next howled in whiteness. [3]The blast streamed and eddied round house, barn and bush; men ventured their lives to feed stock in barns and straw sheds; they staggered indoors to thaw their faces. [4]The storm squirmed through door-cracks, between window and sill in granular curls, prying at the people piling deep with wood their roaring heaters. [5]It blurred pale the frozen face of night.

—RUDY WIEBE[1]

■ **Exercise 2** Revise the following sentences to make them more emphatic. Change the word order when desirable, and delete unnecessary words and phrases.

1. Music has the power to hypnotize, so they say.
2. In fact, only one person could have written all these articles because of their same political slant, I am convinced.
3. There is one stunt woman who earns five thousand dollars for two hours of work.
4. Lewisville finally decided to enforce the old ordinance; there were nearby towns that revived similar laws and began clean-up campaigns, also.
5. It had never before entered her mind to resent her husband's complacent ignorance or to ignore his unreasonable demands, however.

---

[1]From *Peace Shall Destroy Many* by Rudy Wiebe reprinted by permission of The Canadian Publishers, McClelland and Stewart Limited, Toronto.

29b

Gain emphasis by changing loose sentences into periodic sentences.

In a *loose* sentence, the main idea (grammatically a main clause or sentence base) comes first; details or appended elements follow. In a *periodic* sentence, however, the main idea comes last.

> LOOSE   The curtain has fallen on the age of Bumper Sticker Bugling—where people displayed their strongest beliefs, like loud sounds, on the backs of their cars. —ANTOINETTE BOSCO   [The main idea comes first; explanatory details follow the dash.]

> PERIODIC   When you die, when you get a divorce, when you buy a house, when you have an auto accident, not to mention the hundreds of times during your lifetime when you are fleeced in your role as a consumer, a lawyer either must or should be involved. —DAVID HAPGOOD   [The main idea comes last, just before the period.]

Both types of sentences can be effective. The loose sentence is, and should be, the more commonly used. Although the periodic sentence is often the more emphatic, you should take care in your writing not to overuse it to the point of making your style unnatural. Variety is desirable: see Section 30 .

> LOOSE   Such sticky labels do not accurately describe any generation—for example, labels like *lost, beat, now, silent, unlucky,* or *found.*

> PERIODIC   Such sticky labels as *lost, beat, now, silent, unlucky,* or *found* do not accurately describe any generation.

> LOOSE   The Swiss are second only to the Americans, if the chart indicating per capita wealth is dependable.

> PERIODIC   If the chart indicating per capita wealth is dependable, the Swiss are second only to the Americans.

■ **Exercise 3** Study the structure of the following sentences; then label each as either *loose* or *periodic*.

1. Italy remains cheerful, despite everything.
   —AUBERON WAUGH
2. All things are beautiful as long as you get them in the proper order. —JOHN GRIERSON
3. The Milky Way Galaxy is entirely unremarkable, one of billions of other galaxies strewn through the vastness of space. —CARL SAGAN
4. And then she was sweet and apologetic, as always, as she had been all her life, nervously backing away from the arguments she should have had with my father, turning aside from the talks she should have had with me.
   —JOYCE CAROL OATES
5. When schemes are laid in advance, it is surprising how often the circumstances fit in with them.
   —SIR WILLIAM OSLER

■ **Exercise 4** Convert the loose sentences in Exercise 3 to periodic sentences, and the periodic to loose. Notice how your revisions make for varying emphasis.

29c

Gain emphasis by arranging ideas in the order of climax.

Notice in the following examples that the ideas are arranged in the order of importance, with the strongest idea last:

> Urban life is unhealthy, morally corrupt, and fundamentally inhuman. —RENÉ DUBOS [Adjectives in the series arranged in climactic order]

> *Every* man is wise when pursued by a mad dog; *fewer* when pursued by a mad woman; *only* the wisest survive when attacked by a mad notion. —ROBERTSON DAVIES [The three italicized words give the sentence a climactic progression.]

In the language of screen comedians four of the main grades of laugh are the titter, the yowl, the belly laugh and the boffo. The titter is just a titter. The yowl is a runaway titter. Anyone who has ever had the pleasure knows all about a belly laugh. The boffo is the laugh that kills. —JAMES AGEE [First words and then sentences placed in climactic order]

In a sentence like the following, the order of climax depends on the writer's judgment:

Discontented, desperate, vengeful people who no longer fear and even welcome death are the stuff of troublemakers, revolutionaries, assassins. —OSBORN SEGERBERG, JR.

Note: Anticlimax—an unexpected shift from the dignified to the trivial or from the serious to the comic—is sometimes used for special effect.

When I return to Canada from time to time, what I always find most tiresome is the cultural protectionism, the anti-Americanism. No heritage is worth preserving unless it can survive the sun, the mixed marriage, or the foreign periodical. Culture cannot be legislated or budgeted or protected with tariffs. Like potatoes. —MORDECAI RICHLER

■ **Exercise 5** Arrange the ideas in the sentences below in what you consider to be the order of climax.

1. In *Aesop's Fables* the grasshopper is a symbol of self-destruction, irresponsibility, and playfulness.
2. Among the images in the poem are sun-drenched orchards, diamond-eyed children, and golden-flecked birds.
3. He left the city because his health was failing, his taxes were going up, and his pet dog was tired of the leash.
4. Something must be done at once. Unless we act now, the city will be bankrupt in five years. The commission is faced with a deficit.
5. The would-be alderman attended a community festival, autographed books for teenagers, promised prosperity to all, and wrote letters to senior citizens.

29d

Gain emphasis by using the active voice instead of the passive voice.

UNEMPHATIC	Little attention is being paid to cheap, nutritious foods by the average shopper.
EMPHATIC	The average shopper is paying little attention to cheap, nutritious foods.

Exception: If the receiver of the action is more important than the doer, the passive voice is more effective.

There in the tin factory, in the first moment of the atomic age, a human being was crushed by books. —JOHN HERSEY

Freedom can be squashed by the tyrant or suffocated by the bureaucrat. —WILLIAM F. RICKENBACKER

■ **Exercise 6** Make each sentence below more emphatic by substituting the active for the passive voice.

1. Pennies are often pinched by the land-poor.
2. Every Saturday morning, television is being watched by easily influenced children.
3. The wastebasket was being filled with illegible photocopies by a student about to run out of coins.
4. When the play was brought to an end, the actors were greeted with a loud burst of applause by the audience.
5. It is greatly feared by the citizens that adequate punishment will not be meted out by the judge.

29e

Gain emphasis by repeating important words.

Note the effective repetition of *lie, successfully, natural,* and *wonder* in the parallel structures of the following passage. See also **26b** and **31b(3)** .

That we lie successfully to each other is natural; that we successfully lie to ourselves is a natural wonder. And that the three sciences central to human understanding—psychology, anthropology, and sociology—successfully and continually lie to themselves, lie to each other, lie to their students, and lie to the public at large, must constitute a paramount wonder of a scientific century. —ROBERT ARDREY[2]

■ **Exercise 7**   Prepare for a class discussion of the effect of repetition on emphasis in the following paragraph.

We are not only a civilized race, we are the pioneers of civilization; we are not only a religious people, we are the messengers of the religious idea; we are not only submissive sons of the Church, we are, we ought to be, numbered among its zealots, its defenders, and its apostles. Our mission is less to manipulate capital than to change ideas; it consists less in lighting the fires of factories than in maintaining and radiating afar the hearthlight of religion and thought. —LOUIS-ADOLPHE PAQUET[3]

29f

Gain emphasis by occasionally inverting the word order of a sentence. See also **30b**.

Basic to all the Greek achievement was freedom. —EDITH HAMILTON [Compare "Freedom was basic to all the Greek achievement."]

Caution: This method of gaining emphasis, if overused, will make the style distinctly artificial. And of course the order of the parts of the sentence should never be such as to cause ambiguity: see **25a**

---

[2] From *The Social Contract* by Robert Ardrey. Copyright © 1970 by Robert Ardrey. Reprinted by permission of the publisher, Atheneum Publishers.
[3] Quoted in John Robert Colombo, *Colombo's Concise Canadian Quotations* (Edmonton: Hurtig, 1976).

29g

Gain emphasis by using balanced sentence construction.

A sentence is balanced when grammatically equal structures—usually main clauses with parallel elements—are used to express contrasted (or similar) ideas: see Section **26.** A balanced sentence emphasizes the contrast (or similarity) between parts of equal length and movement.

> For many years we had a country with little or no art; now it seems we are to have art without a country.
>
> —A. Y. JACKSON

> Love is positive; tolerance negative. Love involves passion; tolerance is humdrum and dull. —E. M. FORSTER

■ **Exercise 8** Use balanced, emphatic sentences to show the contrast between the following:

(1) summer and winter, (2) youth and age, (3) town and city, (4) hypocrisy and candour.

29h

Gain emphasis by abruptly changing sentence length.

> I suppose each painter has his own way of launching into the adventures in shape, colour, texture and space that we call painting. I mostly fall into them. —DAVID MILNE [The short sentence, which abruptly follows a much longer one, is emphatic.]

■ **Exercise 9** Write a short, emphatic sentence to follow each long sentence below. Then write another pair of sentences—one long and one short—of your own.

1. According to a number of journalists, not to mention many references in official reports, astronauts have seen flying objects in outer space, objects that may have been clouds, satellites, or space debris.

2. For at least four hours, Charles worked with my hair; he painstakingly parted each segment, measured and cut each layer, carefully timed the waving lotion and the neutralizer; finally, after applying a dark rinse, setting and resetting each wave, shuttling me under and out from under a dryer, combing and recombing each curl, he handed me a mirror.

■ **Exercise 10** Revise the following sentences as necessary for greater emphasis.

1. I think that experimenting on fetuses should stop, whether they are dead or alive.
2. These retirees fear death, illness, poverty.
3. Fields of wild flowers were all around us.
4. Fools talk about each other; ideas fill the conversations of the wise.
5. At any rate, the gun fired when the fleeing youth tripped over the policeman's foot.
6. The storm broke in all its fury at the close of a hot day.
7. A quick break was made by Burns from his own end, and after the defense was outpaced by him a spectacular save was made by the goalkeeper.
8. I asked her to marry me, two years ago, in a shop on Tremont Street, late in the fall.
9. The art of the people was crude, but a great deal of originality was shown by some of them.
10. Wilfred Owen's poetry magnified and isolated the ugly side of war, unlike much poetry highlighting only the romantic aspects of human conflict.

Variety

30

Vary the structure and the length of your sentences to make your whole composition pleasing and effective.

Occasionally, as the example below illustrates, a series of brief, subject-first sentences may be used for special effect:

> He stumbled, recovered, picked up his pace. Now he was running. He broke out of the ring. People were throwing things at him. An egg hurtled past his head. A tomato hit someone nearby and splattered onto his suit.   —GERRY NADEL
> [The short sentences suggest staccato action.]

A long compound-complex sentence may also be appropriate. See, for example, the second sentence of John Steinbeck's paragraph on page 239.

Inexperienced writers tend to rely too heavily—regardless of content or purpose—on a few comfortable, familiar structures. For that reason, Section **30** recommends sentence variety and cautions against monotonous repetition of any one-type of sentence.

Note: If you have difficulty distinguishing various types of structures, review the fundamentals of the sentence treated in Section **1**, especially **1d**.

30a

As a rule, avoid a series of short simple sentences. Vary the length. See also 29h.

MONOTONOUS

She picked her way toward the garden chairs beside the front porch. She poured out a customary torrent of complaint. Her eyesight was failing. She found herself swatting raisins on the kitchen table. She thought they were flies. She brought her stick down on spiders. These turned out to be scurrying tufts of lint. Her hearing was going. She suffered from head noises. She imagined she heard drums beating. [Series of short, choppy sentences]

VARIED

As she picked her way toward the garden chairs beside the front porch, she poured out a customary torrent of complaint. Her eyesight was failing. She found herself swatting raisins on the kitchen table, thinking they were flies, and bringing her stick down on spiders that turned out to be scurrying tufts of lint. Her hearing was going, and she suffered from head noises. She imagined she heard drums beating.
—PETER DE VRIES[1] [Interspersed with longer sentences, the short sentences are emphatic.]

Rather than present your ideas in a series of choppy, ineffective sentences, learn how to relate your ideas precisely in a longer sentence.

CHOPPY   The sticky crowd was sluggish. It flowed up and down Broadway. He was swallowed up in this crowd.

EFFECTIVE   He was swallowed up in the sticky crowd flowing sluggishly up and down Broadway.
—HARVEY SWADOS [Effective use of modifiers]

---

[1]From *The Vale of Laughter* by Peter De Vries. Published by Little, Brown and Company, 1967. Copyright © 1953, 1962, 1964, 1967 by Peter De Vries. Reprinted by permission of Little, Brown and Company.

CHOPPY He was a small boy. He had to drown three newborn puppies. The blind, tiny creatures struggled
for life in the bucket. This conveyed to him a vivid
sense. In everything there is an "I." This "I" deserves respect.

EFFECTIVE When he was a small boy, he had to drown three
newborn puppies, and the blind, tiny creatures
struggling for life in the bucket conveyed to him a
vivid sense that in everything there is an "I" which
deserves respect. —PETER STANSKY [The conjunctions *when, and, that,* and *which* connect and
relate ideas.]

■ **Exercise 1** Study the structure of the sentences in the following paragraph, giving special attention to the variety of sentence lengths.

[1] He listened to her moving around, going from the bathroom
to the kitchen. [2] Lying back, closing his eyes, he searched for
something he thought he had seen in her face. [3] If he went
closer to her in her stillness, would the effect be broken, the
effect inside himself? [4] A girl who could give him this sudden
sense of harmony—surely she had some view of her own life.
[5] Something moving, something significant, must have happened to her. [6] There had to be a structure behind it. [7] How
aware was she of herself? [8] Could she explain her effect on
him? [9] Of course not. [10] Could he explain it himself? [11] He
knew he had always been good at measuring the achieved
effects of painters and writers. [12] Information. [13] Get all the
information. [14] He had the tool he trusted: analysis. [15] He had
never had any patience with mysteries. [16] Everything could be
explained. —MORLEY CALLAGHAN[2]

■ **Exercise 2** Convert each of the following series of short
simple sentences to one long sentence in which ideas are carefully related.

[2]From *A Fine and Private Place* by Morley Callaghan, The Macmillan Co.
of Canada Ltd., 1975. Copyright © 1975 by Morley Callaghan. Reprinted
by permission.

1. There were thirty seconds of play left. Harrison intercepted the pass and raced downfield. He dropped the ball at the five-yard line.
2. Her speech had an interesting thesis. Salespersons should solve the existing problems of their customers. They should also point out new problems in order to solve them.
3. Bennett's Comet appeared in 1969. It disappeared again in 1970. It will not be visible again for thousands of years.
4. Ellen Dolan did not buy a second car. She bought a Piper. It is a cub plane. It flies at almost a hundred miles an hour.
5. J. Allen Boone is the author of *Kinship with All Life*. In his book Boone describes his ability to communicate with animals. He converses mentally with a dog. He orders ants to leave his home. They obey his orders. He even tames an ordinary housefly.

30b

Avoid a long series of sentences beginning with the subject. Vary the beginning.

Most writers begin about half their sentences with the subject—far more than the number of sentences begun in any other one way. But overuse of the subject-first beginning results in monotonous writing. If you tend to use this sentence pattern almost exclusively, make an effort to vary the word order of your sentences.

(1) Begin with an adverb or an adverb clause.

> ADVERB *Suddenly* the professor walked in.
> ADVERB CLAUSE *Although Bruce has good manners now,* he was a bungler then.

(2) Begin with a prepositional phrase or a participial phrase.

> PREPOSITIONAL PHRASE *At that moment* Professor Morrison walked in.

PARTICIPIAL PHRASE   *Waiting patiently for help,* a man lay
    beside the road.

(3) Begin with a conjunction such as *and, but, or, nor, for,* or *yet.*

An effective sentence can often begin with a coordinating
conjunction, but only when the conjunction shows the
proper relation of the sentence to the preceding sentence:
see **31b(4)**

COORDINATING CONJUNCTION   *But* the injured man, lying be-
    side the road, waited patiently for help. [The *but*
    makes a contrast with something in the preceding sen-
    tence, such as "The young woman wept and wrung her
    hands."]

COORDINATING CONJUNCTION   *And* the injured man, lying be-
    side the road, waited patiently for help. [The *and* makes
    a simple addition to the preceding sentence.]

Note: Though effective occasionally, declarative sentences
with inverted word order (see **29f**) do not often appear in
modern expository writing.

    Friends they still were, but only on the surface.
    In walked the professor with his wife.

■ **Exercise 3**   Prepare for a class discussion of the types of
sentence beginnings in the following two paragraphs.

¹ Whenever the east-west context of the Canadian outlook
begins to weaken, separatism, which is always there, emerges as
a political force. ² Every part of Canada has strong separatist
feelings: there is separatism of the Pacific Coast, of the Prairies,
of the Maritimes, of Newfoundland, as well as of Quebec.
³ Ontario, of course, began with a separatist movement from the
American Revolution. ⁴ But since the rise of the great ideologi-
cal revolutionary movements of our time, whether communist,
fascist, imperialist, Islamic or what not, separatism has been an
almost wholly destructive force. ⁵ The successful separatings,

like that of Norway and Sweden in 1905, took place before the rise of these movements. [6] In India and Pakistan, in the Arab-Jewish world, and in many other centres divided by language, colour or religion, separatism has seldom if ever stabilized the prejudices which gave rise to it, but has steadily increased them. [7] Even where there is no political affiliation, the separation of Cuba from the American sphere of influence, or of Yugoslavia from the Russian one, cannot be a politically neutral act.

—NORTHROP FRYE[3]

[1] Mounting the spiraled staircase, he heard the voices roll in a steady wave, then leap to crescendo, only to die away, but always remaining audible. [2] Ahead of him glowed red letters: E—X—I—T. [3] At the top of the steps he paused in front of a black curtain that fluttered uncertainly. [4] He parted the folds and looked into a convex depth that gleamed with clusters of shimmering lights. [5] Sprawling below him was a stretch of human faces, tilted upward, chanting, whistling, screaming, laughing [6] Dangling before the faces, high upon a screen of silver, were jerking shadows. [7] "A movie," he said with slow laughter breaking from his lips. —RICHARD WRIGHT[4]

■ **Exercise 4** Each of the sentences below begins with the subject. Recast each sentence twice to vary the beginnings, as shown in the following example.

EXAMPLE
Two businessmen dropped by the dean's office and re quested reasons for the inefficiency of the school's gradu ates.
a. *Dropping by the dean's office, two businessmen re quested reasons for the inefficiency of the school's graduates.*
b. *In the dean's office, two businessmen requested reasons for the inefficiency of the school's graduates.*

---

[3]From *The Bush Garden: Essays on the Canadian Imagination* by Northrop Frye, House of Anansi Press Ltd., Toronto, 1971. Copyright © Northrop Frye, 1971. Reprinted by permission.

[4]From *Eight Men* by Richard Wright. Published by Paul R. Reynolds, Inc 1944. Reprinted by permission.

1. We still need a better understanding between management and labour.
2. Reporters interviewed the newly appointed ambassador and asked him some sticky questions about world affairs.
3. Hundreds of students will line up in order to register in a floating university, the *Queen Victoria*.
4. Jesse enjoyed the course in science-fiction literature most of all.
5. The green fireballs travelled at great speed and fascinated sky watchers throughout the country.

30c

Avoid the loose, stringy compound sentence. See also 24b.

To revise an ineffective compound sentence, try one of the following methods.

(1) Convert it into a complex sentence.

COMPOUND The Mississippi River is one of the longest rivers in the world, and in the springtime it often overflows its banks, and the lives of many people are endangered.

COMPLEX The Mississippi River, which is one of the longest rivers in the world, often overflows its banks in the springtime, endangering the lives of many people.

(2) Use a compound predicate in a simple sentence.

COMPOUND He put on his coat, and next he picked up his hat and umbrella, and then he hurried from the house.

SIMPLE He put on his coat, picked up his hat and umbrella, and hurried from the house.

(3) Use a modifier or an appositive in a simple sentence.

COMPOUND The town was north of the Red River, and a tornado struck it, and it was practically demolished.

SIMPLE The town, located north of the Red River, was struck by a tornado and practically demolished.

COMPOUND She was the mayor of the town, and she was an amiable person, and she invited the four students into her office.

SIMPLE The mayor of the town, an amiable person, invited the four students into her office.

(4) Use phrases in a simple sentence.

COMPOUND The streets were icy, and we could not drive the car.

SIMPLE Because of the icy streets, we could not drive the car.

COMPOUND He arrived in Hull at 1:30 A.M., and then he made a collect call.

SIMPLE After arriving in Hull at 1:30 A.M., he made a collect call.

■ **Exercise 5** Using the methods illustrated in **30c**, revise the loose, stringy compound sentences below.

1. The small car hugs the road, and it is easy to drive in traffic, but it is not comfortable.
2. The Johnsons grew tired of city smog and noise pollution, so they moved to the country, but there they had no fire department or police protection.
3. North Americans at first traded their products, and then they began to use money and bank cheques, and now they use the all-inclusive plastic credit card.
4. Harvey kept criticizing middle-class values, and he mentioned such things as marriage and two-car garages, but he did not define upper-class or lower-class values.

30d

Vary the conventional subject–verb sequence by occasionally separating subject and verb with words or phrases.

SUBJECT–VERB	*The auditorium is* across from the park, and *it is* a gift of the alumni. [Compound sentence]
VARIED	*The auditorium,* across from the park, *is* a gift of the alumni. [Simple sentence]
SUBJECT–VERB	*The crowd sympathized* with the visitors and *applauded* every good play.
VARIED	*The crowd,* sympathizing with the visitors, *applauded* every good play.
SUBJECT–VERB	*Her ability to listen is* an acquired skill that attracts many friends.
VARIED	*Her ability to listen,* an acquired skill, *attracts* many friends.

30e

Vary a series of declarative statements by using an occasional exclamation, command, or question.

What if everyone did actually write his story, and what if everyone's story were Xeroxed? Imagine millions and millions of welterweight Norman Mailers, each making himself the center of existence and each describing his feelings as the only trustworthy view of the world's ways. Imagine it! What would all that writing, the whole of it, amount to? It might be life. It might be what no artist can conceive, bigger than the biggest visions of poets and madmen. That's it. That's what The Universal Xerox Life Compiler Machine could do for us, something "now" and "total," so to speak.

—WILLIAM JOVANOVICH[5]

---

[5] From "The Universal Xerox Life Compiler Machine" by William Jovanovich. Copyright © 1970 by William Jovanovich. All rights reserved.

■ **Exercise 6** The following sentences all have structures tha usually contribute to variety in composition. By referring to specific parts of Section **30**, prepare for a class discussion o these structures.

1. At its most effective a symbol is like a many-faceted jewel: i flashes different colors when turned to the light.
   —LAURENCE PERRINE

2. To those who think that the law of gravity interferes with their freedom, there is nothing to say. —LIONEL TIGER

3. Interestingly enough, Ortega's definition of the "mass man" is identical with Plato's definition of the tyrant.
   —IRVING KRISTOL

4. Reading *The Penguin Book of Saints,* I am sorry to learn that St. Catherine of the catherine wheel never existed.
   —W. H. AUDEN

■ **Exercise 7** Prepare for a class discussion of sentence variety in the following paragraphs.

[1] *Hamlet* has obsessed the Western mind for 369 years. [2] Why? [3] It is not because most people love great works of art. [4] On the contrary, most people find great works of art oppressive, since such works invariably center on the nature of human destiny, and that destiny is tragic. [5] Quite simply, *Hamlet* is a world, and like the world, it cannot be ignored. [6] Every man has lived some part of the play, and to be a man is to be inextricably involved in the play. [7] *Hamlet* probes and grips the profound themes of existence—death, love, time, fidelity, friendship, family, the relationships of a man and a woman, a son and father, a mother and son, murder and madness. [8] Above all, it probes the value of existence, man's most anguishing question put in the form that every man knows from the time he first hears and ponders it—to be or not to be.

[9] Far from being a surefire part, the role of Hamlet dwarfs most actors, for the magnitude of the role requires a corresponding size and scope in the actor who plays it. [10] Technique is not

enough. [11] Verbal violin play, a graceful carriage, a handsome profile—these suffice for the ordinary Hamlet. [12] The great Hamlet is coached by life itself, schooled by life to think, listen, grow, love, hate, suffer and endure. [13] So rigorous is this demand that in these more than three and a half centuries there have been no more than a dozen great Hamlets. —TIME[6]

From "Elsinore of the Mind," *Time*, January 12, 1970. Reprinted by permission from *Time*, The Weekly Newsmagazine; Copyright Time Inc., 1970.

LARGER ELEMENTS

The Paragraph

31

Make paragraphs unified and coherent; develop them adequately.

A paragraph is a distinct unit of thought—usually a group of related sentences, though occasionally no more than one sentence—in a written or a printed composition. The form of a paragraph is distinctive: the first line is indented, about one inch in longhand and five spaces in typewritten copy.

Below is an example of a unified, coherent, adequately developed paragraph.[1] As you read it, observe the clear statement of the controlling idea in the first sentence (often called the *topic sentence*). Notice how this idea is developed: every sentence that follows illustrates the vitality of George Poliakoff, the man the author is describing.

1 He came unannounced, and the little room vibrated with his vitality. He was tall, pale, with an enormous marble brow fronting a head at the back of which sparse hair still grew. He had dark magnetic eyes, and very white teeth, and a yellow skin. In a sinister sort of way, he was good looking. He was voluble, friendly, overwhelming. He would

---

[1] For easy reference, all thirty-five of the specimen paragraphs in this section are numbered.

not take a chair; he was not that kind of man; he was too physically exuberant. He strode up and down the little room while we broke the ice of our first encounter. He kept glancing at me with his large brown eyes, and smiling at me with his handsome mouthful of teeth, and I felt that he was summing me up. I smiled in return.   —LOVAT DICKSON[2]

Since each paragraph in a composition is a distinct unit of thought, the beginning of a new paragraph is an important signal to the reader. It serves as a signpost marking an approaching curve in the avenue of thought. Below, for example, is another paragraph from the same book. Unlike the preceding paragraph, which describes Poliakoff, this paragraph gives the author's summation of the kind of relationship that he had with him.

2   I must always have been rather a disappointment to Poliakoff; he would have been so much better repaid for his trouble if I had been a good conversationalist, or an entertaining table companion, or even, perhaps, a suitable son-in-law. I proved never to be any of these things, but Janet Courtney was right. He was given to enthusiasms, and for some reason, probably because he was essentially kind-hearted, he saw my inexperience and perceived that I needed help. He had plenty to do, but he could not resist a dumb call of this nature, and for the next three years, while I was on *The Fortnightly,* he proved an invaluable and always kind friend, and he contributed considerably to my education.   —LOVAT DICKSON[3]

---

[2]Abridged from *The House of Words* by Lovat Dickson. Reprinted by permission of The Macmillan Company of Canada.

[3]From *The House of Words* by Lovat Dickson. Reprinted by permission of The Macmillan Company of Canada.

Expository or argumentative paragraphs in contemporary books and magazines are usually from 50 to 250 words in length, with the average perhaps 100 words. Paragraphs tend to run longer in books and shorter in the narrower columns of newspapers. Shorter paragraphs are more frequent in narrative writing, especially dialogue, in which each speech is paragraphed separately. For an example of dialogue, see 16a(3).

Very short stories or anecdotes may be used in expository writing to illustrate a point. The rules and examples in this section, however, deal primarily with the types of paragraphs that are often emphasized in university writing.

31a
Give unity to the paragraph by making each sentence contribute to the central thought.

A paragraph is said to have unity when each sentence contributes to the central thought. Any sentence that violates the unity of the paragraph should be deleted. In expository writing, the main idea of a paragraph is most often stated at or near the beginning, as in the example below, although it may appear anywhere in the paragraph.

3   Organized crime supplies goods or services wanted by a large number of people—desperately needed cash, narcotics, prostitutes, the chance to gamble. These are its principal sources of income. They are consensual crimes for the most part, desired by the consuming public. This fact distinguishes the main activities of organized crime from most other crime. Few want to be mugged, have their assets embezzled or their cars stolen, but it is public demand that creates the basis for the activities of organized crime. Where this demand is great, law enforcement is working against the strong desires of a significant sector of the

populace and will not therefore prevail in a free society—or
for long under any circumstances. —RAMSEY CLARK[4]

To achieve unity, you may find it helpful to make a plan for
your paragraph. The preceding paragraph, for instance,
reveals this plan:

> *Topic:* The public demand for certain types of crime
> 1. Demand for drugs, prostitutes, etc. (not for muggings, etc.)
> 2. Demand—the basis for organized crime
> 3. Demand—a barrier to law enforcement

When the controlling idea is stated early in the paragraph,
it may be restated at the end, thus pointing up its importance. In the following paragraph compare "the intolerable
has become normal" with the final "Ugliness is accepted, no
longer even noticed."

4   In the towns and cities of Ulster, the intolerable has
become normal. The civic environment is scarred. In
Belfast and Derry, it is hard to find a shop with windows;
shopkeepers have had so many broken that they are content
to leave the boards up. Burned-out houses and shops are left
as abandoned hulks. The army has run out its barbed wire,
concrete and corrugated iron in dozens of checkpoints,
barricades and gun emplacements. Ugliness is accepted, no
longer even noticed. —PAUL HARRISON[5]

Occasionally, the most important idea of a paragraph is
stated in the last sentence, especially when the writer pro-
gresses from particulars or a specific example to a generalization.

---

[4]From *Crime in America* by Ramsey Clark. Copyright © 1970, by Ramsey
Clark. Reprinted by permission of Simon & Schuster, Inc.

[5]From "The Dark Age of Ulster" by Paul Harrison, *Human Behavior,*
October 1975. Copyright © 1975 *Human Behavior* Magazine. Reprinted
by permission.

5   In the film, we see a broad stream upon which float hundreds of boxes filled with people. Human beings have cut themselves off from each other in a system of isolated nationalistic boxes. Each box floats aimlessly, bumping, swamping others, drifting toward some uncertain future collision. Later in the film, some hope is suggested when eyes appear looking out of the boxes to indicate a growing awareness of the others and a faint beginning toward imagining alternative possibilities. Dozens of films based on similar symbolic visual premises, and specifically conceived for instructional purposes, are being made from Calcutta to Zagreb. Animation artists around the world are breaking out of the limitations of the fairy tale to confront contemporary issues.   —JOHN HUBLEY[6]

When not expressly stated, the controlling idea of a unified paragraph is distinctly implied. The implied idea of paragraph 6 ("These are steps in the embalming process") can be clearly understood from the context of Jessica Mitford's complete description. (The quotations are from a textbook about embalming.)

6   About three to six gallons of a dyed and perfumed solution of formaldehyde, glycerin, borax, phenol, alcohol and water is soon circulating through Mr. Jones, whose mouth has been sewn together with a "needle directed upward between the upper lip and gum and brought out through the left nostril," with the corners raised slightly "for a more pleasant expression." If he should be bucktoothed, his teeth are cleaned with Bon Ami and coated with colorless nail polish. His eyes, meanwhile, are closed with flesh-tinted eye caps and eye cement.

—JESSICA MITFORD[7]

"The next step," writes Jessica Mitford in the first sentence of her next paragraph, "is to have at Mr. Jones with a thing called a trocar."

Caution: Do not make rambling statements that are only vaguely related to your topic. As you write a paragraph, hold to the main idea. For instance, if the controlling idea of a paragraph is "My roommate Bill Jones cannot keep a secret," irrelevant sentences about Bill Jones or about secrecy will disrupt the unity. Every statement should pertain to Bill Jones's inability to keep a secret.

If the paragraphs in your compositions tend to lack unity, use the following checklist to help you in revision.

Checklist for Revising a Faulty Paragraph

1. *Is the central idea of the paragraph clearly stated or implied?* If not, add a clear statement of the controlling idea.

2. *Does the subject of the paragraph shift one or more times?* If so, either develop each main point in a separate paragraph or restate the central idea so that it will closely relate all the points discussed.

3. *Are all sentences in the paragraph relevant to the central idea?* If not, cross out each irrelevant sentence. If any sentence is related to the central idea but not clearly so, revise it to make the relationship clear.

Revision of a Faulty Paragraph

A helping hand, ~~always~~ sometimes loses its little finger. For example, ~~My~~ my friend Michelle often lends her textbooks, her class notes, and even her clothes. Borrowers seldom return them. [Controlling idea supplied— with transition]

(Of course, some people are luckier than Michelle.) The other day, when two "hungry" boys asked my roommate for spare dimes, he quickly reached for his billfold, but they beat him to it and then ran off. ~~I myself give to institutional charities!~~ Again, [An aside placed in parentheses]

[Irrelevant— deleted]

when ^a motorist ran out of gasoline, ~~When~~ my sister Alicia stopped to help him; she parked too near the mainstream of traffic. Her brand-new Honda got sideswiped. ¶ A helping hand, though, is not always appreciated. Consider meddlers and nosey people. [Subordination used to place focus on main idea]

[Different facet of subject— new paragraph needed for development]

■ **Exercise 1** Point out, or supply, the controlling idea for paragraphs 9, 10, and 12 on pages 307, 308, and 309 and for any other paragraphs assigned by your instructor.

■ **Exercise 2** Revise the following faulty paragraph to improve unity. Be prepared to give the reasons for your revisions.

At my place last night, a tornadic wind played several mischievous pranks. Whistling loudly through the weather stripping, it sprayed dirty water all over the freshly mopped kitchen floor. Next, as though chiding me for my earlier complaints about stuffy air, it created enormous drafts by breaking half a dozen window panes. The moment an announcer on television started reading a special bulletin from the weather bureau, the wind knocked down my television antenna; just as I reached for the radio, it blacked out the whole house. Later I learned that a pilot flying above the turbulent weather had reported that he had never seen such a violent thunderstorm. The wind levelled a two-car garage belonging to Mr. Fulton, my neighbour. Travelling at ninety miles an hour, it also turned on an outdoor water tap, flooding my flower bed; overturned the dog house, imprisoning my fox terrier; and dumped a stolen boat into the back yard, after ripping the motor off and breaking the oars. After that savage storm, my family and I are grateful to be alive and uninjured.

31b

Give coherence to the paragraph by so interlinking the sentences that the thought flows smoothly from one sentence to the next. Provide transitions between paragraphs as well as between sentences.

A paragraph is said to have coherence when the relationship between sentences is clear and when the transition from one sentence to the next is easy and natural. The reader should be able to follow the thought without difficulty. To achieve coherence, arrange sentences in a clear, logical order. Also provide transitions between sentences (not only within the paragraph but between paragraphs) by the effective use of pronoun reference, repetition, conjunctions, transitional phrases, and parallel structure. The choice of transitional devices is a matter of judgment. Usually, several of these aids to coherence are found in a single paragraph (although each is treated separately in this section).

ARRANGEMENT OF SENTENCES

(1) Arrange the sentences of the paragraph in a clear, logical order.

There are several common, logical ways to order the sentences in a paragraph. The choice of an appropriate order depends on the context and on the writer's purpose. Perhaps the simplest and most common order is *time order*.

7 I was born at Swanmoor, Hants, England on December 30, 1869. I am not aware that there was any particular conjunction of the planets at the time, but should think it extremely likely. My parents migrated to Canada in 1876, and I decided to go with them. My father took up a farm near Lake Simcoe, in Ontario. This was during the hard times of Canadian farming, and my father was just able by a great diligence to pay the hired men and, in years of plenty, to raise enough grain to have seed for the next year's crop without buying any. By this process my brothers and I were inevitably driven off the land, and have become professors, business men, and engineers, instead of being able to grow up as farm labourers. Yet I saw enough of farming to speak exuberantly in political addresses of the joy of early rising and the deep sleep, both of body and intellect, that is induced by honest manual toil. —STEPHEN LEACOCK[8]

Narrative paragraphs often have a chronological arrangement.

8 Smith's first blow bent the spike badly. Frank Brothers, the road-master, pulled it out and replaced it with another.

[8]From *Sunshine Sketches of a Little Town* by Stephen Leacock reprinted by permission of The Canadian Publishers, McClelland and Stewart Limited, Toronto.

Smith posed with the uplifted hammer. The assembly froze. The shutter clicked. Smith lowered the hammer onto the spike. The shutter clicked again. Smith began to drive the spike home. Save for the blows of the hammer and the sound of a small mountain stream there was absolute silence. Even after the spike was driven home, the stillness persisted. "It seemed," Sandford Fleming recalled, "as if the act now performed had worked a spell on all present. Each one appeared absorbed in his own reflections." The spell was broken by a cheer, "and it was no ordinary cheer. The subdued enthusiasm, the pent-up feelings of men familiar with hard work, now found vent." More cheers followed, enhanced by the shrill whistle of the locomotives. —PIERRE BERTON[9]

Other types of paragraphs often have a time element that makes a chronological arrangement both possible and natural. For example, in explaining a process—how something is done or made—the writer can follow the process through, step by step, as in the following paragraph.

9   In *engraving,* the artist grooves out clean strips of metal from the plate with a steel instrument called a burin. The artist is actually drawing with the burin. After the picture is engraved, printing ink is rubbed over the entire plate. The surface is then wiped clean, leaving ink in the incised portions of the copper. A dampened sheet of paper is placed over the plate and together they are run through a roller press. The paper is dampened to retain the ink better and to avoid cracking or tearing, since a great deal of pressure must be exerted to force the paper into the incised areas. —MARVIN ELKOFF[10]

[9]From *The Last Spike* by Pierre Berton reprinted by permission of The Canadian Publishers, McClelland and Stewart Limited, Toronto.

[10]From "Collecting Original Art Prints" by Marvin Elkoff, *Holiday,* December 1965. © 1965 The Curtis Publishing Company. Reprinted by permission of *Travel/Holiday* Magazine.

Passages that have no evident time order can sometimes be arranged in *space order*, in which the paragraph moves from east to west, from near to distant, from left to right, and so on. This order is used especially in descriptive writing.

10   The Eskimos knew something of the geography of these lands. Toward the evening sun lay a great water, but it was said that it pushed within the land. White men called it Hudson Bay. It was said that other Eskimos lived on the other side. Toward the morning sun, after four days of crossing the tundra, was a desolate barren land, a stony country with terrible winters. In the country of the North Star there was again water, then immense islands under eternal snow. To the south, after the mossy tundra, lay 'the tree country.   —YVES THERIAULT[11]

Another good arrangement of sentences is in the *order of climax*. Here the least important idea is stated first, and the others are given in order of increasing importance, as in the following paragraph. See also **29c**.

11   An ant cannot purposely try anything new, and any ant that accidentally did so would be murdered by his colleagues. It is the ant colony as a whole that slowly learns over the ages. In contrast, even an earthworm has enough flexibility of brain to enable it to be taught to turn toward the left or right for food. Though rats are not able to reason to any considerable degree, they can solve such problems as separating round objects from triangular ones when these have to do with health or appetite. Cats, with better brains, can be taught somewhat more, and young dogs a great deal. The higher apes can learn by insight as well as by trial and error.   —GEORGE RUSSELL HARRISON[12]

---

[11] From *Agaguk* by Yves Theriault. Copyright © 1967. Reprinted by permission of McGraw-Hill Ryerson Limited.

[12] Reprinted by permission of William Morrow & Co., Inc. from *What Man May Be* by George Russell Harrison. Copyright © 1956 by George Russell Harrison.

Sometimes the movement within the paragraph may be from the general to the particular, from the particular to the general, or from the familiar to the unfamiliar. A paragraph may begin with a general statement or idea, which is then supported by particular details (as in paragraph 12). Reversing the process, it may begin with a striking detail or series of details and conclude with a summarizing statement (as in paragraph 13).

12   What's wrong with the student-union bookshop? Everything. It's interested in selling sweatshirts and college mugs rather than good books. Its staff often is incompetent and uncivil. The manager may not be intelligent enough even to order a sufficient number of copies of required textbooks for the beginning of a term. As for more lively books—why, there are masses of paperbacks, perhaps, that could be procured at any drugstore; there are a few shelves or racks of volumes labeled "Gift Books," usually lavishly illustrated and inordinately costly, intended as presents to fond parents; but there are virtually no *book* books, of the sort that students might like to buy.   —RUSSELL KIRK[13]

13   When we watch a person walk away from us, his image shrinks in size. But since we know for a fact that he is not shrinking, we make an unconscious correcting and "see" him as retaining his full stature. Past experience tells us what his true stature is with respect to our own. Any sane and dependable expectation of the future requires that he have the same true stature when we next encounter him. Our perception is thus a prediction; it embraces the past and the future as well as the present.

—WARREN J. WITTREICH[14]

---

[13] From "From the Academy: Campus Bookshops" by Russell Kirk, *National Review*, December 19, 1975. Reprinted by permission.

[14] From "Visual Perception and Personality" by Warren J. Wittreich, *Scientific American*, April 1959. Copyright © 1959 by *Scientific American*, Inc. All rights reserved. Reprinted by permission.

Paragraphs 7 through 13 illustrate five of many possible types of clear sentence arrangement within the paragraph. Any order of sentences, or any combination of orders, is satisfactory as long as it makes the sequence of thought clear. Proper arrangement of the sentences is the first, the basic, step to ensure good transitions from sentence to sentence.

■ **Exercise 3**   Determine the type of sentence arrangement used in paragraph 5, page 302, and in paragraph 28, page 324.

TRANSITIONS BETWEEN SENTENCES

(2) Link sentences by means of pronouns referring to antecedents in the preceding sentences. See also Section **28**.

In the following paragraph, italics are used to indicate the pronouns serving as links between sentences. Such pronouns near the beginning of the sentence are often especially useful for paragraph coherence.

14   The brain is the controller, the organizer, the information-processing center of the body. *It* is the boss. *It* runs the show. And *it* acts like the boss, freely exercising *its* privileges and prerogatives. Though *it* makes up only 2 percent of the body's weight, *it* hogs 20 percent of the blood supply. Like the leader of a pride of lions, *it* also "eats" first—that is, *it* takes *its* share of nutrients from the blood, no matter what goes elsewhere. In case of malnutrition, *it* is the last to starve.   —ALBERT ROSENFELD AND KENNETH KLEVINGTON[15]

■ **Exercise 4**   Underline the pronouns used to link sentences in paragraph 3, page 300; in paragraph 13, page 309; or in any other paragraphs assigned by your instructor. Check the antecedent (in a preceding sentence) to which each pronoun refers.

---

[15] From "Inside the Brain: The Last Great Frontier" by Albert Rosenfeld and Kenneth Klevington, *Saturday Review*, August 9, 1975. Copyright 1975 Saturday Review, Inc. Reprinted by permission.

(3) Link sentences by repeating words or ideas from the preceding sentences.

Notice in the next paragraph how repetition of key words binds together the sentences.

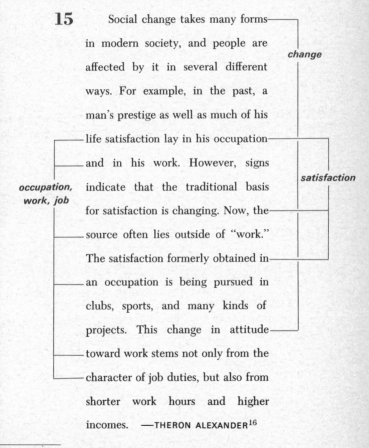

15   Social change takes many forms in modern society, and people are affected by it in several different ways. For example, in the past, a man's prestige as well as much of his life satisfaction lay in his occupation and in his work. However, signs indicate that the traditional basis for satisfaction is changing. Now, the source often lies outside of "work." The satisfaction formerly obtained in an occupation is being pursued in clubs, sports, and many kinds of projects. This change in attitude toward work stems not only from the character of job duties, but also from shorter work hours and higher incomes.   —THERON ALEXANDER[16]

change

satisfaction

occupation, work, job

---

[16]From "The Individual and Social Change" by Theron Alexander, *Intellect*, December 1974. Reprinted by permission.

¶

■ **Exercise 5** Link the sentences in each of the following pairs by revising the second sentence to repeat a word or an idea in the first sentence. Follow the pattern of the examples.

EXAMPLES

Radio and television perpetuated myths. The majority was not silent in the 1960s.

Radio and television perpetuated myths. One myth spread by the media was that the majority was silent in the 1960s.

A family reunion makes my parents happy. But I have a sudden yearning to travel overseas.

A family reunion makes my parents happy. But the mere thought of dozens of relatives in our house makes me suddenly yearn to travel overseas.

1. William likes to read the editorials in the *Greenview Herald*. His brother prefers original advertisements.
2. Living in a high-rise apartment house can be boring. There is no lawn to keep.
3. Marian attends only professional hockey games. She can boo with a clear conscience.
4. Enrolment in universities suddenly began to drop. The values of the young shifted.

(4) Link sentences by using such transitional expressions as the following.

1. <u>*Addition:*</u> moreover, further, furthermore, besides, and, and then, likewise, also, nor, too, again, in addition, equally important, next, first, second, third, in the first place, in the second place, finally, last

2. <u>*Comparison:*</u> similarly, likewise, in like manner

3. <u>*Contrast:*</u> but, yet, and yet, however, still, nevertheless, on the other hand, on the contrary, even so, notwithstanding, for all that, in contrast to this, at the same time, although this may be true, otherwise

4. *Place:* here, beyond, nearby, opposite to, adjacent to, on the opposite side

5. *Purpose:* to this end, for this purpose, with this object

6. *Result:* hence, therefore, accordingly, consequently, thus, thereupon, as a result, then

7. *Summary, repetition, exemplification, intensification:* to sum up, in brief, on the whole, in sum, in short, as I have said, in other words, that is, to be sure, as has been noted, for example, for instance, in fact, indeed, to tell the truth, in any event

8. *Time:* meanwhile, at length, soon, after a few days, in the meantime, afterward, later, now, in the past

Note Theron Alexander's use of the transitional expressions *for example, in the past, however,* and *now* in paragraph 15. Also observe Peter Farb's use of introductory transitional words or phrases in paragraph 30.

■ **Exercise 6** Insert an appropriate transitional expression in the second sentence of each item below.

1. The students were elected to the senate by majority vote. The actions of the elected senate members did not reflect the thinking of the majority of the students.
2. Some comic books provide a painless education for the young. Many adults could profit from reading educational comic books.
3. Fees went up by almost sixty per cent. Thousands of students flocked to the Parliament Buildings to protest.
4. It was a year of natural disasters. Earthquakes shook Italy and China.
5. Bad weather, careless workmanship, and theft of materials have added to the difficulty of building the Alaskan pipeline. The cost of the construction is in the billions.

(5) Link sentences by means of parallel structure—that is, by repetition of the sentence pattern.

Notice how parallelism serves as a cohesive force in the first, long sentence of the following two-sentence paragraph. See also Section 26.

16   The environmental crisis is the result of success—success in cutting down the mortality of infants (which has given us the population explosion), success in raising farm output sufficiently to prevent mass famine (which has given us contamination by pesticides and chemical fertilizers) success in getting people out of the noisome tenements of the 19th-century city and into the greenery and privacy of the single-family home in the suburbs (which has given us urban sprawl and traffic jams). The environmental crisis, in other words, is largely the result of doing too much of the right sort of thing.   —PETER F. DRUCKER[17]

■ **Exercise 7**   Prepare to develop the following topics orally in class; use parallel structure to link ideas. (In brackets after each topic is a suggested point of departure.)

1. There are two types of students, the conformists and the nonconformists.
   [*One* _____; *the other* _____.]

2. We fear the unknown.
   [*When* _____, *then* _____.]

3. Job shortages are a result of failure.
   [They are a result of *failure to* _____, *which can cause* _____.]

4. Fiction is full of stereotypes.
   [A cowboy is *a person who* _____; a detective is *one who* _____.]

[17] From "Saving the Crusade" by Peter F. Drucker, *Harper's*, January 1972. Copyright © 1971 Minneapolis Star and Tribune Company. Reprinted by permission of *Harper's* Magazine.

■ **Exercise 8** Prepare for a class discussion of the specific linking devices (transitional words, repetition, parallel structure, and so on) used in paragraph 17.

17   One of these necessities of life is security. Of course, there's no such thing as absolute security. What we mean here is protection for your dependents if you die prematurely and protection for yourself if you live to extreme old age. In the former case, you might leave your children with little chance of higher education and your wife with an unpaid mortgage. In the latter case, you'd probably be faced with insufficient funds to live out your years gracefully. The conventional way to acquire security against either situation is through insurance.   —ALBERT VOLKER[18]

■ **Exercise 9** Revise the following paragraph so that the thought flows smoothly from one sentence to the next. Use a variety of linking devices as necessary.

Perhaps Mr. Brandon should resign from the planning committee. He should at the least be severely censured. He is responsible for the report on the new freeway. Errors were made by him in his report that are inexcusable. Also serious omissions that don't look like accidents. It was argued by him that only ten houses would be expropriated for the road. Fifty is more like it. His cost estimates are way out of line too.

TRANSITIONS BETWEEN PARAGRAPHS

(6) Provide clear transitions between paragraphs.

Transitions from one paragraph to the next are even more necessary than those between sentences within the paragraph. Notice below how Theron Alexander made a transition to a new facet of his discussion of social change. The beginning and the end of paragraph 15 are given first (see page 311) and then the opening of the next paragraph:

---

[18]From *How You Can Make a Fortune in Canada* by Albert Volker—published by PaperJacks Ltd. Used by permission of General Publishing Co. Limited, 30 Lesmill Road, Don Mills, Ontario.

> →Social change takes many forms. . . .
>
> This change in attitude toward work stems not only from the character of job duties, but also from shorter work hours and higher incomes.
>
> →Another social change taking place is in family life. . . .

The repetition of *change* not only links the beginnings of the two paragraphs but also links the last sentence of the first paragraph with the first sentence of the second.

At or near the beginnings of paragraphs, such transitional words as *first, then, next,* and *finally* and phrases like *just as significant, more important,* and *most important of all* are useful—especially when the paragraphs are arranged according to time order or the order of climax.

Sometimes a paragraph is used to make a transition. The transitional paragraph below first refers to the author's foregoing discussion (what a woman's role in marriage was) and then sets forth an idea to be developed in the paragraphs that follow (important social forces and their influence on changes in the male/female relationship).

18   Against this background then, consider the conjunction of forces which have radically altered the male/female relationship. —MAGGIE TRIPP

■ **Exercise 10** Prepare for a class discussion of the various types of transitions you find in the composition on the following pages.

Upstream by Leaps and Bounds

19   At the foot of a roaring waterfall, the restless fish stack up like logs under the water, waiting for precisely the right moment. Then, almost as if on signal, as many as a half-dozen at a time vault through the swirling foam. Many land with stunning impact on the rocks and ledges above. Eventually, though, almost all of the fish—some weighing ten pounds or more—manage to battle their way up the turbulent river to spawn. But these are not the famous Pacific salmon on their annual inland run. They are rainbow trout, braving an icy stream in northern Vermont called the Willoughby. And unlike their gallant western cousins, the hardy rainbows do not die after spawning. Instead, they merely turn about and swim back downstream to their home in Lake Memphremagog.

20   When Willoughby's rainbows start their extraordinary run, just after the ice begins to melt, the waters become a mass of darting shadows. At first, the drive is slow, led by anxious males. Later, as the water temperatures increase, larger females bulging with roe begin to swarm upstream. By then, the Willoughby is lined elbow-to-elbow with hopeful anglers. But the dauntless rainbows are preoccupied with the lively currents, and few strikes are made.

21   In the picturesque village of Orleans, a thundering waterfall poses the major obstacle to the upstream procession. Here, hundreds of spectators gather annually to watch the jumping rainbows jackknife from pool to pool. Fishing is not allowed at the Orleans falls, nor is it permitted a few miles upriver, where the actual spawning takes place. At that point, shallow gravel beds and thickets provide ideal protection for spawning. Under tangles of evergreens, the female trout whisk out nests (redds) with their tails, while their escorts dart to and fro, chasing other males away. Then, the two males position themselves on either side of the female while she lays the eggs. After they are fertilized, the female swishes loose gravel over them.

22   Exactly what triggers the rainbows' urgent spring runs is not known. But this much is certain: they will go on surging up the Willoughby, year after year, so long as they continue to thrive in Lake Memphremagog, or until the falls at Orleans thunder no more.

—CLYDE H. SMITH[19]

31c
Develop the paragraph adequately.

Many short paragraphs are adequately developed. A one-sentence paragraph such as the following supplies enough information to satisfy the reader.

23   Used in combination with such other devices as exhaust gas recirculation systems, air pumps and elaborate carburetion controls, the muffler-like catalytic converter is effective in cutting back on the three pollutants that most worry environmentalists: hydrocarbons (HC), carbon monoxide (CO) and oxides of nitrogen (NOx).

—FINANCIAL POST[20]

Sometimes, however, short paragraphs (especially a series of them) suggest inadequate development of the idea. If such paragraphs deal with the same topic, they should be combined into one or more longer paragraphs. If they deal with different topics, each paragraph should be expanded to the point where the thought is adequately developed.

---

[19]"Upstream by Leaps and Bounds" by Clyde H. Smith. Copyright 1974 by the National Wildlife Federation. Reprinted from the June–July issue of *National Wildlife* Magazine.

[20]From "Schizophrenia Detroitensis," *The Financial Post Magazine*, October 30, 1976. Reprinted by permission.

PARAGRAPHS THAT SHOULD BE COMBINED

The line of demarcation between capitalism and socialism is sharp and clear.

Capitalism is that form of organization in which the means of production—and by that is meant the machine and the funds required to utilize the machine—are controlled by private individuals or by privately owned organizations.

Under a socialistic regime the control of the means of production, the control of capital—for even socialists concede the need for capital—is by the group. Under capitalism the profits accrue to the private individual; under socialism, to the group.

Taken separately, these three paragraphs are short and choppy; if combined, they would form a paragraph of average length adequately developing a controlling idea stated in the first sentence and clarified in the last.

The following paragraphs stop before supplying enough information to satisfy an interested reader.

PARAGRAPHS THAT SHOULD BE EXPANDED

Many adoptees searching for their natural parents have similar experiences. A few of the stories they tell, however, are unique.
[Which kinds of experiences are similar? Which kinds unique?]

Forestry work is healthful, educational, and financially rewarding. A forester, for example, soon learns how to prevent and to fight forest fires.
[The reader expects to find out about three aspects of forestry work, but the writer comments briefly on only one. How is the work healthful? What else does a forester learn? What are the financial rewards?]

If the paragraphs in your compositions tend to be inadequately developed, study the seven methods of paragraph development described and illustrated in 31d.

Note: Excessively long paragraphs, especially those that belabour one point or combine too many points, are generally avoided by modern writers.

31d
Master various methods of paragraph development.

You can learn to write good paragraphs by studying the various techniques that professional writers use to develop ideas. The more you read, the more you will find that no one method, or no one combination of methods, is better than another except as it fits the needs of a given paragraph. As you analyze the following illustrations of good paragraphs, notice how each controlling idea (stated in the first sentence of all paragraphs except paragraph 29) is developed by the other sentences in the paragraph.

(1) Supply relevant, specific details to develop the controlling idea.

The controlling idea of a paragraph often brings specific details to mind. Take, for example, "Thomas Boultbee thought of Easter Sunday which was only two days away, and of his wife, who had died of pneumonia." Two very different ideas are juxtaposed in one sentence, and this raises a number of questions: Why is he thinking of these things at the same time? How does the approaching Easter affect the way Boultbee remembers his dead wife? What special significance does the death of his wife give to the coming holiday? By answering these questions and selecting details carefully, the writer effectively develops this central idea in the following paragraph.

24   All the way home from work that evening Thomas Boultbee thought of Easter Sunday, which was only two days away, and of his young wife, Elsie, who had died of pneumonia and been buried in the last winter month. As Thomas Boultbee started to climb the stairs to his apartment he felt very lonely. His feet felt heavy. By the time he got to the landing he seemed unreasonably weary and he rested to take a deep breath. He had been thinking how all the church bells would ring on Easter Sunday while the choirs sang of the Lord who had risen from the dead, and he hoped it would be a crystal-clear, sunlit day. Last Easter, at a time when he and Elsie had been married only a few weeks, they had gone to the church together and he had held her hand tightly even while they knelt down to pray. "I guess there's no use thinking of that," he said, as he started to climb the stairs again, yet he went on thinking stubbornly that all over the country on Sunday there would be a kind of awakening after the winter, in the city the church choirs would chant that the dead had returned to life, and for some reason it stirred him to feel that Elsie was so alive and close to him in his thoughts.

—MORLEY CALLAGHAN[21]

■ **Exercise 11** Write a paragraph in which you develop one of the following topics by using carefully selected specific details.

1. Our local butcher is an expert at cutting up meat and reputations.
2. I know what it feels like to be on the wrong end of a gun (OR to operate an elevator, to wait outside an emergency room).
3. It is a season (OR place) that seems full of contradictions.
4. When I visualize life in the 1990s, I get excited (OR worried, impatient, full of ideas).

(2) Use several closely related examples or one striking example to illustrate the controlling idea.

Examples are especially useful for developing a generalization that a reader might question or might not understand. To be convincing, an example given in support of a generalization needs to be truly representative.

25   Natural frontiers exist between nations, but the border between Canada and the United States is not one of them. Birds fly over it, fish swim through it, ore bodies lie under it, stands of timber straddle it, rivers traverse it. As in the

---

[21] Abridged from "Rocking-Chair" by Morley Callaghan, *Morley Callaghan's Stories*, Macmillan of Canada, Toronto. Copyright Morley Callaghan 1959. Reprinted by permission.

movement of trade, so in the disposition of resources. The continent is an economic unit. Its bisection is political, not geographic. —JAMES EAYRS[22]

[A number of specific examples illustrate the generalization stated in the first sentence.]

26   Ed Wynn and Fields, as rival comedians, were constantly vying for laughs. During one performance, Wynn concealed himself beneath the pool table and tried to steal the scene by smirking and winking at the audience. Fields became uneasily aware that his laughs were coming at the wrong places, and his eye caught a suspicious movement under the table. He waited until Wynn, on all fours, carelessly stuck his head out too far. With a juggler's perfect timing, Fields swung the butt of his cue in a half-circle and lowered it into his rival's skull. Wynn sagged to the floor while Fields continued his game serenely amid boisterous applause. Every time that Wynn struggled back to consciousness and emitted a low moan, the audience laughed louder. —COREY FORD[23]

[The controlling idea is developed by one striking example: the competitive behaviour of the comedians during one performance.]

■Exercise 12   Write a paragraph using either several examples or one striking example to develop one of the following topics.

1. Almost anything can be a symbol.
2. The Canadian temperament is like the Canadian temperature.

---

[22] From James Eayrs, "Sharing a Continent: The Hard Issues," in *The United States and Canada*, ed. John Sloan Dickey (Englewood Cliffs, N.J.: Prentice-Hall, 1964).

[23] From *The Time of Laughter* by Corey Ford. Published by Little, Brown and Company. Copyright © 1967 by Corey Ford. Reprinted by permission of Little, Brown and Company.

3. Even the rich have serious problems.
4. It is easy to be a coach (OR a judge, the premier) at a distance.
5. We are living in a decade of crises.

(3) Formulate and develop a definition.

A formal definition has two parts: first the thing being defined is put into a class of similar things; then it is differentiated from all other things in that class. Notice in the following paragraph that Kenneth Rexroth first classifies the ballad as a narrative folk song and then points out its distinguishing characteristics—its brevity, dramatic situation, rhetoric, measure, and so on.

27   The ballad has been defined as a folk song which tells a story, concentrating on the dramatic situation of the climax, rather than a long narrative unfolding action and reaction. The tale is presented directly in act and speech with little or no comment by the narrator. Although the most violent passions may be shown by the characters, the maker of the ballad remains austerely unmoved. So does the performer. Emotional comment, where it occurs, comes through a special kind of rhetoric peculiar to the ballad, often, especially in some of the refrains, dependent upon the use of rather remote metaphors to intensify the psychological situation. Most ballads are in "ballad measure," four lines of alternating eight and six syllables—really fourteen syllables or seven stressed syllables with a strong pause after the eighth—rhyming usually at the end of each fourteen syllables. However, this pattern varies constantly even within the same song. What varies it is the fluency of the music clustered around a simple melodic pattern, which a good ballad singer seldom, stanza for stanza, repeats exactly.
—KENNETH REXROTH[24]

[24] From "The English and Scottish Ballad" by Kenneth Rexroth, *Saturday Review,* December 14, 1968. Copyright 1968 Saturday Review, Inc. Reprinted by permission.

■ **Exercise 13** Write a paragraph presenting a definition of one of the following:

(1) tomato, (2) government, (3) happiness, (4) needlepoint, OR (5) tattooing.

(4) Use classification to relate ideas.

To classify is to divide into categories. Some classifications are based on similarities: for instance, such trees as the black oak, the sycamore, and the cottonwood may all be classified as *deciduous*. Other classifications are based on differences: the black oak, the sycamore, and the cottonwood may be differentiated from the cedar, the fir, and the pine by the labels *deciduous* and *evergreen* trees. A classification relates ideas by listing and characterizing the members of a group.

28   There are three kinds of book owners. The first has all the standard sets and best-sellers—unread, untouched. (This deluded individual owns woodpulp and ink, not books.) The second has a great many books—a few of them read through, most of them dipped into, but all of them as clean and shiny as the day they were bought. (This person would probably like to make books his own, but is restrained by a false respect for their physical appearance.) The third has a few books or many—every one of them dog-eared and dilapidated, shaken and loosened by continual use, marked and scribbled in from front to back. (This man owns books.)   —MORTIMER J. ADLER[25]

[Adler divides book owners into three main categories and then lists and describes each type.]

■ **Exercise 14** Write a paragraph on one of the following topics in which you use classification to relate ideas.

----

[25] From "How to Mark a Book" by Mortimer J. Adler, *Saturday Review*, July 6, 1940. Copyright 1940 The Saturday Review Company, Inc.; renewed 1967 Saturday Review, Inc. Reprinted by permission.

1. There are various kinds of home owners (OR automobile mechanics, flight attendants, campus lecturers).
2. As the controversy raged, letters to the editor fell into two (OR three, four) categories.

(5) Use contrast or comparison to develop the controlling idea.

To contrast is to point out differences between members of the same class—for example, differences between two kinds of terror.

29   Most of us enjoy the gooseflesh and the tingle along the spine produced by the successful ghost story. There is something agreeable in letting our blood be chilled by bats in the moonlight, guttering candles, creaking doors, eerie shadows, piercing screams, inexplicable bloodstains, and weird noises. But the terror aroused by tricks and external "machinery" is a far cry from the terror evoked by some terrifying treatment of the human situation. The horror we experience in watching the Werewolf or Dracula or Frankenstein is far less significant than that we get from watching the bloody ambition of Macbeth or the jealousy of Othello. In the first, terror is the end-product; in the second, it is the natural accompaniment of a powerful revelation of life. In the first, we are always aware of a basic unreality; in the second, reality is terrifying.   —LAURENCE PERRINE[26]

[The key idea is stated at the end of the paragraph.]

The comparison in the next paragraph, unlike the contrast, is between members of two different classes: language and games.

30   The language game shares certain characteristics with all other true games. First of all, it has a minimum of two players (the private, incomprehensible speech of a schizo-

---

[26]From *Literature: Structure, Sound, and Sense*, 2nd edition by Laurence Perrine. Published by Harcourt Brace Jovanovich, Inc., 1974. Reprinted by permission.

phrenic is no more a true game than is solitaire). Second, a person within speaking distance of any stranger can be forced by social pressure to commit himself to play, in the same way that a bystander in the vicinity of any other kind of game may be asked to play or to look on. Third, something must be at stake and both players must strive to win it—whether the reward be a tangible gain like convincing an employer of the need for a raise or an intangible one like the satisfaction of besting someone in an argument. Fourth, a player of any game has a particular style that distinguishes him as well as the ability to shift styles depending upon where the game is played and who the other players are. In the case of the language game, the style might be a preference for certain expressions or a folksy way of speaking, and the style shift might be the bringing into play of different verbal strategies when speaking in the home, at the office, on the street, or in a place of worship.

—PETER FARB[27]

■ **Exercise 15** Write a paragraph in which you develop by contrast or comparison one of the following topics or one of your own choice.

1. supermarkets and corner shops
2. compulsive liars and compulsive thieves
3. personal freedom and social responsibility
4. fads today and yesterday

(6) Show cause or effect to develop the controlling idea.

A paragraph developed by causal analysis must not only raise the question *why* but answer it to the satisfaction of the reader. The cause or causes must satisfactorily explain the result. Notice that paragraph 31 is developed by explaining why the opening statement is true.

---

[27] From *Word Play: What Happens When People Talk* by Peter Farb. Published by Alfred A. Knopf, Inc., a Division of Random House, Inc. Copyright © 1973 by Peter Farb. Reprinted by permission.

31   But in the long run every advantage lay with the British. The French empire was far too big to hold on so small a basis as the population of New France. Stretched out too thin, with the fur trade its only real resource, French Canada gradually exhausted itself. The British Colonies, occupying a relatively small area, had been able to build up a thickly populated community with many and varied resources. They were capable of far greater effort. There were, after all, more than twenty British colonists for every French Canadian. And if many of the thirteen colonies would not effectively support the struggle with the French, Massachusetts, which was active, alone had a larger population than all New France.   —J. M. S. CARELESS[28]

[In stating that "in the long run every advantage lay with the British," the opening sentence implies that a British victory was the most likely result of an Anglo-French struggle in North America. The sentences that follow explain what those advantages were and, thus, why a British victory was likely.]

■ **Exercise 16**   Write a paragraph that begins with one of the following statements. Develop the paragraph by showing why the opening statement is true.

1. One might wonder why such a small percentage of Canadians created such a major national problem.
2. In the past few years, higher education has become more (OR less) important to young people than it was previously.
3. Childhood experiences shape personality.
4. Survivors of the next war may have to live underground.

(7) Use a combination of methods to develop the controlling idea.

Many good paragraphs are developed not by any one specific method but by a combination of methods. Some good paragraphs almost defy analysis. The important considera-

---

[28]From *Canada: A Story of Challenge* by J. M. S. Careless. Reprinted by permission of The Macmillan Co. of Canada Ltd.

tion is not the specific method used but the adequacy of the development.

32   It is sometimes argued that terrorism is bound to decrease once society becomes less repressive. Such an assessment rests on an overly optimistic view of the rationality of human behavior. However just the social order, however democratic the political regime, there will always be disaffected, alienated, and highly aggressive people claiming that the present state of affairs is intolerable and that any change will be for the better. In the past, society was less exposed to such attacks, simply because the means of destruction were far less effective. Under present conditions, on the other hand, a handful of madmen or fanatics can cause a great deal of havoc, and the end is not yet in sight. The hijacking of aircraft was an early and, on the whole, ineffective prelude to a new age of terror. (In 1969–70 some 164 civil aircraft were hijacked, in 1973–74 only a mere handful.) But it seems only a question of time before weapons like the SAM-7, which weighs a mere 25 pounds, costs less than $1,000 to produce, and can be operated by a child, will be used against civilian planes. The first recorded attempt, at Ostia near Rome, was thwarted in time. One day the terrorists may be more successful.

                                            —WALTER LAQUEUR[29]

[The first sentence presents a viewpoint, which serves as a "straw man" (an idea to be refuted). Then Laqueur gives reasons why he believes the opening viewpoint to be false. Following this, a concrete example and specific details are used to develop the paragraph.]

33   The question of why snowflakes are different remains one of the classic puzzles of science, but that they *are* different is part of our culture. Who has not heard, and believed without a thought, that no two snowflakes are alike? All snowflakes *look* very much alike; like little white

---

[29] From "Guerrillas and Terrorists" by Walter Laqueur. Reprinted from *Commentary*, by permission; copyright © 1974 by the American Jewish Committee.

dots. No doubt, if one examines them closely enough, there are differences to be found, but surely there is nothing remarkable about that. A single ice crystal might well contain some ten sextillion molecules: Considering all the ways those molecules can be arranged, the odds against any two completely identical snowflakes having fallen since the atmosphere formed some four billion years ago are enormous. But by the same analysis, no two grains of sand on the beach, no two waves in the ocean, no two hairs on the head are identical. Why all the fuss, then, over snowflakes?

—FRED HAPGOOD[30]

[The first sentence states a fact. Next comes a rhetorical question—followed by specific details, a reason, a comparison, and a second rhetorical question.]

■ **Exercise 17** Prepare for a class discussion of paragraphs 34 and 35. Be able to point out controlling ideas, methods of development, types of organization or arrangement of sentences, and devices used for transition.

34   Television homogenizes its audiences, arrests the assimilation process and introduces a new sense of community to cultural groups. Scotland, Wales, the Basque countries, Corsica and Brittany have pulled back from the precipice of oblivion, reviving language and national pride so vestigial the rest of the world had forgotten their existence. The phenomenon coincided with the plugging of every household and tavern into an audiovisual network to which anyone had instant access for the price of a dynamite stick, a syringeful of mercury or merely a violent remark. None learned to use the power of television more quickly than the more desperate and inventive members of minorities suffering oppression or discrimination.   —DAVID THOMAS[31]

[30] From "When Ice Crystals Fall from the Sky" by Fred Hapgood. Copyright Smithsonian Institution 1975, from *Smithsonian* magazine January 1976.

[31] From "If you still don't believe the medium is the message, talk to René Lévesque" by David Thomas, *Maclean's,* March 20, 1978, © 1978 by Maclean's Magazine. Reprinted by permission.

35   Laboratory fertilization, though, is just a first and
indispensable step toward greater leaps against mankind.
The most formidable is cloning. It should not be necessary
to reiterate the arguments against such an attack on human
individuality, sexuality, and identity. The ability to make
unlimited copies of any human reduces the uniqueness and
sanctity of the individual. Apart from all the psychological
complications of having an exact replica as a parent or
child, the social benefits of this practice redound chiefly to
the technocratic state. The state would have to decide
which genotypes were most worthy of reproduction. This
power is too great to invest in any human authority. It is
power not merely over the immediate arrangements of
human life but also over all future generations.

—GEORGE F. GILDER[32]

■ **Exercise 18**   Using paragraph 12, 34, or 35 (or any other
paragraph selected by your instructor) as a model, write a para
graph setting forth and developing a personal opinion (or an
argument) on a topic of your choice.

■ **Exercise 19**   Indicate an appropriate method or combination
of methods for developing four of the following statements.

1. Everything is wrong with the typical bathroom.
2. National identity cannot survive without cultural identity.
3. Lifestyles will change drastically.
4. It is 2084, and Johnny still cannot read.
5. There is no substitute for the printed word.
6. Man is the slave of the machines that were once his serv
   ants.
7. The development of an international language has disad
   vantages as well as advantages.

---

[32]Copyright © 1973 by George F. Gilder. Reprinted by permission of
Quadrangle/Times Books from *Sexual Suicide* by George F. Gilder.

Planning and Writing the Whole Composition

32

Arrange and express your ideas effectively.

A paragraph is usually a series of sentences developing one controlling idea: see Section **31**. A whole composition is usually a series of paragraphs developing several closely related facets of one controlling, or central, idea.

As you read the following composition, observe how Patricia Follmer effectively arranges and expresses her ideas as she explains the attitudes and traditions of the nomadic Gypsies (her central idea). Notice that every paragraph sticks to the subject and refers to the title. Give special attention to the close relationship between the beginning and the ending of the composition.

The Gypsies

1   When spring comes, the *drom* ("road") beckons all Roms, as the Gypsies call themselves. Whether they are nomads who have stopped for the winter or sedentary Gypsies living in cities, their hearts are awakened. They believe that all land under their feet is their own.

2   José, a Gypsy of Arles, in Provence, once told me about his youth before World War II, when he traveled with his large family in a horse-drawn caravan to Switzerland, Ger-

plan

many, the Netherlands, the west coast of France, through the Pyrenees, Montpelier, and then back to Arles again by autumn, making the same circuit year after year, selling horses and rugs and doing metalwork. "We went everywhere. We stopped in the fields, amused ourselves in the trees. If we wanted a fruit, we ate it. We were savage. We were free."

3   The Gypsies, it is thought, wandered out of Central Asia about 4,000 years ago. They have never stopped moving. They arrived in Europe in the late Middle Ages, and used the annual religious pilgrimages they found there as pretexts for large tribal gatherings, since they ordinarily traveled in small groups to avoid the authorities. At the gatherings, they conducted family business—baptisms, marriages, trials—and exchanged news.

4   This tradition continues today. Every May, Gypsies from all over Europe gather in the village of Les Saintes Maries-de-la-Mer, in the south of France, to venerate their patron saint, Sara-Kali. The campgrounds are filled with trailers, clotheslines, and cooking fires. Inside each caravan, the entire family sleeps crowded together on the floor under feather quilts. Although they live communally, Gypsies preserve their privacy through mutual respect and strict codes of behavior; they feel there is something wrong with a man who needs to hide behind walls.

5   The Gypsy is happiest in the natural world, where he can hear the rain at night on his caravan and smell the woods. He lives from day to day, and he likes uncertainty. He has known practically from infancy that sudden changes from comfort to discomfort are essential for a healthy life. As a result, he has a deep sense of self-reliance.

6   Today many Gypsies have moved into the cities (there are communities in Boston, New York, Newark, and Los Angeles) or have been forced into "settlements." But they paint their ceilings blue to remind themselves of the sky, and they cover their walls with rugs to bring back the

feeling of a tent. "We don't like fancy houses," José says. "We like an old house with a fireplace for heat and cooking. We eat with the fingers—no need for forks or spoons. We are free like that, and it is because of this that the Romany will never change. We will always stay as we were born."

—PATRICIA FOLLMER[1]

A unified composition, whether only one paragraph or a series of paragraphs, does not fall into order by chance. Order is the result of careful planning.

32a
Choose an appropriate subject and limit it properly.

A subject is appropriate if it appeals to you and if it is acceptable to the intended reader. A subject is properly limited if you can treat it adequately (according to your purpose) in the time and space at your disposal.

Here are two examples of ways that a subject may be limited:

sports → the Olympics → the winter games → contests on ice → speed skating

domestic arts → food preparation → additives → cyclamates → cyclamate-sweetened peaches

Deciding on the degree of limitation is a matter of the writer's judgment.

PURPOSE

Before making a final decision regarding the specific topic, you should consider your purpose in writing the composition. Suppose, for example, that you have chosen (or have

---

[1] "The Gypsies" by Patricia Follmer. Copyright © 1974 by *Harper's Magazine.* All rights reserved. Reprinted from the July 1974 issue by special permission.

been assigned) "North American Burial Customs" as a subject for a short paper. If your main purpose is to inform the reader, either "Kinds of Floral Arrangements for Coffins" or "Some Burial Customs Are Dying Out" would be appropriate. If, however, you decide you want to argue against the idea of burial, you might choose a title such as "Why Not Give the Body to Science?" or "Cremation Is Better." Or if you decide to describe a scene, you might give a word picture of a military burial or a funeral procession—with its colour, movement, sounds, silences. If your primary aim is to inform as you entertain, a suitable topic might be "Pay Now—Die Later" or "A Lay-Away Plan." To arouse interest, you might write a story (as a part of this composition or as a complete, separate composition) about a person who has trouble arranging for his or her own burial—perhaps by mail order.

Although you may have secondary aims, each of the primary purposes you might select corresponds to one of the four main types of writing as they are conventionally classified in rhetoric:

Type of writing	*Primary purpose*
Exposition	To inform or explain
Argumentation	To convince or persuade
Narration	To entertain or interest
Description	To describe or picture

Exposition (often combined with description and/or bits of narration) is the most common type of nonfiction and the kind most frequently written by university students. "How-to" compositions, for instance, are expository. Dealing with facts and ideas, expository compositions may define, identify, classify, illustrate, compare, contrast, or explain a process. *Argumentation* (often blended with exposition, as well as with other types of writing) is concerned with the validity of a theory, thesis, or proposition and gives reasons why it is true or false. *Narration* (generally blended with description) focusses on action: simple stories (like newspaper stories) present events in chronological order; narratives with plots involve setting, characterization, conflict. *Description* (seldom written independently, but usually a part of narration, exposition, argument) presents a picture with details that convey a sensory impression. Few compositions are a single form of discourse. Most are mixtures in which one form predominates.

CENTRAL IDEA

After deciding on your purpose, you will find it helpful to set down, in a single sentence, the central or controlling idea for your paper. In fact, if in the beginning you can set down a central idea containing logically arranged main points (see the first example below), you will already have the main plan and perhaps eliminate the need for a formal outline.

1. *Purpose:* To inform by pointing out ways to appraise a used car   [Exposition]
   Title: How to Buy a Good Used Car
   Central idea: Before selecting a used car, a wise buyer will carefully inspect the car, talk to the former owner of the car, and engage a good mechanic to examine its motor.

2. *Purpose:* To convince the reader of a need for change in the examination system   [Argument]
   Title: Why Have Final Examinations?
   Central idea: Final examinations should be abolished.

3. *Purpose:* To tell a story about a true experience   [Narration]
   Title: Dangerous Waters
   Central idea: Looking for dolphin twenty miles out, I steered my light fishing boat into dangerous waters and spent hours battling high winds before being rescued.

4. *Purpose:* To describe my sister and show how she manages to get her own way with others.   [Exposition, description, narration]
   Title: Who Can Say No to Her?
   Central idea: My sister gets her way because of her "endearing young charms."

■ **Exercise 1** Select a subject that interests you; then if it is too broad, limit it. Decide on your purpose. Consider the possibility of writing for two different types of readers. Using the examples on page 335 as a guide, write your purpose, a suitable title, and the central idea. You may wish to choose one of the following subjects.

1. CB radio
2. fads in dress
3. trying out for a play
4. endangered species
5. overpopulation—fact or fiction?

32b

Develop a working plan, or a rough outline, before writing a composition.

Although a formal outline (see **32c**) may not be required for every paper, a working plan contributes to the unity of a composition and makes the actual writing easier.

The first step in the preparation of a rough outline is the jotting down of ideas on the topic. Suppose, for example, that a student has chosen to write a paper on the mood and attitudes of the youth of today. The writer has strong feelings about the way his generation of students is compared with the previous one. The purpose of the paper will be both to inform and persuade the reader. Next the student chooses a tentative title, "The Youth of Two Generations," and then jots down ideas related to the title, without much concern for order.

Sixties	*Today*
mass movements	individual action
questioned society as whole	part of society
group sense of identity	no group identity
dismissed value of education	education valued
optimistic	pessimistic

Ideas on a list such as this often overlap; some are general, and some are specific. But it is the beginning of a plan.

The student then formulates a central idea, singles out key ideas, and arranges them in a logical order (see **32e**), decides on the title, and writes out the plan.

WORKING PLAN

> *Title:* Where Have All the Flowers Gone?
> *Central idea:* Today's youth are often compared unfavourably—but unfairly—with the youth of the sixties.
>
> 1. The sixties—unfocussed group optimism, anger against society
> 2. Today—focussed individual concern; individuals, as part of society, must share the blame for its problems

For a short paper, a plan of this type may be adequate. Often, however, a formal outline can result in a more carefully organized paper, especially with regard to specific details.

32c

Use a formal outline of the type specified by your instructor. See also 33c.

The types of outlines most commonly used are the sentence outline, the topic outline, and the paragraph outline. Topic outlines and sentence outlines have the same parts and the same groupings; they differ only in the fullness of expression employed. In a paragraph outline no effort is made to classify the material into major headings and subheadings: the controlling idea (stated or implied) of each paragraph is simply listed in the order in which it is to come. Paragraph outlines are especially helpful in writing short papers. Topic or sentence outlines may be adapted to papers of any length.

337

SENTENCE OUTLINE

Where Have All the Flowers Gone?

Central idea: Today's youth are often compared unfavourably—but unfairly—with the youth of the sixties.

Introduction: The comparison of the idealism of the sixties and the cynicism of today is a misleading one.

I. The youth of the sixties had a strong group identity and anger.
   A. Society was the enemy that could be fought and defeated.
   B. Youth in the sixties knew who they were and where they were going.
II. Today's youth cannot express and solve their problems through group action.
   A. "The enemy" is not something outside ourselves.
   B. We must solve our own problems as individuals.

Conclusion: Enlightened pessimism is perhaps more valuable in today's world than unfocussed optimism.

TOPIC OUTLINE (See also pages 343–44).

Where Have All the Flowers Gone?

Central idea: Today's youth are often compared unfavourably—but unfairly—with the youth of the sixties.

Introduction: The comparison of the idealism of the sixties and the cynicism of today is a misleading one.

I. Group identity and anger of sixties youth
   A. Society as the enemy
   B. Sense of identity and destiny
II. Today's youth—individual action
   A. "The enemy" as part of ourselves
   B. Solving problems as individuals

Conclusion: Enlightened pessimism is perhaps more valuable in today's world than unfocussed optimism.

PARAGRAPH OUTLINE

1. The comparison of the idealism of the sixties and the cynicism of today is misleading.

2. The sixties was a time of mass movements and society was the enemy.
3. Hand in hand with an awareness that society was to blame for everything that was wrong was a strong sense of group identity for the youth of the sixties.
4. Today's youth do not find it so easy to blame "society" for their problems because they see themselves as being a part of that society.
5. Enlightened pessimism is as valuable in our time as un-focussed optimism was in the sixties.

■ **Exercise 2** Observing the flow of ideas, first read through the composition that follows; then write down the central idea; finally, make a sentence or a topic outline that reveals Lowell Thomas's plan.

Glacier Bay: Alaska's Frozen Dreamland

1   While I have spent more than my share of time plowing through desert sands and humid jungles, I confess to a bias toward chilly climes. Hence, it is not surprising that one of my favorite wonders is Alaska's little-known Glacier Bay, where the mountains rise higher from the sea than at any other place on earth.

2   Backdropped by the storm-ridden, ironically misnamed Fairweather Range, Glacier Bay's 4400 square miles is a frozen dreamland of glaciers, immense perpendicular ice walls shimmering in the sun and magnificent fjords. The waters of the bay are strewn with huge blocks of floating ice and fossilized tree stumps that scientists say were growing before the Pyramids were built.

3   Here virtually all varieties of arctic wildlife abound. One can see, for example, close at hand and unafraid of man, whales blowing their geyser-like breath, seals riding floating icebergs, bears of various breeds, blacktail deer, moose, wolves and wolverines, and huge flocks of snowbirds and waterfowl.

4   There is nothing fixed or static at Glacier Bay. It is a world constantly in flux, providing scientists a unique laboratory of earth processes. The great glaciers form slowly, build to fantastic dimensions and then slide majestically toward the sea, overrunning great forests and leaving behind new soil—where the cycle of growth begins all over again. As one scientist commented, "Watching these changes is like being in on the Creation."

—LOWELL THOMAS[2]

■ **Exercise 3** Make a paragraph outline of "The Gypsies" (pages 331–33).

32d

Make sure that the outline covers the subject.

An adequate outline is essential to a successful composition. The major headings (I, II, III, and so on) must be sufficient in number and in scope to satisfy the expectations aroused by the title. Just as the central idea must be covered by the major headings, each of these headings must in turn be covered by its subheadings.

INADEQUATE COVERAGE	ADEQUATE COVERAGE
The Grading System	The Grading System
I. What a *B* means	I. Differences between an *A* and a *B*
II. What a *C* means	II. Differences between a *C* and a *D*
	III. Meaning of *F*

A writer might prefer to leave the main headings on the left above unchanged and to alter the title to agree—for example, "The Meaning of *B* and *C* in the Grading System."

In reality, making an outline is a process of thinking through the paper. Ordinarily, if your outline does not fit the

---

[2] Excerpt from "Nature's Seven Greatest Wonders," by Lowell Thomas, *The Reader's Digest,* July 1974.

rules for an outline, there is something faulty about the plan itself—a missing element, a misstated title, or an inadequate purpose. Thus an outline can help you give focus to your paper and can sometimes show the need for further limitation of your topic.

32e
Make sure that your ideas are logically arranged in your outline.

Logical arrangement is second in importance only to adequacy of coverage. If the outline is disorganized and ineffective, the paper that follows it will also be disorganized and ineffective. See also **31b** .

(1) Group related ideas.

Although you may begin your outline by jotting down as many ideas on your topic as possible, without regard to order, you should later bring related ideas together, grouping them under major headings. Compare the first list of ideas for a composition on the youth of two generations (page 336) with the groupings in the finished outlines (pages 338–39).

(2) Arrange the parts in a natural, logical order.

The nature of the subject will suggest an appropriate arrangement, such as time order, space order, or order of climax: see pages 306–09.

TIME ORDER	ORDER OF CLIMAX
Building a Storm Cellar	Types of Wars
I. Choosing the site	I. Civil
II. Digging the hole	II. International
III. Pouring the cement	III. Interplanetary
IV. Adding the door	

■ **Exercise 4** Make a list of three, four, or five main points closely related to one of the following subjects; then arrange the items in a natural, logical order. (In parentheses are suggestions for appropriate arrangements.)

1. a brush with the law (*time order*)
2. ways to influence legislation (*order of climax*)
3. a walk across the campus (*space order*)
4. the trials of being a freshman (*order of climax*)

(3) Do not allow headings to overlap.

Overlapping often occurs when a writer attempts an arrangement based on more than one principle.

MIXED ARRANGEMENT

Advertising on Television

I. Since the advent of colour [Arrangement by time]
II. Its effect on sales [Arrangement by cause and effect]
III. Pain relievers [Arrangement by classification]

CONSISTENT ARRANGEMENT

Advertising on Television

Time	*Cause and Effect*	*Classification*
I. Before colour	I. Creates demand	I. Detergents
II. After colour	II. Influences sales	II. Appliances
	III. Affects economy	III. Pain relievers

(4) Do not use a subheading for an idea that belongs in a main heading, and vice versa.

ILLOGICAL

Wonder Products on TV

I. Detergents
   A. Appliances
II. Washing machines
III. Remedies for headaches
   A. Pain relievers
   B. Pills for arthritis

LOGICAL

Wonder Products on TV

I. Detergents
II. Appliances
   A. Washing machines
   B. Refrigerators
III. Pain relievers
   A. For headaches
   B. For arthritis

(5) Do not use single headings or subheadings any-where in the outline.

Headings and subheadings stand for divisions, and a division denotes at least two parts. Therefore, to be logical, each outline should have at least two main headings, I and II. If it has a subheading marked A, it should also have a subheading marked B; if it has a 1, it should also have a 2.

Title: Endangered Species

INCOMPLETE	COMPLETE
I. On land	I. On land
A. Wild mustangs	A. Wild mustangs
II. In the sea	B. Prairie dogs
	II. In the sea

32f

Check your topic and sentence outlines for details of notation and indention. Check topic outlines for parallel structure.

Any intelligible system of notation is acceptable. The one used for both the topic outline and the sentence outline in **32c** is in common use. This system, expanded to show subheadings of the second and third degrees, is as follows:

  I. . . . . [Used for major headings]
    A. . . . . [Used for subheadings
    B. . . . .   of the first degree]
      1. . . . . [Used for subheadings
      2. . . . .   of the second degree]
        a. . . . . [Used for subheadings
        b. . . . .   of the third degree]
  II. . . . .

Seldom, however, will a short outline—or even a longer one—need subordination beyond the first or second degree.

Use parallel structure for parallel parts of the topic outline to clarify the coordination of parts. (See Section **26** and note

343

the parallel structure of the outline on page 338.) In topic outlines, the major headings (I, II, III, and so on) should be expressed in parallel structure, as should each group of subheadings. But it is unnecessary to strive for parallel structure between different groups of subheadings—for example, between A, B, and C under I and A, B, and C under II. (Parallel structure is not a concern in either the sentence outline or the paragraph outline.)

■ **Exercise 5** Make an outline (of the type specified by your instructor) on the subject you used for Exercise 1, page 336. Then check your outline against the principles set forth in **32d–f**.

32g
After you have decided on your approach, write the paper according to your plan or formal outline.

Just as point of view is important in narration, a consistent approach is desirable in expository writing. Point of view refers to the writer's relation to the subject of the composition. Writers of formal compositions often prefer the omniscient point of view, and therefore consistently use third-person pronouns (*one, they,* and so on—and sometimes the impersonal *you* or *we*). Writers have a choice, though, and use the *I* or the impersonal *you* approach when it best suits their purposes. (If you choose the second-person point of view, make sure that each impersonal *you* refers to readers in general, not to just a few. Use with discretion the *you* in sentences such as "The people in that area are just as uneducated and common as you are." See also Section **27**.)

Your working plan or formal outline should contribute to the orderly flow of ideas in your composition. But be sure to supply transitions not only between sentences but also between paragraphs: see **31b(2)–(6)**. As you write, cover all items in the outline. The actual writing of the paper, of

course, may very well suggest the need for changing parts of
the plan.

Notice how the following composition is related to the
sample outlines on pages 338–39.

Where Have All the Flowers Gone?

1   It has become fashionable to compare the "silent seventies" and the "vibrant sixties" to show that the youth of
the past decade were superior to the youth of our own. The
youth of the sixties, we are told, were buzzing with idealism, cared passionately about the injustices of society, and
had a clear vision of the world they wanted. Our generation, by contrast, is criticized for its cynicism, apathetic
insensitivity to the tyranny of progress, and lack of concern
with anything in the future other than graduation, safe jobs,
and financial security. This is an easy generalization, but if
one examines the issue, not in the vociferous sweeping
statements of the sixties but with some of the quiet detach-
ment of the seventies, the situation becomes less clear.

2   The sixties were undoubtedly a time of mass movements. The youth of North America threw itself into causes
of one kind or another, often with very little sense of
discrimination. The "enemy" was the amorphous "they."
"They" were the technocratic society that "we" were fighting. "They" were the universities that did military research,
that kept dehumanizing information in their computers,
and that manufactured human cogs for the great social
machine. "They" were all the past generations that had sold
out to society in return for material comfort, and therefore
"they" were responsible for pollution, war, the consumer
society, and so forth.

3   And with this sense of who the enemy was, went a
clear sense of who "we" were. Could there be any doubt
about it? "We" were the thousands who turned out for
demonstrations in Toronto, Montreal, and Vancouver. "We"
knew that war was "not healthy for children and other
living things." "We" knew that higher education was a

fraud and that degrees were not worth the paper they were written on. "We" wore our hair long, made love not war and *knew* that the times "they were a changin'."

4   But the times have changed. For us, the youth of the seventies, there is no such certainty of whom to blame for what is wrong. The technocratic society survives intact while the "counter-culture" that was to provide an alternative to it is alive and well and living comfortably within the society it claimed to oppose. Education, which could be dismissed lightly and scathingly by the youth of the opulent sixties, cannot be dismissed so readily in our time. Education is no longer the key to luxury, it is the key to survival. Even the symbols of revolt in the last decade are now thoroughly socialized. Our long hair is cut in unisex boutiques, our jeans are pre-faded, and our peace signs are the products of a massive consumer industry.

5   Yes, the seventies are different from the sixties. But the difference is not simply between involvement and apathy, idealism and cynicism. The sixties were a time of group optimism, group anger. The seventies are a time of individual pessimism, individual action. We now know that society cannot be simply polarized into "good guys and bad guys." "We have met the enemy and they is us," as a character in a well-known comic strip says. Rather than being able to wallow in the unfocussed idealism of collective action, as the youth of the sixties did, we are becoming steadily aware that we cannot rely on the group to bring change, just as we cannot lay the blame on "society" as a whole. And if that is apathy and cynicism, then perhaps we should wear it as a symbol of our identity, not of our shame.

—PELHAM DAVIS

---

[3] Reprinted by permission of the author.

■ **Exercise 6** The composition "Where Have All the Flowers Gone?" is the opinion of one student. Write a composition on the youth of today, perhaps comparing your perception of today's generation with Davis' "enlightened pessimists." Or you might enjoy writing a paper on what you think the next generation of students will be like.

EFFECTIVE BEGINNINGS AND ENDINGS

Every composition needs an effective beginning and ending.

One of the best ways to begin is with a sentence that not only arouses the reader's interest but also sets forth the first main point and starts its development.

Title: Three Preferred Jobs

If I had no one but myself to consider, my first choice of an occupation would be stunt flying because I could take all kinds of exciting risks and be paid for having fun. For example, I could. . . .

Another way to begin a composition is to write an introductory paragraph that arouses interest and states the central idea of the composition but does not start the development of the first main point.

Title: Carousel—A New Experience

All of us enjoy wearing a new pair of shoes, eating a dish we have not had before, seeing a movie with an unusual plot, or touring in a new section of the country; in other words, we like experiences which are novel, different. I happen to be one of those people who enjoy discovering an unfamiliar poem by a famous poet, reading a good book, or attending a choral or band concert. I like new and different cultural outlets, and a few weeks ago my English assignment brought me face to face with just such an experience: Carousel, theatre-in-the-round. The play which I attended was an Irish drama by Paul Vincent Carroll, entitled *Shadow and Substance,* and I would like to use it as the vehicle in my description of Carousel itself—the interior of the theatre, the actors, the techniques used.

347

Still another way to begin is with a question. The answer to it may set forth the main points to be discussed later. A transitional paragraph may intervene between the introduction and the discussion of the first main point.

> What is it that we really require from the scientists and technologists? I should answer: We need methods and equipment which are
>
> —cheap enough so that they are accessible to virtually everyone;
> —suitable for small-scale application; and
> —compatible with man's need for creativity.
>
> Out of these three characteristics is born non-violence and a relationship of man to nature which guarantees permanence. If only one of these three is neglected, things are bound to go wrong. Let us look at them one by one.
> Methods and machines cheap enough to be accessible to virtually everyone—why should we assume that our scientists and technologists are unable to develop them? This was a primary concern of Gandhi. . . .
>
> —E. F. SCHUMACHER[4]

A composition should end; it should not merely stop. Two ways to end a composition effectively are to stress the final point of the main discussion by using an emphatic last sentence and to write a strong concluding paragraph. Often a concluding paragraph clinches, restates, or stresses the importance of the central idea or thesis of the composition. An effective ending may also present a summary, a thought-provoking question, a solution to a problem, or a suggestion or challenge. (See the endings of the compositions on pages 317–18, 331–33, 339–40, and 345–46.)

Caution: Do not devote too much space to introductions and conclusions. A short paper often has only one paragraph for

---

[4] From *Small Is Beautiful* by E. F. Schumacher. Reprinted by permission of the publishers, Harper & Row, and Blond and Briggs.

a beginning or an ending; frequently one sentence for each is adequate. Remember that the bulk of your composition should be the development of the central idea, the discussion of the main headings and subheadings in your outline.

■ **Exercise 7** Giving special attention to the beginning and ending, write a composition based on the outline you prepared for Exercise 5, page 344.

■ **Exercise 8** Read the following composition in preparation for a discussion of (1) its title, (2) its purpose and central idea, (3) its arrangement and development of main points, (4) its beginning and ending. Also be ready to compare "O Tannenbaum" (its diction, tone, and so on) with "Where Have All the Flowers Gone?" (page 345) and "The Gypsies" (page 331).

O Tannenbaum

1   I don't know what to do with the Christmas tree. Christmas is over and there it sits in my yard, tinsel gleaming, leaning up against the hedge. If I haul it away in my car, then the car will fill with needles and tinsel tidbits no vacuuming could remove. And I refuse to spend an entire winter weekend morning pinching after each tidbit with my fingers. If I try to burn the thing, Mr. Swanson will call the police and an embarrassed patrolman will arrive at my door to point out reluctantly, as Swanson watches from his lawn across the street, that outdoor burning is against local ordinances. Even if I got by the vigilant Swanson, the fire would leave a charred patch on my lawn which would have to be reseeded in the spring. And even then the tinsel would remain, evading rakes, tangling in the grass, and waiting for a queasy cat to choke come summer.

2   The tree was bought late from a temporary stand on a safety island in the parking lot of the Big Buy Shopping Plaza. The tree man kept reminding me that if I had come a few days earlier I could have had my pick of the best trees of the season. The ground was littered with bits of string and little piney scraps. I selected the tallest of the remaining trees and talked the man down to fifteen dollars. "You're robbing me," he said as I loaded my tree into the station wagon. "But what the hell, it's Christmas."

3   I could chop the tree into kindling and pile it neatly by the kitchen door. It would look well there, split and stacked. But my wife is afraid of fires, and I am forgetting the tinsel. I just can't see hiring someone to dispose of the tree; it's such a simple thing and I have a terror of men in trucks. "It's around here," I'd say, leading them to the rear of the house. "I'd take care of the thing myself, but it's the tinsel that's the real rub, here." They would give me a suspicious look with the word "rub." I would try to help them load the tree onto their truck, but I see myself uselessly grasping the limp top of the tree as they struggle with the trunk and bulk of the thing. "That's twenty bucks," they'd tell me, refusing coffee, and I would shell it out quickly, as if I had been waiting all year to pay someone twenty bucks. "Believe me," I'd say, "it's worth every dime to me."

4   What I could try is to take several of those plastic bags you get from dry cleaners and wrap the tree up in them. I could lay the bags on the ground and then just roll the thing up, tuck it into the station wagon, and haul it away. I may have something here. All I'd have to do is wrap it up and haul it away. But if it's wrapped in plastic, how will I carry it? I wouldn't be able to reach in and grab the trunk, and if I tried to hug the thing to the car then the plastic would tear and there I am back with the tinsel.

5   I don't know what I'm going to do with the Christmas tree.

—ANDREW WARD[5]

[5]"O Tannenbaum" by Andrew Ward, *Atlantic Monthly,* January 1976. Copyright © 1976 by Andrew Ward. Excerpted with permission of Andrew Ward and The Atlantic Monthly Company.

Library Paper

33

Learn how to prepare a library paper.

A library paper (sometimes called a research or term paper)
is usually a formal, well-documented composition. It is different from the short composition (see Section **32**) in that it
generally has a flyleaf (giving the title of the paper and the
name of the writer), numbered footnotes (referring to sources
used or cited in the paper and/or providing additional information), and a bibliography (a list of works consulted). All
documentation may be placed at the end of the paper, or the
footnotes may be put at the bottom of pages in the text.

To obtain a general idea of what a library paper looks like,
thumb through "Lord Durham's Legacy" and "The Albatross as a Symbol in *The Rime of the Ancient Mariner*," at the
end of this section.

The rules in this section describe the usual steps in writing
a library paper, from the selection of the subject to the
preparation of the final bibliography.

33a
**Choose a subject that is suitable for a library paper
and then limit it appropriately.** See also 32a.

First, select a subject that you are interested in—not just any
subject, but one that you want to learn more about through

reading. You might begin by selecting a general topic like music, the media, literature, organic farming, spacecraft, Canadian history, psychology.

Next, start reading about your subject and decide what facets of it you could develop in a library paper. How much you limit your subject depends on the assigned length of the paper and on the availability and the adequacy of relevant books, newspapers, magazines, and so on. Below are examples of possible ways a general subject may be limited:

> Canadian history → Canada before Confederation → steps towards Confederation → the Durham Report
>
> literature → tales about the sea → *Jaws,* Joseph Conrad's stories, *Moby Dick, The Old Man and the Sea, The Rime of the Ancient Mariner* → symbols in these favourites → the albatross as a symbol in the *Ancient Mariner*

Report or thesis   The type of library paper you write will depend on your purpose. Suppose, for example, that you are writing a library paper on the nature of dreams. You discover in Patricia Garfield's book *Creative Dreaming* the idea that we can control the content of our dreams because "As a man believes, so shall he dream" and "each image in the dream is a part of you." If you develop your subject in an organized presentation of the views of Patricia Garfield, and of other writers as well, you will be writing a *report* paper. If, however, you present evidence to support your idea that we cannot control the content of our nightmares nor of our precognitive dreams, then you will be writing a *thesis* paper. Although with either purpose in mind you should be able to write an effective paper, the purpose you select will influence your collecting of facts and should therefore be determined as soon as possible.

■ **Exercise 1**   Select a subject that would be suitable for a library paper. Then check the availability of materials. (If you cannot find enough books, periodicals, and so on, try another subject.) As you skim through the information, perhaps beginning with an encyclopedia, single out facets of the subject that you would like to investigate further. Finally, limit the subject so that you can develop it in a paper of the assigned length according to your purpose.

33b
Making good use of the materials in the library, prepare a preliminary bibliography. Learn an acceptable form for bibliographical entries.

A preliminary bibliography contains information (titles, authors, dates, and so on) about the materials (books, magazines, newspaper articles, microforms,[1] and the like) that you are likely to use as sources. Use the card catalogue, indexes to periodicals, and reference books (as explained on the following pages) to make a preliminary bibliography by writing down the most promising titles you can find. Copy each title on a separate card (generally 7.5×12.5 cm) in an acceptable form: see page 367. You should keep these cards in alphabetical order until you complete your paper, adding useful titles as you find them and discarding those that prove useless. The final bibliography, to be typed at the end of your paper, will most often include only the works that help in the actual writing—usually those cited in the footnotes.

(1) Use the card catalogue.

The card catalogue is the index to the whole library. It lists all books and all bound magazines, whether they are housed in the stacks, on the open shelves of the reference room, or in any other part of the building. In many libraries one general card catalogue lists all books owned by the college or uni-

---

[1] *Microform* refers to all reduced materials—such as microfilm, microfiche, micro-opaques, microprints.

versity and shows whether the book is in the general library or in a special collection in another building.

Usually the card catalogue consists of cards arranged alphabetically in drawers. These may be "author" cards, "title" cards, or "subject" cards, for in most libraries each book is listed alphabetically in at least three places, once according to its author, again according to its title, and again according to its subject or subjects. These cards are identical except that the title card and the subject card have extra headings.

SAMPLE CATALOGUE CARDS

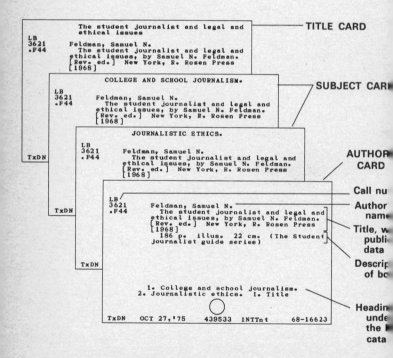

Note: After using the card catalogue, you may wish to refer to the *Cumulative Book Index, Books in Print, Canadian Books in Print* and *Paperbound Books in Print* to find titles that are closely related to your subject. Or you may wish to read what others have written about a book, perhaps one your library does not have, in the *Book Review Digest* or in a periodical referred to by a book such as *Book Review Index*.

(2) Use indexes to periodicals.

When preparing your bibliography, remember that the periodical indexes do for articles what the card catalogue does for books in the library. You will probably find the *Readers' Guide,* the *New Serial Readers Guide,* and the *British Union Catalogue of Periodicals* the most useful of these indexes. Below is a sample entry from the *Readers' Guide.* The editor chose it to familiarize users with the forms of reference. Beneath the sample entry is the editor's explanation.[2]

Sample entry: ADULT education
      Mother goes back to school. B. Farber. il
      Parents Mag 49:46-7+ Ja '74

      An illustrated article on the subject ADULT
      education entitled "Mother goes back to
      school," by B. Farber, will be found in
      volume 49 of Parents' Magazine, pages 46-7
      (continued on later, or preceding pages of
      the same issue) the January 1974 number

Indexes to Periodicals

General

Poole's Index. 1802–1907. (Subject index only)
Nineteenth Century Readers' Guide. 1890–99. (Author, subject)
Readers' Guide. 1900—. (Author, title, subject)

---

[2] *Readers' Guide to Periodical Literature* Copyright © 1974, 1975 by The H. W. Wilson Company. Material reproduced by permission of the publisher.

International Index. 1907–65. Succeeded by *Social Sciences and Humanities Index.* 1965–73. Succeeded by *Social Sciences Index.* 1974—. *Humanities Index.* 1974—. (Author, subject)

New York Times Index. 1913—. (A useful guide for finding the dates of important events, which can then be looked up in the *Times,* often available on microfilm, or in other newspapers)

Special

Art Index. 1929—.

Biography Index. 1946—.

Biographie Universelle. 1854; 1970.

Current Index to Journals in Education. 1969—.

Canadian Periodical Index. 1938—.

Education Index. 1929—.

Hawlice, P. P. *Index to Literary Biography.* 1975.

Industrial Arts Index. 1913–57. Succeeded by *Applied Science and Technology Index.* 1958—. *Business Periodicals Index.* 1958—.

Music Index. 1949—.

Periodicals in the Social Sciences and Humanities currently received by Canadian Libraries. 1968—.

Watters, Reginald Eyre and Inglis Freeman Bell. *On Canadian Literature 1806–1960.* 1966; 1967.

See also the various abstracts, such as *Abstracts of English Studies,* 1958—; *Biological Abstracts,* 1926—; *Chemical Abstracts,* 1907—; *Psychological Abstracts,* 1927—.

(3) Use reference books.

Learn the general location of the chief classes of reference books in order that you may turn to them without loss of time. For a detailed list of such books, with a short description of each, consult Constance M. Winchell's *Guide to Reference Books.* Since many reference books, especially some of the encyclopedias, are kept up to date by frequent revisions, you should remember to cite the latest copyright date of the edition you are using. A few of the more important reference books are listed on the following pages (with abbreviated bibliographical information).

Reference Books

General dictionaries (unabridged)

A Dictionary of American English on Historical Principles. 4 vols. 1938–44.

New Standard Dictionary of the English Language. 1947, 1952, 1966.

The Oxford English Dictionary. 13 vols. 1933. Originally issued as *A New English Dictionary on Historical Principles.* 10 vols. and Supplement. 1888–1933. *The Compact Edition.* 2 vols. 1971. (photo-reproduction)

The Random House Dictionary of the English Language. 1966, 1967.

Webster's Third New International Dictionary. 1961, 1971.

Special dictionaries

Avis, W. S. *A Dictionary of Canadianisms on Historical Principles.* 1967.

Barnhart, C. L., et al. *A Dictionary of New English.* 1963–72.

Chambers Dictionary of Science and Technology. 1972.

Dictionary of the History of Ideas. 4 vols. 1973.

Follett, Wilson. *Modern American Usage.* 2nd ed. 1974.

Fowler, H. W. *Dictionary of Modern English Usage.* 2nd ed. Rev. Sir Ernest Gowers. 1965.

Hayakawa, S. I., and the Funk & Wagnalls dictionary staff. *Modern Guide to Synonyms and Related Words.* 1968.

Miller, Madeline, and J. Lane. *Harper Bible Dictionary.* 1973.

Morris, W., and M. D. Morris. *Dictionary of Word and Phrase Origins.* 3 vols. 1971.

The New Roget's Thesaurus in Dictionary Form. 1974.

Oxford Dictionary of English Etymology. 1966.

Partridge, Eric. *Dictionary of Slang and Unconventional English.* 7th ed. 1970.

Webster's Collegiate Thesaurus. 1976.

Webster's New Dictionary of Synonyms. 1968.

Wentworth, Harold, and Stuart B. Flexner. *Dictionary of American Slang.* 2nd ed. 1975.

General encyclopedias

Collier's Encyclopedia.
Encyclopedia Americana.
Encyclopædia Britannica.
Encyclopedia Canadiana.
Encyclopedia International. 20 vols.

Special encyclopedias

Duyckink, E. A., and George L. Duyckink. *Cyclopedia of American Literature.* 1973.
Ebel, R. L. *Encyclopedia of Educational Research.* 1969.
Edwards, Paul. *Encyclopedia of Philosophy.* 4 vols. 1973.
Encyclopedia of Education. 10 vols. 1971.
Encyclopedia of Sociology. 1974.
Encyclopedia of World Art. 15 vols. 1959–68.
Eysenck, H. J. *Encyclopedia of Psychology.* 3 vols. 1972.
Grove's Dictionary of Music and Musicians. 5th ed. 9 vols. 1954. Supplement. 1961.
International Encyclopedia of the Social Sciences. 17 vols. 1968.
Klein, Barry, and D. Icolari. *Reference Encyclopedia of the American Indian.* 2nd ed. 1974.
Langer, William L. *An Encyclopedia of World History.* 5th ed. 1972.
McGraw-Hill Encyclopedia of Science and Technology. 15 vols. 3rd ed. 1971.
Munn, Glenn G. *Encyclopedia of Banking and Finance.* 7th ed. 1973.
Story, N. *The Oxford Companion to Canadian History and Literature.* 1967. (Supplement 1973)
Thompson, O. *International Cyclopedia of Music and Musicians.* 10th ed. 1974.

Atlases and gazetteers

Columbia Lippincott Gazetteer of the World. 1962.
Medallion World Atlas. 1971.
The National Atlas of Canada. 4th ed. Rev. 1974.
National Geographic Atlas of the World. 4th ed. 1975.

Rand-McNally New Cosmopolitan World Atlas. Rev. ed. 1971.
The Times Atlas of the World. 1975.
World Atlas of Agriculture. 5 vols. 1972–75.

Yearbooks—current events

Annual Register. 1758—.
Britannica Book of the Year. 1938—.
Canadian Annual Review. 1960–70. Succeeded by *Canadian Annual Review of Politics and Public Affairs.* 1971—.
Facts on File. 1940—.
Guinness Book of World Records. 1955—.
Information Please Almanac. 1947—.
Statesman's Year-Book. 1864—.
World Almanac and Book of Facts. 1868–76/1886—.

Biography

Canadian Who's Who. 1910; 1936—.
Contemporary Authors. 1962—.
Current Biography. 1940—.
Dictionary of American Biography. 20 vols. and Index. 1928–43. (Supplements to date)
Dictionary of Canadian Biography. 1966—.
Dictionary of National Biography (British). 22 vols. 1938. (Supplements to date)
International Who's Who. 1935—.
McGraw-Hill Encyclopedia of World Biography. 12 vols. 1973.
Marquis Who's Who Publications: Index to All Books. 1974.
Wakeman, John. *World Authors, 1950–1970.* 1975.
Wallace, W. Stewart. *The Macmillan Dictionary of Candian Biography.* 4th ed. 1978.
Who's Who. 1848—.

Literature—mythology

Bartlett's Familiar Quotations. 14th ed. 1968.
Bateson, F. W. *Cambridge Bibliography of English Literature.* 5 vols. 1941–57.
Benét, William Rose. *The Reader's Encyclopedia.* 2nd ed. 1965.
Brewer's Dictionary of Phrase and Fable. 1972.

Bulfinch, Thomas. *Bulfinch's Mythology.* 2nd. rev. ed. 1970.

Colombo, John Robert. *Colombo's Canadian Quotations.* 1974.

Davis, N. *Oxford History of English Literature.* 12 vols. 1945–69.

Essay and General Literature Index. 7 vols. 1960–69. (With annual cumulations)

Evans, Bergen. *Dictionary of Quotations.* 1968.

Fiction Catalog. 8th ed. 1971.

Frazer, Sir James G. *The Golden Bough.* 3rd ed. 13 vols. 1955.

Frye, Northrop. *The Bush Garden.* 1971.

Gayley, C. M. *Classic Myths in English Literature and in Art.* 1911; rpt. 1974.

Hart, James D. *Oxford Companion to American Literature.* 4th ed. 1965.

Harvey, Sir Paul. *Oxford Companion to Classical Literature.* 1937.

——————. *Oxford Companion to English Literature.* 4th ed. 1967.

Modern Humanities Research Association. *Annual Bibliography of English Language and Literature.* 1920—.

Oxford Classical Dictionary. 2nd ed. 1970.

Short Story Index. 1953. (Supplements)

Klinck, Carl F. *Literary History of Canada: Canadian Literature in English.* 1965.

Tatlock, Jessie M. *Greek and Roman Mythology.* 1975.

Thrall, William Flint, Addison Hibbard, and C. Hugh Holman. *A Handbook to Literature.* 3rd ed. 1972.

(4) Use a standard bibliographical form.

Put each item of your bibliography on a separate card (preferably 7.5 × 12.5 cm) so that you can readily drop or add a card and can arrange the list alphabetically without recopying it. Follow exactly and consistently the bibliographical form you are instructed to use. The form illustrated by the models below (and by the footnote forms on pages 376–82) is based on the revised style sheet of the Modern Language Association (MLA).

Bibliographical entries often consist of only three units, which are separated by periods:

1. *Name of the author.* Give the last name first to make alphabetization easy.

2. *Title of the book.* Underline (italicize) the title, and capitalize it in accordance with **9c**. Always include the book's subtitle.

3. *Publication data.* Include the place of publication, the publisher, and the latest copyright date as shown on the copyright page. You may give a shortened form of the publisher's name as long as it is clear.

```
Creighton, Donald G.  The Empire of the
     St. Lawrence.  Toronto: Macmillan, 1956.

Frye, Northrop.  The Bush Garden: Essays on the
     Canadian Imagination.  Toronto: Anansi Press,
     1971.
```

Some entries, however, require more than three units. These must be given special treatment. As you study the following model bibliographical entries, which cover most of the special problems you are likely to encounter, observe both the arrangement of information and the punctuation. See also pages 375–76 for a list of abbreviations that are permissible in bibliographies, footnotes, and tables.

Model Bibliographical Entries

Books

```
Aiken, Michael, Lewis A. Ferman, and Harold L.
     Sheppard.  Economic Failure, Alienation, and
     Extremism.  Ann Arbor: Univ. of Michigan Press,
     1968.
```

[A book by three authors. Notice that the name of the first author is inverted, but the names of the other two authors are given in the normal order.]

Ardrey, Robert. The Social Contract. New York: Dell,
    Laurel Edition, 1974.

[Documentation refers to the publisher of the paperback, not to
the publisher of the original edition, because of possible revisions and differences in pagination.]

Baron, Salo Wittmayer. A Social and Religious
    History of the Jews. 2nd ed. 14 vols. New
    York: Columbia Univ. Press, 1952–69.

[A multivolume work published over a seventeen-year period]

Bebout, John E., and Ronald J. Grele. Where Cities
    Meet: The Urbanization of New Jersey. New
    Jersey Historical Series, Vol. 22. Princeton:
    Van Nostrand, 1964.

[A book by two authors; also a book in a series. Notice that the
volume number of a book in a series is given in Arabic rather
than Roman numerals.]

Brown, Milton P., et al. Problems in Marketing. New
    York: McGraw–Hill, 1968.

[A book by more than three authors]

Agriculture Canada, Food Advisory Division.
    Food--à la Canadienne. Ottawa: Supply and
    Services Canada, 1970.

[A book with corporate authorship]

Pratt, Robert A., et al., eds. Masters of British
    Literature. 2 vols. Boston: Houghton, 1958.

[A work with more than three editors]

Sartre, Jean–Paul. Literary Essays. Trans. Annette
    Michelson. New York: Philosophical Library,
    1957.

[A translation]

Trilling, Diana. "The Image of Women in Contemporary Literature." <u>The</u> <u>Woman</u> <u>in</u> <u>America</u>. Ed. Robert Jay Lifton. Boston: Houghton, 1965.

[A specific article from an edited anthology]

Undset, Sigrid, et al. <u>The</u> <u>Achievement</u> <u>of</u> <u>D.</u> <u>H.</u> <u>Lawrence</u>. Ed. Frederick J. Hoffman and Harry T. Moore. Norman: Univ. of Oklahoma Press, 1953.

[A work with more than three authors and two editors]

Zimmern, Alfred. <u>America</u> <u>and</u> <u>Europe</u> <u>and</u> <u>Other</u> <u>Essays</u>. 1920; rpt. Freeport, N.Y.: Books for Libraries Press, 1969.

[A reprint of a book first published in 1920. Notice that the state in which the book was published is given along with the city to avoid confusion with other cities named Freeport.]

Magazines and newspapers

"Case for the Defence." <u>Financial</u> <u>Post,</u> 15 July 1978, p. 6, cols. 1–2.

[An unsigned article in a well-known weekly newspaper. The column numbers are supplied for ease of reference.]

"Sinclair Becomes Hero to Embattled America." <u>London</u> (Ontario) <u>Free</u> <u>Press</u>, 29 November 1973, p. 6.

[An unsigned article in a newspaper that is not widely known. The name of the city is part of the newspaper title. To avoid confusion with the other London, the name of the province is inserted in parentheses. In an entry of a foreign newspaper, the name of the city appears after the title: *Times* (London).]

Elson, John T. "Much Ado." <u>Time</u>, 19 Jan. 1976, p. 71.

[A signed article in a weekly magazine. The names of months consisting of over five letters are usually abbreviated.]

Gray, Ralph. "How Do You Move the Mountain into the
Classroom?" <u>NEA</u> <u>Journal</u>, 55, No. 3 (1966), 34–
36.

[An article from a journal in which pages are numbered separately for each issue. Notice that both *Vol.* and *pp.* are omitted when both the volume and the page numbers are given. The issue number follows the volume number when the month or season of publication is not specified on the title page.]

"Ontario Grants for French Textbooks." <u>Quill</u> <u>and</u>
<u>Quire</u>, April 1978, p. 1.

[An unsigned article in a monthly magazine]

Beales, R. C. "The Rise and Decline of National
Identity." <u>Canadian</u> <u>Review</u> <u>of</u> <u>Studies</u> <u>in</u>
<u>Nationalism</u>, 4 (Spring 1977), 147–66.

[An article from a journal in which pages are numbered continuously through each year]

Span, Paula. "Woods Hole, Mass.––A Kind of Purga–
tory." <u>New</u> <u>York</u> <u>Times</u>, 27 June 1976, Sec. 10,
p. 7.

[A signed article (filling all columns) in a large newspaper. The name of the city is part of the newspaper's title.]

Note: Sometimes a magazine article is printed on pages that are separated by other articles; for example, the first part appears on pp. 137–39, the last on pp. 188–203. As a rule, only the number of the first page need be given in a bibliographical entry.

Encyclopedias and almanacs

"Country and Western." <u>Encyclopaedia</u> <u>Britannica</u>,
1974.

"Hockey in 1974–75." <u>World</u> <u>Almanac</u> <u>and</u> <u>Book</u> <u>of</u> <u>Facts</u>,
1975.

[Unsigned articles. Notice that it is unnecessary to give full publication information for familiar reference works.]

Ryther, John H. "Marine Biology." <u>World Book Encyclopedia</u>, 1976.

B[rock], M. G. "Durham, John George Lambton." <u>Encyclopaedia Britannica</u>, 1972.

[Signed articles. Brackets are used in giving the full name of a contributor who used initials. A list of contributors is ordinarily supplied in the index volume or in the front matter of an encyclopedia. The title "Durham, John George Lambton" indicates that the article is listed under *D.*]

Bulletins and pamphlets

<u>Mushroom Collecting for Beginners</u>. Canada Department of Agriculture, Information Division Publication 861. Ottawa: Supply and Services Canada. 1977.

The <u>Velvetbean Caterpillar</u>. Dept. of Agriculture, Bureau of Entomology and Plant Quarantine Leaflet No. 348. Washington, D.C.: Government Printing Office, 1953.

Miscellaneous works
(unpublished or available only in microform)

Rushworth, John. <u>Historical Collections, 1618–29. Private Passages of State, Weighty Matters in Law, Remarkable Proceedings in Five Parliaments</u>. London, 1721–22. 8 vols. Washington, D.C.: Microcard Editions, 1971.

[Titles of works available only in microform are usually underlined (italicized).]

Taylor, Robert John. "The Darwinian Revolution: The Responses of Four Canadian Scholars." Diss. McMaster University, 1976.

[An unpublished dissertation]

NOTES ON THE FINAL BIBLIOGRAPHY

Note 1: If you use two or more works by the same author in your paper, list each work separately in your final bibliography, but do not repeat the author's name. To indicate the omission of the name, use seven hyphens (or a straight line) followed by a period. Notice that entries of this type are alphabetized by title.

> Erikson, Erik H. <u>Childhood</u> <u>and</u> <u>Society</u>. Rev. ed. New York: Norton, 1964.
>
> ———————. <u>Gandhi's</u> <u>Truth</u>. New York: Norton, 1969.

Note 2: Spacing of the entries in final bibliographies should be consistent. Each entry, like the preceding examples, may be single-spaced (with hanging indention); double-spacing separates the entries. See the bibliography of "The Albatross as a Symbol in *The Rime of the Ancient Mariner*," at the end of this section. Or all lines in the final bibliography may be double-spaced (with hanging indention). See the bibliography of "Lord Durham's Legacy" at the end of this section.

Note 3: Although the final form may not be required for preliminary-bibliography cards, it is a helpful practice to use from the beginning a form that is appropriate for the final bibliography. (You may wish to add a call number to help you relocate a book in the library.)

BIBLIOGRAPHY CARDS

Each department of a college or university ordinarily suggests a particular style for documentation. One department may recommend Kate L. Turabian's *Manual for Writers of Term Papers, Theses, and Dissertations*, 4th ed. (Chicago:

Univ. of Chicago Press, 1973); another may prefer the form described in the Chicago *Manual of Style*, 12th ed. rev. (Chicago: Univ. of Chicago Press, 1969). If your instructor does not specify a different style, you may use the one described in this handbook. Whatever style you use for your bibliographical entries and for your footnotes, follow it consistently.

Scott, Susan. "Willie, the Picnic and a Place in History." *Nashville Sound*, Sept. 1976, pp. 25-29.

Highet, Gilbert *The Immortal Profession: The Joys of Teaching and Learning.* New York: Weybright and Talley, 1976.

LB
1025.2
.H5

■ **Exercise 2** Select a subject (the one you chose for Exercise 1 on page 352 or a different one) and prepare a preliminary bibliography. (Often you will find helpful bibliographies in the books that you consult, especially in encyclopedias and other reference works.)

33c

Make a preliminary outline and develop it as you take notes on readings and as you write your library paper.
See also 32b–f.

After completing a preliminary bibliography and a minimum of general reading on your subject (an encyclopedia article and parts of one or two other works may suffice), make a preliminary outline that will give direction to your investigation. The outline will enable you to discard irrelevant material from your bibliography and to begin spotting valuable passages on which you will want to take notes. If you attempt to take notes without first knowing what you are looking for, your efforts will lead only to frustration.

Be careful, however, not to adhere too rigidly to your preliminary outline. For although the outline will direct your reading, your reading will almost certainly suggest ways in which the outline may be improved. No outline should be regarded as complete until the research paper has been finished. As you take notes, you will probably revise your original outline frequently, adding subheadings to it, changing subheadings to major headings, perhaps dropping some headings entirely.

33d

Take notes on readings (after evaluating the sources).

As you take notes on your readings, learn how to find and evaluate useful passages with a minimum of time and effort. Seldom will a whole book, or even a whole article, be of use as subject matter for any given research paper. To get what is needed for your paper, you will find that you must turn to many books and articles, rejecting most of them altogether and using from others only a section here and there. You cannot take the time to read each book completely. Use the table of contents and the index of a book, and learn to skim the pages rapidly until you find the passages you need.

One important consideration always is the reliability of the source. Do others speak of the writer as an authority? As you read, do you find evidence that the author is competent, well-informed, not prejudiced in any way? Is the work recent enough to provide up-to-date information? Is the edition the latest one available? Use your best judgment to determine the most dependable sources for your paper. You may find in the *Book Review Digest* convenient summaries of critical opinion on a book in your bibliography.

One of the best ways to take notes is on cards of uniform size, preferably 10 × 15 cm. (A smaller card may be used for the bibliography.) Each card should contain a single note with a heading keyed to a significant word or phrase in the preliminary outline. If the paper is to have the customary footnotes, each card must also show the source of the note, including the exact page or pages from which it is drawn.

SOURCE

Lord Durham's Report is generally regarded as one of the most perceptive and significant documents in Canadian history, but at the same time his recommendation that French Canada should be assimilated is deplored as indicative of a regrettable blind spot. In seeking to explain this flaw in the Durham Report one may very easily fall into oversimplification. It is obvious that Durham greatly underestimated the depth and vitality of French-Canadian culture and nationalism. The "miracle" of *la survivance* in the years since 1841 and the ever-increasing strength of the French fact in Canada reveal the recommendation to have been unrealistic—assimilation was an unobtainable objective. While this may be acceptable as an ultimate conclusion, it leaves a great deal unexplained.

When did Durham decide that assimilation was necessary, and why? What grounds did he have for thinking that assimilation, however necessary, could be accomplished? Why did he recommend a legislative union of the Canadas as the means of achieving this objective, especially after he had condemned such a union throughout his stay in Canada? How could he maintain that an immediate answer must be found to the French political threat in Lower Canada, and still advocate that assimilation proceed at a rate which would not offend French-Canadian sensibilities? Until these questions are answered it is impossible either to resolve the apparent contradictions in the Report or to discover the rationale behind Lord Durham's recommendation.[3]

NOTE CARD

Analysis of the Durham Report – regarded as "perceptive and significant" but with "regrettable blind spot" – namely recommendation that French Canada shd. be assimilated. But to oversimplify by stating that Durham underestimated French-Canadian national and cultural strength, is to leave important questions unanswered. 1. When did he decide assimilation was necessary? 2. Why? 3. Why did he decide it was possible? 4. Why did he choose "legislative union" as means of accomplishing it? 5. Why did he say it must take place slowly?

Answering these questions will allow us to "resolve the contradictions in the report" and to "discover the rationale behind Durham's recommendation." Ormsby, p. 37

(Good summary of questions that the paper must deal with)

Except for the note-taker's postscript inside parentheses, the note card above is a concise summary, or précis. Copied words are inside quotation marks and words omitted from a quotation are indicated by an ellipsis mark: see **17a(3)**.

Another way to take notes is to use regular notebook paper, perhaps adding photocopies of materials that are not copyrighted. On a photocopy you may underline quotable material, add words in brackets that you would insert, and jot down your own ideas as you study the source. On a full page there is usually room to add a related note.

---

[3]Reprinted from *On Canada: Essays in Honour of Frank H. Underhill*, edited by Norman Penlington, by permission of University of Toronto Press. © University of Toronto Press, 1971.

PHOTOCOPIED SOURCE, WITH RELATED NOTES

—from Coleridge's <u>Rime</u> in <u>Poems</u>:

Their beauty and their happiness.	O happy living things! no tongue *p.198*
	Their beauty might declare:
[the snakes]	<u>A spring of love gushed from my heart,</u>
He blesseth them in his heart.	<u>And I blessed them unaware:</u> 285
	Sure my kind saint took pity on me,
	And I blessed them unaware.
The spell begins to break.	The self-same moment <u>I could pray;</u>
	<u>And from my neck so free</u>
	<u>The Albatross fell off,</u> and sank 290
	Like lead into the sea.

And ever and anon throughout his future life an agony constraineth him to travel from land to land;	Since then, at an uncertain hour, *p.208*
	That agony returns:
	And till <u>my ghastly tale</u> is told, *very strange*
	This heart <u>within me burns.</u> 585
	I pass, like night, from land to land;
	I have strange power of speech;
	That moment that his face I see,
	I know the man that must hear me:
	To him my tale I teach. 590

— from Gilbert Highet's <u>Explorations</u> (Oxford, 1971), p. 313:

When talking about "The Ancient Mariner's Association, Inc.," G. H. says that Coleridge didn't understand the sailor's story—and added a "moral" (my quotes)—"if you love water snakes you can love anything and so your soul will be saved." The old mariner? Just one of thousands of compulsive story tellers!

Direct quotations   Any quotations that you use in your paper should be convincing and important ones. When you discover such a passage in your reading, you should take it down verbatim—that is, copy every word, every capital letter, and every mark of punctuation exactly as in the original. Be sure to enclose the quoted passage in quotation marks. When you are quoting, quote accurately. When you are not quoting, use your own sentence structure and phraseology, not a slightly altered version of your source.

Note: As you write your library paper, keep a few guidelines in mind when you are quoting the exact words of another. Pay close attention to form, punctuation, and spacing: see **16a**. Use periods appropriately to indicate ellipsis: see **17a(3)**. But don't use ellipsis periods before quotations that are only parts of sentences. To avoid these periods at the beginning of a quotation (especially one that begins a paragraph), use a word like *that* or an introductory word group before the quotation. You may use a period to end a quotation that is a grammatically complete sentence, even though the source may have a semicolon or another mark of punctuation.

Plagiarism   If you fail to acknowledge borrowed material, then you are plagiarizing. Plagiarism is literary theft. When you copy the words of another, be sure to put those words inside quotation marks and to acknowledge the source with a footnote. When you paraphrase the words of another, use your own words and your own sentence structure, and be sure to give a footnote citing the source of the idea. A plagiarist often merely changes a few words or rearranges the words in the source. As you take notes and as you write your paper, be especially careful to avoid plagiarism.

■ **Exercise 3**   Carefully read paragraphs 8 (page 306) and 11 (page 308) in Section **31**. Then write a précis of each paragraph, using as your model the specimen note card on page 370. Unless you are quoting directly, avoid entirely the sentence patterns of the source. To convey the ideas in the source exactly, choose your words carefully.

33e
Using the outline, the bibliography, and the notes, write a properly documented library paper.

After you have made your outline as complete as possible and have taken a number of notes on every major heading and every subheading of the outline, you are ready to begin writing. Arrange your notes in the order of the outline, and then use them as the basis of your paper. Naturally you will need to expand some parts and to cut others, and you will need to provide transitional sentences—sometimes even transitional paragraphs. Write the material in the best way you can—in your own style, in your own words.

(1) Footnotes and footnote form Since you will get your material for the library paper largely from the published work of others, you will need to give proper credit in the paper itself. To do so, use footnotes numbered consecutively throughout the paper and placed at the bottoms of the appropriate pages or in one list at the end of the paper, if your instructor so directs (see the library papers on pages 385 and 399). Footnote numerals in the text should come immediately after the part of the sentence to which the footnote refers and should come *after* all punctuation except the dash. The number of footnotes needed will vary with the paper. Every quotation must have its footnote, and so must all the chief facts and opinions drawn from the work of others. From one to four footnotes for each page will be needed for proper documentation of the average library paper.

As the following model forms show, the first footnote reference to a source is similar to, but not identical with, the bibliographical entry. Notice differences in indention and punctuation. Notice also that the author's name is inverted in the bibliographical entry but not in the footnote reference, and that the subtitle of the book is included in the bibliography but may be omitted in the footnote.

BIBLIOGRAPHICAL ENTRIES

Adair, Patricia M. The Waking Dream: A Study of
     Coleridge's Poetry. London: Arnold, 1967.

"No time for apathy on Canada." Toronto
     Star, 30 June 1978, Sec. C, p. 2, cols.
     1-2.

Robertson, Heather. "Grey Liberation."
     Saturday Night, Jan./Feb. 1978, pp. 19-25.

FIRST FOOTNOTE REFERENCES

   [1] Patricia M. Adair, The Waking Dream (London:
Arnold, 1967), p. 57.

   [2] "No time for apathy on Canada," Toronto Star,
30 June 1978, Sec. C, p. 2, cols. 1-2.

   [3] Heather Robertson, "Grey Liberation," Saturday
Night, Jan./Feb. 1978, p. 21.

Points to Remember About First
Footnote References

1. The first line is indented five spaces. (Normal paragraph indention is used instead of the hanging indention used to make each entry stand out in a bibliography.)
2. Footnote numbers are typed slightly above the line, followed by a space.
3. The names of authors and editors are given in the normal order, first names first. (Since footnotes are never alphabetized, there is no need to give the last name first.)

4. Commas are used between the main items (but not before parentheses).

5. In references to books, parentheses enclose the publication data. In references to journals, parentheses enclose the month and year of publication (except when the day of month is given).

6. Each footnote ends with a period.

7. Such abbreviations as the following may be used. (These abbreviations are also appropriate in bibliographies and in tables, but they are inappropriate in the text of a library paper.)

Assn.	Association
bk., bks.	book, books
cf.	compare
ch., chs.	chapter, chapters
col., cols.	column, columns
Dept.	Department
Diss.	Dissertation
ed.	edition OR edited by, editor
eds.	editions OR edited by, editors
et al.	and others
f., ff.	and the following page, pages (Inclusive page numbers are preferred: "pp. 5–13" instead of "pp. 5 ff.")
ibid.	in the same place; in the source cited in the immediately preceding footnote
l., ll.	line, lines
MS, MSS	manuscript, manuscripts
n.d.	no date (of publication)
n., nn.	(foot)note, (foot)notes (for example, "p. 6, n. 2")
No., Nos.	Number (of issue), Numbers
n.p.	no place (of publication)
p., pp.	page, pages
pt., pts.	part, parts
rev.	revision OR revised, revised by
rpt.	reprinted, reprint
sec., secs.	section, sections
trans.	translated by, translator

Univ.   University
vol., vols.   volume, volumes

Standard abbreviations for months of publication and for
names of states and countries (sometimes given to prevent
confusion of cities such as Cambridge, Mass., and Cambridge, Eng.)

Compare the following model footnotes to the sample
bibliographical entries on pages 361–65 to see exactly how
the treatment differs.

Model Footnotes—First References

Books

[1] Donald G. Creighton, The Empire of the St.
Lawrence (Toronto: Macmillan, 1956), p. 389.

[2] The Bush Garden (Toronto: Anansi Press, 1971),
pp. 31–33.

[The author's name may be omitted if it appears in full in the text
of the paper. Notice that the subtitle, *Essays on the Canadian
Imagination,* is also omitted.]

[3] Michael Aiken, Lewis A. Ferman, and Harold L.
Sheppard, Economic Failure, Alienation, and Extremism
(Ann Arbor: Univ. of Michigan Press, 1968), pp. 184–
86.

[A book by three authors]

[4] Robert Ardrey, The Social Contract (New York:
Dell, Laurel Edition, 1974), p. 17.

[Documentation refers to the publisher of the paperback, not to
the publisher of the original edition, because of possible revisions and differences in pagination.]

[5] Salo Wittmayer Baron, A Social and Religious
History of the Jews, 2nd ed., XIV (New York: Columbia
Univ. Press, 1969), 281–85.

[The number of volumes in a multivolume work (one with a definite limit, one that is or will become a finished set) is not given in a reference to a specific passage. Notice that the volume number precedes the publishing information when the various volumes of the work have been published in different years. Notice also that both *Vol.* and *pp.* are omitted when both volume and page numbers are given.]

⁶ John E. Bebout and Ronald J. Grele, <u>Where Cities Meet</u>, New Jersey Historical Series, Vol. 22 (Princeton: Van Nostrand, 1964), pp. 61–62.

[A book by two authors; also a book in a series (a work without a specific limit, one that can be continued indefinitely). Notice that the volume number of a book in a series is given in Arabic rather than Roman numerals.]

⁷ Milton P. Brown et al., <u>Problems in Marketing</u> (New York: McGraw–Hill, 1968), p. 43.

[A book by more than three authors]

⁸ Agriculture Canada, Food Advisory Division, <u>Food—à la Canadienne</u> (Ottawa: Supply and Services Canada, 1970), p. 23.

[A book with corporate authorship]

⁹ Robert A. Pratt et al., eds., <u>Masters of British Literature</u> (Boston: Houghton, 1958), I, 15.

[A work with more than three editors. Notice that the volume number follows the publishing information when the various volumes of a multivolume work were published in the same year.]

¹⁰ Jean–Paul Sartre, <u>Literary Essays</u>, trans. Annette Michelson (New York: Philosophical Library, 1957), p. 29.

[A translation]

[11] Diana Trilling, "The Image of Women in Contemporary Literature," in The Woman in America, ed. Robert Jay Lifton (Boston: Houghton, 1965), p. 70.

[A specific article from an edited anthology]

[12] Sigrid Undset et al., The Achievement of D. H. Lawrence, ed. Frederick J. Hoffman and Harry T. Moore (Norman: Univ. of Oklahoma Press, 1953), p. 7.

[A work with more than three authors and two editors]

[13] Alfred Zimmern, America and Europe and Other Essays (1920; rpt. Freeport, N.Y.: Books for Libraries Press, 1969), p. 23.

[A reprint of a book first published in 1920. Modern paperback books that are reprints of previously published works are footnoted in this way.]

Magazines and newspapers

[14] "Case for the Defence," Financial Post, 15 July 1978, p. 6, col. 2.

[An unsigned news story. Column numbers may be supplied for ease of reference.]

[15] Ron Base, "A Legend in the Making," Maclean's, 10 July 1978, p. 33.

[A signed article in a weekly magazine]

[16] Ralph Gray, "How Do You Move the Mountain into the Classroom?" NEA Journal, 55, No. 3 (1966), 35.

[An article from a journal in which pages are numbered separately for each issue. Notice that both *Vol.* and *pp.* are omitted when both the volume and the page numbers are given. The issue number follows the volume number when the month or season of publication is not specified on the title page.]

17 "Ontario Grants for French Textbooks," <u>Quill</u> <u>and</u> <u>Quire</u>, April 1978, p. 1.

[An unsigned article in a monthly magazine]

18 R. C. Beales, "The Rise and Decline of National Identity," <u>Canadian</u> <u>Review</u> <u>of</u> <u>Studies</u> <u>in</u> <u>Nationalism</u>, 4 (Spring 1977), 148–49.

[An article from a journal in which pages are numbered continuously through each year]

19 Paula Span, "Woods Hole, Mass.—A Kind of Purgatory," <u>New</u> <u>York</u> <u>Times</u>, 27 June 1976, Sec. 10, p. 7.

[A signed article from a newspaper]

Encyclopedias and almanacs

20 "Country and Western," <u>Encyclopaedia</u> <u>Britannica</u>, 1974.

21 "Hockey in 1974–75," <u>World</u> <u>Almanac</u> <u>and</u> <u>Book</u> <u>of</u> <u>Facts</u>, 1975.

[Unsigned articles. Volume numbers and page numbers are omitted in references to alphabetically arranged articles.]

22 John H. Ryther, "Marine Biology," <u>World</u> <u>Book</u> <u>Encyclopedia</u>, 1976.

23 M. G. B[rock], "Durham, John George Lambton," <u>Encyclopaedia</u> <u>Britannica</u>, 1972.

[Signed articles]

Bulletins and pamphlets

24 <u>Mushroom</u> <u>Collecting</u> <u>for</u> <u>Beginners</u>, Canada Department of Agriculture, Information Division Publication 861 (Ottawa: Supply and Services Canada, 1977), pp. 18–19.

25 The Velvetbean Caterpillar, Dept. of Agriculture, Bureau of Entomology and Plant Quarantine Leaflet No. 348 (Washington, D.C.: Government Printing Office, 1953), p. 3.

Miscellaneous works
(unpublished or available only in microform)

26 John Rushworth, Historical Collections, 1618–29, II (Washington, D.C.: Microcard Editions, 1971), 13.

27 Robert John Taylor, "The Darwinian Revolution: The Responses of Four Canadian Scholars," Diss. McMaster University, 1976, p. 75.

The models below show second (or later) footnote references in an appropriately abbreviated form. Compare them with the first footnote references to see exactly how they have been shortened. Pay special attention to the use of *ibid.*, which means "in the same place" or "in the source just cited." Notice that two or more short footnotes may be given on the same line.

Model Footnotes—Second References

Books

28 Creighton, p. 29.   29 Sartre, pp. 14–15.

30 Aiken, Ferman, and Sheppard, p. 188.

31 Bebout and Grele, p. 65.

32 Ibid.

[Exactly the same source as the immediately preceding footnote]

33 Pratt et al., I, 14.

34 Bebout and Grele, p. 67.

[*Ibid.* as footnote 34 would refer to the work by Pratt et al.]

³⁵ Baron, XIV, 290.

³⁶ Ibid., p. 150.

[Baron's work, also Vol. XIV, but a different page]

³⁷ Ibid., IX, 112–13.

[Baron's work, but a different volume and page. When the various volumes of a work have been published in different years, be sure that the first reference to each new volume cited is a complete reference, giving the specific date of publication of that particular volume.]

Magazines and newspapers

³⁸ Gray, pp. 35–36.

³⁹ Beales, p. 161.

⁴⁰ "Ontario Grants for French Textbooks," p. 1.

[If more than one article from the same newspaper or magazine is used, however, then the full reference must be repeated.]

Encyclopedias and almanacs

⁴¹ "Country and Western."

⁴² Ryther, "Marine Biology."

Bulletins and pamphlets

⁴³ <u>Mushroom Collecting</u>, p. 28.

[Notice that a title may be shortened as long as it is easily identified.]

⁴⁴ <u>Velvetbean Caterpillar</u>, p. 3.

[Notice that the initial *The* is omitted.]

Miscellaneous works
(unpublished or available only in microform)

> 45 Rushworth, II, 8.

If you refer in your paper to two or more works by the same author, include titles (in shortened form if the title is long) in your second footnote references.

> 46 Sartre, <u>Literary</u> <u>Essays</u>, pp. 102–04.

> 47 Sartre, <u>Essays</u> <u>in</u> <u>Aesthetics</u>, p. 14.

If you refer to works by two authors with the same last name, repeat the full name of the author in second references.

> 48 Salo Wittmayer Baron, p. 285.

> 49 Roger Baron, p. 246.

If you use articles with the same title from two or more encyclopedias, include the name of the encyclopedia in your footnote.

> 50 "Jenkins, Robert," <u>Encyclopaedia</u> <u>Britannica</u>, 1967.

> 51 "Jenkins, Robert," <u>Encyclopedia</u> <u>Americana</u>, 1964.

Note 1: Information related to the central idea of the paper but not directly supporting it may be presented in a footnote: see footnote 3, page 402.

Note 2: Occasionally, footnotes credit nonwritten sources of information—such as an interview, a TV program, or a movie. Two examples of such footnotes follow:

¹ Jules Leger, CBC, "Getting to Know You," July 1, 1978.

² John Diefenbaker, interview at Parliament Hill, Ottawa, June 17, 1968.

Whatever footnote form you adopt, use it consistently. Unless your instructor directs you to use a different style, you may adopt the one that is described in this handbook.

(2) Final outline and paper   After writing the first draft of your paper, complete with footnotes, read it over carefully, correcting all errors in spelling, mechanics, and grammar. Check to be sure that the arrangement is logical and that the writing is as clear, concise, and pleasing in style as you can possibly make it. You will probably rewrite some sentences, strike out others, and add still others. Your outline, which should have developed steadily throughout the note-taking and the first draft of the paper, will now be in its final form. It serves primarily, of course, as a guide to the writing of the paper; but it can also serve, if copied in its final stage, as a guide to the contents of the paper.

After you have proofread and revised your first draft, and after you have put your outline in final form, write the final draft of your paper. Use a typewriter if possible. If not, use pen and ink, writing legibly and neatly.

(3) Final bibliography   You should have assembled a preliminary bibliography early in your research. As you pursued your investigation, you probably eliminated some items and added others. Not until you have completed your paper can you know which items should make up your final bibliography. Once your paper is complete, look through your footnotes. Every book or article appearing even once in a footnote belongs in the bibliography. Once you have determined which items should be included, you can easily arrange the bibliography cards in alphabetical order and copy them, either in one alphabetical list or in a list classified according to your instructor's directions.

Students are often asked to submit, along with the completed paper, both the final and the preliminary outlines; the notes, on cards; and the rough draft of the paper, with footnotes.

■ **Exercise 4** On the following pages are two completed library papers—the first on the Durham Report and the second on a literary subject. As you study these two papers, give special attention to content and form, organization, and documentation. Prepare for a class discussion of the strengths *and weaknesses* of either one or both of the papers, as your instructor directs.

LORD DURHAM'S LEGACY

by

Sarah C. Anson

OUTLINE

Title: Lord Durham's Legacy

Central Idea: The Durham Report is one of the most
important documents in Canadian history. The issues
it tried to deal with are still central to Canada
today. Its recommendations and the effect of these
recommendations provide a valuable lesson for modern
Canada.

Introduction: Attitudes to the Report and problems that
must be dealt with in studying it.

   I. Brief background to the Report.

      A. The 1837 Rebellions.

      B. Lower Canada, the key to the conflict.

  II. Outline of the Report itself: its major
      recommendations.

      A. Responsible government.

      B. The assimilation of the French–Canadian
         population.

III. The Report in retrospect.

      A. Its major achievements.

      B. Its major shortcomings.

Conclusion: Many of the problems facing Canada today
are the problems Durham tried to deal with in his
Report. What have we learned from both his
achievements and his mistakes?

Lord Durham's Legacy

On January 15, 1838, in the wake of the Rebellions
of 1837 in Upper and Lower Canada, John George Lambton,
Earl of Durham, was appointed Governor-General of
Canada. In November of the same year he resigned from
the post and returned to England. The following year,
in February, he handed down to the House of Commons the
document that was to become known as the Durham Report.

The Report was immediately hailed as being of
profound importance, but it also sparked a great deal of
controversy. The British commercial classes in Canada
praised it, and the French-speaking population of Lower
Canada, disunited in the wake of the failure of the 1837
Rebellion, regrouped to oppose it. Modern historical
opinion of the Report is similarly divided. While no
one doubts the importance of the Report, very few people
agree as to its merits.

Donald Creighton, for example, says of Lord Durham
that although he was

> the author of the greatest report in British
> colonial history, he occupies an accepted, a
> renowned, but nonetheless a slightly ambiguous
> position in the evolution of the Canadian
> provinces. He proposed responsible government, a
> political device which became the hope of the

Canadian radicals; but he also advocated the union of the provinces, which for two generations had been the objective of the Canadian commercial classes.[1]

William Ormsby, arguing along similar lines, but with a slightly different emphasis, says:

Lord Durham's Report is generally regarded as one of the most perceptive and significant documents in Canadian history, but at the same time his recommendation that French Canada should be assimilated is deplored as indicative of a regrettable blind spot.[2]

Léandre Bergeron, the Quebec Marxist historian, on the other hand, says of Durham that he

is an imperialist, a racist and a liberal. He is an imperialist to the extent that the solutions he proposes serve the interests of the Metropolis—get rid of the Canayens and let the English colonialists participate in government to tighten the ties with the Empire. He is a racist according to the nature of his solution for the Canayen problem. He considers the English race superior and sees an opportunity for the Canayens to raise themselves to the level of a civilized people through assimilation. He is a liberal inasmuch as he grants responsible government to the English colonialists.[3]

Clearly there is a middle ground between these positions. It will be the purpose of this paper to examine the Durham Report in its historical context, to examine its major achievements and its shortcomings, and to examine its relevance to both the weaknesses and the strengths of Canada today.

When Durham came to Canada, he expected, he says in the Report, "to find a contest between a government and a people. I found two nations warring in the bosom of a single state: I found not a struggle of principles but of races . . ."[4] While there is some doubt as to whether Durham ever expected to see anything other than an ethnic conflict when he came to Canada, it is the second part of his observation—that he found a struggle of races, not of principles—that needs to be examined here.

The flow of English settlers into Lower Canada in the late eighteenth and early nineteenth centuries posed a definite threat to the French way of life. Under the seigneurial system, a legacy of the French colonization, the largely rural French population owned, or rather leased, tax-free, large tracts of land. However, the French population of Lower Canada had grown sevenfold since the English conquest of Canada, and already the seigneurial system was stretched to the breaking point.[5] The influx of English settlers, many of them demanding land, stretched it still further, and with the English demand for land came also English demands for the replacement and reform of many of the traditional French socio-economic institutions. The new settlers demanded the abolition of the system of notaries and its replacement with a system of registry offices, and they exerted pressure to have a system of land taxes instituted, an idea that struck at the heart of the seigneurial system. These demands aggravated a situation already made almost impossible by the fact that many of the French settlers, particularly younger sons of leasehold farmers, were already being forced to give up individual farming and to take jobs as hired labourers on large estates, many of which were owned by absentee English landlords.

Thus, while to a large extent the Rebellion in Upper Canada <u>was</u> a protest against authoritarian and undemocratic rule—in other words a struggle of the kind Durham says he expected to find when he came to Canada —the Rebellion in Lower Canada was much more the culmination of a steadily growing antagonism between two incompatible ways of life. In fact, while the Upper Canada Rebellion was an attack on the political system, the French in Lower Canada were actually using the Assembly, in which they had a majority, to protect their way of life. And this further complicated the issue and heightened the tensions because it brought them into direct conflict with the British commercial faction in

Canada who wanted to see the Upper and Lower Canada Assemblies merged, so as to create, along the whole length of the St. Lawrence, a unified commercial arena.

It was in these circumstances, fraught with tension, that Durham produced his report; a report which recommended that Upper and Lower Canada should be unified as a stepping stone to responsible government—— that is to say, a form of government in which the executive (which today we would call the Cabinet) was responsible not to the Crown as it had been up to this point but to an assembly elected by the people of Canada. And hand in hand with this recommendation, Durham urged that the French-Canadian population should be assimilated into the English-speaking community as swiftly as possible.

These two major recommendations, responsible government via unification and assimilation, are at the heart of the Report. They are often dealt with by historians as separate issues, and Durham is usually praised for the former and condemned for the latter. However, as William Ormsby points out, if the Report is analyzed in this way "one may very easily fall into oversimplification."[6] It is of crucial importance to realise that Durham saw the two issues as being inseparable. Assimilation of the French-Canadian population was not Durham's way of punishing them for the Rebellion of 1837. It is important to realize that Durham saw assimilation as an integral part of, and essential to, his overall plan. As he says in the Report,

> at the root of the disorders of Lower Canada lies the conflict of the two races which compose its population; until this is settled no good government is practicable. . . . Whether the powers of Government be entrusted to the majority or the minority, we may rest assured that, while the hostility of races continues, whichever of then is entrusted with power will use it for partial purposes.[7]

Durham's assessment of the root causes of the "hostility of races" was probably somewhat exaggerated and admittedly contained a bias against French culture, as when he describes the French as a "nationality . . . destitute of all that can invigorate and elevate a people."[8] But his analysis of the situation was basically sound and contained enough impartial evidence for Louis-Joseph Papineau, leader of the Lower Canada Rebellion to write, in 1839,

> Ce n'est plus à moi à porter l'accusateur du gouvernement anglais. . . . Ce gouvernement s'est lui-même confessé coupable dans les cent vingt pages in-folio que vient de publier Lord Durham. Corruption systématique, péculats honteux,

> antipathies contre les peuples, exemples révoltants
> d'irresponsabilité dans les agents du pouvoir,
> accaparement du domaine public, rien ne manque à ce
> tableau des misères du Canada.
> [It is no longer up to me to be the accuser of the
> English Government. This government has admitted
> its own guilt in the 120 folio pages Durham has
> just published. Systematic corruption, shameful
> embezzlement, hostility to the people, disgusting
> instances of irresponsibility by the wielders of
> power, monopolization of the public domain, nothing
> is missing from this portrait of the miseries of
> Canada.][9]

Thus, if we accept the basic accuracy of Durham's

observations as to the situation in Canada, the crucial

question becomes why he advocated the measures he did to

deal with the situation. In this respect the question

of assimilation is by far the most controversial.

It should be noted in this regard that the question

of assimilation was not one that troubled Durham very

much. He was convinced that it was essential to his

overall plan, but he was sure, as were most of his

British contemporaries, that it did not pose any major

problems. With the example of the French in Louisiana

very much in his mind, he felt sure that an isolated

pocket of French culture surrounded by English would die

out of its own accord. Having seen the effects of the

Industrial Revolution in England, he was sure that the

forces of progress in North America would force the

French in Canada to abandon their culture if only to remain in the mainstream of North American economic life. In fact—although some people today find this fact hard to accept—he was firmly convinced that assimilation was for the good of the French in Canada as much as it was for the well-being of the Canadian nation as a whole. Thus, while he himself was in favour of a kind of federation of Upper and Lower Canada, with each province retaining a large amount of control over its own internal affairs, he eventually, under pressure from the British Government and the English commercial classes in Canada,[10] accepted the idea of the unification of the provinces, even though this would inevitably mean that the process of assimilation would be speeded up greatly. If he had had any doubts as to the inevitability of assimilation or any idea of the strength and durability of French nationalism in Canada, it is unlikely that he would have moved so readily from a position of advocating federation, with a large degree of provincial autonomy, to advocating unification, which would destroy the separate identity of Lower Canada.

The effects of the Durham Report were far-reaching. On the positive side, the success of the "experiment" of responsible government led to the granting of dominion status to Canada, and other former British colonies such as Australia and South Africa, far sooner than would probably otherwise have been the case. Also the Report was responsible for providing the political and economic framework for the commercial growth that made possible the vision of a Canada stretching from coast to coast and provided a great deal of impetus for that commercial growth. On the negative side, the Report, by treating French Canadian national aspirations as an issue of no long-term importance and therefore providing for no expression of those aspirations, virtually ensured that they would become an issue of long-term importance and that any constitution for a united Canada would be deficient to precisely the extent to which it ignored the French fact.

What have we learned from the Durham Report and how do the situations that faced him in 1837 compare to the situation facing Canada today? In some ways the similarities between the situations are very striking. The Durham Report was handed down in a situation in which it had become clear that the Constitution of 1791 was no longer adequate to deal with the demands of the society it was designed for. We are living in a time in which changing the constitution is once again a matter

of considerable significance. The Durham Report was
handed down at a time in which the question of French-
English hostility was a potent factor. We are faced
with a similar situation. The Durham Report had to deal
with the crucial question of regional identity and
unity, and how both can be provided within the context
of a single nation. Canada today must deal with the
same problem, not only as regards Quebec, but also with
respect to the Western Provinces and the Maritimes. We
can learn both from Durham's successes and his mistakes.

From his achievements we can learn the importance
of careful analysis of a situation and the importance of
having a clear insight into and a clear vision of where
we want to go--although we would be wise not to fall
into the mistakes that Durham did. From his failures we
can learn perhaps much more. From the way in which he
ignored the power of French nationalism as a living
force we can learn that we cannot afford to do the same.
From his mistake in finally recommending the
unification of the two Canadas as opposed to linking
them in a Confederation which allowed for a fair amount
of regional autonomy we can learn the dangers inherent
in an over-centralized federal government.

It has been said that those who ignore the lesson of history are condemned to repeat its mistakes. The Durham Report provides us with a lesson that we would be wise not to ignore.

NOTES

[1] Donald G. Creighton, The Empire of the St. Lawrence (Toronto: Macmillan, 1956), p. 325.

[2] William Ormsby, "Lord Durham and the Assimilation of French Canada," in On Canada: Essays in Honour of Frank Underhill, ed. Norman Penlington (Toronto: University of Toronto Press, 1971), p. 37.

[3] Léandre Bergeron, The History of Quebec, A Patriote's Handbook (Toronto: NC Press Ltd., 1971), pp. 95-96.

[4] Lord Durham's Report, ed. Gerald M. Craig (Toronto: McClelland and Stewart, 1963), pp. 22-23. All quotations from the Report in this paper are from this edition.

[5] Accounts from which this summary of the development of the French-English conflict was drawn are Ormsby, Bergeron, and Jacques Monet, The Last Cannon Shot—A Study of French Canadian Nationalism 1837-1850 (Toronto: University of Toronto Press, 1969).

[6] Ormsby, p. 37.

[7] Lord Durham's Report, p. 51.

[8] Ibid., p. 150. For further examples of this in the Report see pp. 27-32 and pp. 146-154.

[9] Louis-Joseph Papineau, Histoire de l'insurrection au Canada (Ottawa: Les Editions Leméac, 1968), p. 48.

[10] The outbreak of rebellion in Lower Canada while Durham was returning to England led to the British Government of Lord Melbourne being very reluctant to accept Durham's idea of a loose federation. The final recommendations in the Report reflect, to a large extent, the pressure that was exerted on Durham by the Home Government. For details of this see Peter Burroughs, British Attitudes Towards Canada 1822-1849 (Scarborough: Prentice-Hall, 1971).

A SELECTED BIBLIOGRAPHY

Bergeron, Léandre. _The History of Quebec: A Patriote's Handbook_. Toronto: NC Press Ltd., 1971.

Burroughs, Peter. _British Attitudes Towards Canada 1822-1849_. Scarborough: Prentice-Hall, 1971.

Burroughs, Peter, ed. _The Colonial Reformers and Canada, 1830-1849_. Toronto: McClelland and Stewart, 1969.

Careless, J.M.S. _The Union of the Canadas--The Growth of Canadian Institutions 1841-1857_. Toronto: McClelland and Stewart, 1967.

Creighton, Donald G. _The Empire of the St. Lawrence_. Toronto: Macmillan, 1956.

Lord Durham's Report. Ed. Gerald M. Craig. Toronto: McClelland and Stewart, 1963.

Monet, Jacques. _The Last Cannon Shot--A Study of French Canadian Nationalism 1837-1850_. Toronto: University of Toronto Press, 1969.

Ormsby, William. "Lord Durham and the Assimilation of French Canada." _On Canada: Essays in Honour of Frank Underhill_. Ed. Norman Penlington. Toronto: University of Toronto Press, 1971.

Papineau, Louis-Joseph. _Histoire de l'insurrection au Canada_. Ottawa: Les Editions Leméac, 1968.

Ryerson, Stanley B. <u>Unequal Union: Confederation and the Roots of Conflict in the Canadas, 1815–1873</u>. Toronto: Progress Books, 1968.

Viau, Roger. <u>Lord Durham</u>. Montréal: Editions HMH Ltée, 1962.

THE ALBATROSS AS A SYMBOL

IN <u>THE</u> <u>RIME</u> <u>OF</u> <u>THE</u> <u>ANCIENT</u> <u>MARINER</u>

by

Gavin Shafer

OUTLINE

<u>Central</u> <u>idea</u>: The mysterious role of the albatross in
<u>The</u> <u>Rime</u> <u>of</u> <u>the</u> <u>Ancient</u> <u>Mariner</u> has led to various
interpretations of the bird as a symbol.

<u>Introduction</u>: Coleridge's concept of a symbol and the
variety of interpretations of the albatross

I. The mysterious role of the albatross
   A. Its appearance
   B. Its death
   C. Its impact on the life of the mariner

II. The interpretations of the albatross as a symbol
   A. As the unity in nature
      1. Coleridge's view of the universe
      2. The mariner's recognition of his kinship
         with other creatures
      3. Warren's theory of "One Life"
   B. As the creative imagination
      1. Symbolic association with the moon
      2. Symbolic association with the wind
   C. As the human father
   D. As a totem-animal

<u>Conclusion</u>: The suggestive power of images like the
albatross

The Albatross as a Symbol

in <u>The</u> <u>Rime</u> <u>of</u> <u>the</u> <u>Ancient</u> <u>Mariner</u>

Samuel Taylor Coleridge once wrote: "An IDEA, in the <u>highest</u> sense of that word, cannot be conveyed but by a <u>symbol</u>."[1] Coleridge's ideas are conveyed by many powerful symbols in <u>The</u> <u>Rime</u> <u>of</u> <u>the</u> <u>Ancient</u> <u>Mariner</u>, the tale of an old man's terrifying journey through sin and atonement to redemption. The senseless killing of an albatross, a huge sea bird of the southern hemisphere, is the pivotal symbolic experience of the poem. Yet the question of exactly what the albatross symbolizes is one that has baffled and divided literary critics for almost two hundred years. Perhaps Coleridge had the albatross in mind when he wrote that "all symbols of necessity involve an apparent contradiction."[2]

This paper reports on four of the most interesting and varied critical interpretations of the meaning of

[1] <u>Biographia</u> <u>Literaria</u>, ed. J. Shawcross (Oxford: Clarendon, 1907), I, 100.

[2] Ibid.

the albatross as a symbol.[3] First, the bird has been seen as a symbol of the unity in all nature. Second, it has been called a symbol of the creative imagination. Third, it has been seen as representing the human father. And, finally, it has been seen as a sacred "totem-animal," the select emissary of the gods. No one of these interpretations can answer all the questions a reader may have about the meaning of the albatross. Yet each of them illuminates one aspect of the bird's role as a primary symbol in the poem.

The albatross first appears in the poem when the mariner and his shipmates have been driven southward into the polar sea by a storm:

> At length did cross an Albatross,
> Thorough the fog it came;
> As if it had been a Christian soul,
> We hailed it in God's name. (lines 63-66)[4]

[3] Not every reader considers the albatross as a symbol. Elmer Edgar Stoll, for example, disagrees with the opinions of symbolists like Robert Penn Warren. See "Symbolism in Coleridge," in British Romantic Poets, ed. Shiv. K. Kumar (New York: New York Univ. Press, 1966), pp. 102-18.

[4] Samuel Taylor Coleridge, The Poems of Samuel Taylor Coleridge, ed. Ernest Hartley Coleridge (1912; rpt. London: Oxford Univ. Press, 1961), p. 189. In this paper, all quotations from The Rime of the Ancient Mariner are taken from this edition.

With the bird comes a wind from the south, and the ship
moves northward once again. The joyful men regard the
albatross as a good omen, and they playfully call to it
and feed it as it follows the ship. Then, with no
apparent motive, the mariner kills the friendly bird.

> 'God save thee, ancient Mariner!
> From the fiends, that plague thee thus!--
> Why look'st thou so?'--With my cross-bow
> I shot the ALBATROSS. (lines 79-82)

At first his shipmates blame the mariner for shooting
the bird that brought good fortune; but when the sun
reappears, they begin to praise him, thinking the bird
had brought the mist and fog. Powered by supernatural
forces, the ship speeds on to the equator. But there it
comes to a sudden halt, and drought begins to plague the
stranded crew. The bewildered men, holding the mariner
responsible, hang the dead albatross around his neck as
a sign of guilt.

Then begins the long exile and the dreadful penance
of the ancient mariner. Alone on a rotting ship, he
despises the creatures of the sea and yearns to die; he
finds himself unable to pray. Finally, after many days
and nights of penance, he is blessed with a vision of
the beauty of the water-snakes, and he realizes that his
heart is filled with love. He exclaims,

> The self-same moment I could pray;
> And from my neck so free
> The Albatross fell off, and sank
> Like lead into the sea. (lines 288-91)

The mariner is briefly comforted by sleep and rain. But his sin is not yet atoned for, and his penance soon begins anew. When at last he is absolved of his guilt and is conveyed by an angelic host to his native country, his whole being has been transformed by his experience. He becomes a seer who travels from land to land, compelled by some awful but redemptive force to tell others the strange tale of his journey.

Those who have seen the albatross as symbolic of the unity in nature have found support for their interpretation in Coleridge's own concept of the universe. As David P. Calleo writes,

> When Coleridge imagined the universe, he saw not a dead heap of uniform particles governed by simple, invariable, and mechanical laws. His universe was a vast arena filled with squirming, individual particulars, each with a vitality and purpose of its own. Yet there is a divine energy—a shaping spirit that coaxes individual inclination into general purpose. Nature is not like a machine, but an organism made up of many individual parts . . . all participating in a larger unity. . . . When man applies his mind to the study of Nature, he must be careful to lose sight neither of the general laws nor of the particular parts.[5]

[5] _Coleridge_ _and_ _the_ _Idea_ _of_ _the_ _Modern_ _State_, Yale Studies in Political Science, No. 18 (New Haven, Conn.: Yale Univ. Press, 1966), p. 39.

As a creature with its own vitality and purpose, the albatross thus participates in the larger unity of the natural world. In a world viewed pantheistically, it can be argued that the mariner, by shooting the albatross, "cuts himself off from nature, the unity of life, and love."[6]

In his analysis of _The Rime of the Ancient Mariner_, Max F. Schulz emphasizes the passages that reflect Coleridge's "reverence for life"[7] and his consciousness of "man's oneness with the external world."[8] When the mariner kills the albatross, he destroys a beautiful and happy living creature; later, when he realizes the beauty of the water-snakes, he blesses and loves "happy living things." At this moment, the spell that has bound him begins to break, and the dead albatross falls symbolically from his neck. The redemption of the mariner begins with his recognition of his own close relationship to other creatures.[9]

---

[6] Coleman O. Parsons, "The Mariner and the Albatross," _Virginia Quarterly Review_, 26 (1950), 119.

[7] _The Poetic Voices of Coleridge_ (Detroit: Wayne State Univ. Press, 1963), p. 57.

[8] Ibid., p. 64.

[9] Humphry House, _Coleridge_ (1962; rpt. London: Hart-Davis, 1969), p. 102.

Robert Penn Warren, who considers the motiveless
shooting of the albatross symbolic murder and who
relates the mariner's crime to the Fall of Man, believes
that the theme of "One Life"—of one being shared by all
the creatures of the universe—is the primary motif of
The Rime of the Ancient Mariner. Thus, in killing the
albatross, the mariner commits a crime against nature.
But Warren also points to a secondary theme in the poem:
a linking of the albatross with the imagination.[10]

According to Warren, the albatross may be
considered as a kind of "moon-bird." When it first
appears, it is associated with mist and fog, with snowy
haze, which Warren calls the "symbolic equivalent of
moonlight."[11] The moon first appears in the poem almost
immediately after the albatross:

> In mist or cloud, on mast or shroud,
> It [the albatross] perched for vespers nine;
> Whiles all the night, through fog-smoke white,
> Glimmered the white Moon-shine. (lines 75-78)

In the poem, the killing of the albatross is followed
immediately by the rising of the sun (lines 82 and 83),

[10] "A Poem of Pure Imagination (Reconsiderations VI)," Kenyon Review, 8 (1946), 398 and 402.

[11] Ibid., p. 407.

the prevailing image through the subsequent period of torture and drought that constitutes the mariner's first penance. With the death of the albatross, in effect, the moon disappears from the poem for 128 lines.

Similarly, as Warren shows, the albatross is closely associated with the wind. In the poem, the south wind begins to blow immediately after the albatross arrives at the ship, and the crew links the bird with the welcome breezes. Warren sees the wind as symbolic of creativity and the moonlight as symbolic of the imagination. Because the albatross is associated with both, the bird is part of what Warren calls a "symbolic cluster" representing the creative imagination. Thus, when the mariner shoots the albatross, he also commits a "crime against the imagination."[12]

Whether considered as a symbol of the unity of nature, or as a symbol of the creative imagination, or as both, the albatross is clearly a symbol of guilt. (Indeed, this meaning of the albatross is made clear by Coleridge himself, who explains in a marginal note that

[12] Ibid., pp. 407-08.

the shipmates hang the dead bird around the mariner's
neck as a sign of his guilt.) As John Ciardi points
out, however, the mariner's release from the "guilty
weight of the Albatross" is not a sign of his
forgiveness: further penance must be undergone.[13] Such
prolonged and terrible penance has suggested to some
critics that the mariner must be guilty of a crime of
the greatest magnitude—the murder of his own father, or
the slaying of a sacred totem-animal.

Some who have studied the life of Coleridge contend
that the poet suffered from an "Oedipal struggle"—
repressed desire for his mother and unconscious
hostility toward his father.[14] Coleridge's own Oedipal
complex could then be reflected in the mariner's crime,
which is only superficially motiveless:[15] the albatross
symbolizes the human father, and the mariner, in killing
it, is motivated by a "primeval instinct" that is a

---

[13] _How Does a Poem Mean?_ Pt. 3 of _An Introduction
to Literature_, ed. Gordon N. Ray et al. (Boston:
Houghton, 1959), p. 721.

[14] Mary Jane Lupton, "'The Rime of the Ancient
Mariner': The Agony of Thirst," _American Imago_, 27
(1970), 150-51.

[15] House, p. 95.

"part of the unconscious heritage of man, of Sophocles as well as Coleridge."[16]

Others, drawing on the work of Sir James G. Frazer, have seen the albatross as a "totem-animal," a sacred bird with a soul. Among many primitive peoples, the killing of a totem-animal against the gods' will is considered an extremely serious offense and is punished by exile and excommunication.[17] The killer—like the ancient mariner—cannot return to society until he has undergone long and severe rituals of penance.

All these interpretations of the albatross, although sometimes overlapping and often contradictory, can be justified in some measure through a close reading of the poem. What _does_ the albatross symbolize? There is no simple answer to the question, and to insist on one would be to underestimate the complexity of Coleridge's own moral view of the world.[18] Moreover, as Donald A. Stauffer has written, "A good poem resists to

[16] Lupton, p. 153.

[17] Ibid., p. 155.

[18] Patricia M. Adair, _The Waking Dream_ (London: Arnold, 1967), p. 68.

the death its reduction to a flat statement; and verse
which is made up of such flat statements is already dead
as poetry."[19] Perhaps, indeed, it is precisely because
of the stubborn suggestive power of images like the
albatross that _The Rime of the Ancient Mariner_ has so
steadfastly refused to die.

[19] "Poetry as Symbolic Thinking," _Saturday Review_,
22 March 1947, p. 10.

BIBLIOGRAPHY

Adair, Patricia M. The Waking Dream: A Study of
    Coleridge's Poetry. London: Arnold, 1967.

Calleo, David P. Coleridge and the Idea of the Modern
    State. New Haven, Conn.: Yale Univ. Press, 1966.

Ciardi, John. How Does a Poem Mean? Pt. 3 of An
    Introduction to Literature. Ed. Gordon N. Ray et
    al. Boston: Houghton, 1959.

Coleridge, Samuel Taylor. Biographia Literaria. 2
    vols. Ed. J. Shawcross. Oxford: Clarendon, 1907.

--------. The Poems of Samuel Taylor Coleridge. Ed.
    Ernest Hartley Coleridge. 1912; rpt. London:
    Oxford Univ. Press, 1961.

House, Humphry. Coleridge: The Clark Lectures, 1951-52.
    1962; rpt. London: Hart-Davis, 1969.

Lupton, Mary Jane. "'The Rime of the Ancient Mariner':
    The Agony of Thirst." American Imago, 27 (1970),
    140-59.

Parsons, Coleman O. "The Mariner and the Albatross."
    Virginia Quarterly Review, 26 (1950), 102-23.

Schulz, Max F. The Poetic Voices of Coleridge: A Study
    of His Desire for Spontaneity and Passion for
    Order. Detroit: Wayne State Univ. Press, 1963.

Stauffer, Donald A. "Poetry as Symbolic Thinking."
    Saturday Review, 22 March 1947, pp. 9-10.

Stoll, Elmer Edgar. "Symbolism in Coleridge." British
    Romantic Poets: Recent Evaluations. Ed. Shiv K.
    Kumar. New York: New York Univ. Press, 1966.

Warren, Robert Penn. "A Poem of Pure Imagination
    (Reconsiderations VI)." Kenyon Review, 8 (1946),
    391-427.

Note: Some instructors prefer to receive handwritten rather than typewritten papers. Below is a sample page from a handwritten library paper.

6

But Warren also points to a secondary theme in the poem: a linking of the albatross with the imagination.[10]

According to Warren, the albatross may be considered as a kind of "moon-bird". When it first appears, it is associated with mist and fog, with snowy haze, which Warren calls the "symbolic equivalent of moonlight."[11] The moon first appears in the poem almost immediately, after the albatross:

> In mist or cloud, on mast or shroud,
> It [the albatross] perched for vespers nine;
> Whiles all the night, through fog-smoke white,
> Glimmered the white Moon-shine.' (lines 75-78)

In the poem, the killing of the albatross is followed immediately by the rising of the sun (lines 82 and 83).

[10] "A Poem of Pure Imagination (Reconsiderations VI)," Kenyon Review, 8 (1946), 398 and 402.
[11] Ibid., p. 407.

Business Letters

34

Follow standard practices when you are writing business letters and addressing envelopes for them.

Business letters are usually typed on only one side of white, unlined paper, size 21 × 28 cm. (Letterhead stationery, of course, varies in both size and color.) The standard business envelope measures 9 × 16 cm or 10 × 25 cm.

34a
Follow standard practices when you are writing business letters.

A business letter has six parts: the heading, the inside address, the salutation, the body of the letter, the complimentary close, and the signature (handwritten and then typed).

Standard business-letter stylings vary. In the full block all parts of the letter, as well as the first lines of paragraphs, are flush with the left margin. The letter on the next page is modified block: the heading and the closing are not flush with the left margin. Carefully observe its general appearance. Note the arrangement, the spacing, the punctuation. (For examples of four main types of styling, see "Style in Business Correspondence" in the back of *Webster's New Collegiate Dictionary*.)

MODEL BUSINESS LETTER

HEADING $\left\{\begin{array}{l}\text{375 Clinton Drive}\\\text{Mississauga, Ontario L5A 3M8}\\\text{March 1, 1978}\end{array}\right.$

Mr. Richard A. McGowen
Manager, The Pines Motel   **INSIDE ADDRESS**
142 Watchill Road
Kitchener, Ontario N2L 5E7

Dear Mr. McGowen: **SALUTATION**

BODY

This letter is an answer to your advertisement in the
spring issue of <u>Summer Jobs for Students</u> for an
office assistant. I wish to apply for this position
and thus gain valuable on-the-job experience.

As a business major at the University of Toronto,
I have completed three years of general business
courses, including one in accounting and another in
electronic data processing. Last week, I was invited
to join the honorary society for business majors.
At present, I am working as a student assistant in
the registrar's office.

I refer you to Ms. Barbara York. She has my
permission to send you my résumé, as well as up-to-
date letters of recommendation, which she has on
file:

> Ms. Barbara York, Director
> Student Employment Service
> University of Toronto
> Toronto, Ontario M5G 1X8

Should you wish an interview, I could come to see you
on almost any weekend or during the spring break,
which begins on March 13 and ends on March 21. (My
telephone number is 416-555-1867.)

CLOSING

Complimentary Close Yours sincerely,

Signature *Eugene Stewart*

Typed name Eugene Stewart

(1) The heading gives the full address of the writer and the date of the letter.

Notice that the heading in the business letter on page 416 is blocked and has no end punctuation. If letterhead stationery is used, the date is often centred two or three spaces below the printed matter, although it may be written flush with either margin (depending on the letter styling).

(2) The inside address gives the name and full address of the addressee.

Four or six spaces usually separate the heading from the inside address, which is consistent in form with the heading. As you do for your address in the heading, follow customary practices for writing such addresses as *121 West Fourth Avenue, 121 N.W. 183rd Street,* or *121—50th Avenue.*

(3) The salutation greets the addressee appropriately.

The salutation is written flush with the left margin two spaces below the inside address and is followed by a colon. The salutation should be consistent with the tone of the letter, the first line of the inside address, and the complimentary close.

When it is known, the surname of the addressee is used in the salutation of a business letter, as in the following examples.

```
Dear Dr. Davis:
Dear Mr. Miller:
Dear Dean Hix:

Dear Ms. Tyler:
OR
Dear Miss Tyler:

Dear Ms. Joseph:
OR
Dear Mrs. Joseph:
```

In salutations, *Ms.* is used instead of *Miss* or *Mrs.* when the marital status of a woman addressee is not known or when she (whether married or not) uses or prefers the *Ms.* (*Mmes.* is the plural of *Mrs.; Messrs.,* of *Mr.*).

In letters to organizations, or to persons whose names you do not know, such salutations as the following are among the conventional greetings:

```
Dear Sir or Madam:
OR
Dear Sir:
OR
Dear Madam:

Gentlemen:
To whom it may concern:
```

For the appropriate forms of salutations and addresses in letters to governmental officials, military personnel, and so on, check the front or back matter of your dictionary or refer to Howard Measures, *Styles of Address*, 3rd ed. (Toronto: Macmillan, 1969).

(4) The body of the letter should follow the principles of good writing.

Typewritten business letters are usually single-spaced, with double spacing between paragraphs. All paragraphs should begin flush with the left margin (full or modified block styling), as in the model business letter on page 416, or should begin with an equal indention (other stylings). The subject matter should be well organized and well paragraphed, but the paragraphs will frequently be shorter than in ordinary writing. The style should be clear and direct. Indirect, abbreviated, or outdated phrasing should be avoided.

```
INDIRECT   Permit us to report that we now have. . . .

DIRECT     We now have. . . .


ABBREVIATED  Hope to mail credentials to you within
             week.

BETTER       I hope to mail my credentials to you
             within a week.
```

(5) The complimentary close should be businesslike and follow conventional style.

Business letters usually have such complimentary closes as *Yours truly, Yours very truly,* or *Very truly yours; Yours sincerely, Sincerely yours,* or *Sincerely; Cordially yours* or *Yours cordially.*

(6) The handwritten signature should be placed between the complimentary close and the typed name of the writer.

Ordinarily, neither professional titles nor degrees should be used with the signature, but the writer's official capacity should be indicated after the typed name:

Yours sincerely,   Yours sincerely,

Christopher Johnson   *Ann Ames*

Christopher Johnson   Ann Ames, President
Assistant Editor

A woman has the option of placing *Ms., Miss,* or *Mrs.* inside parentheses before her typed name. A married woman may choose to add (inside parentheses) below her name *Mrs.* followed by her husband's name.

Yours truly,

Gene Bly

(Ms.) Gene Bly

Yours truly,

Cleo Sale

(Mrs.) Cleo Sale

Yours truly,

Cleo Sale

Cleo Sale
(Mrs. John Sale)

34b
Follow standard practices when you are addressing envelopes. Fold the letter to fit the envelope.

The address that appears on the envelope is identical to the inside address. The return address regularly gives the full name and address of the writer.

MODEL ADDRESSED ENVELOPE

```
Eugene Stewart
375 Clinton Drive
Mississauga, Ontario L5A 3M8



            Mr. Richard A. McGowen
            Manager, The Pines Motel
            142 Watchhill Road
            Kitchener, Ontario N2L 5E7
```

With a postal code, special postal abbreviations not followed by periods may be used for names of provinces:

Winnipeg, MB R3B 1Z9

Below are the steps for folding a business letter to fit the long standard envelope (about 10 × 25 cm in size) and for placing it inside the envelope.

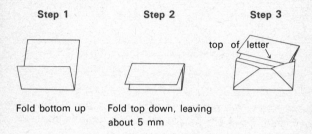

Step 1

Fold bottom up

Step 2

Fold top down, leaving about 5 mm

Step 3

top of letter

Fold the standard-sized paper to fit a small business envelope (about 9 × 16 cm in size) as follows:

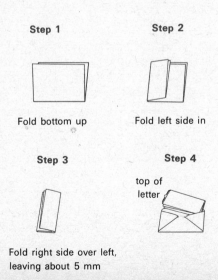

Step 1

Fold bottom up

Step 2

Fold left side in

Step 3

Fold right side over left, leaving about 5 mm

Step 4

top of letter

let

■ **Exercise 1** Write a letter of application for a position that you are competent to fill. Be sure to include a brief, specific description of the job desired and of your qualifications. (See the model business letter on page 416.)

■ **Exercise 2** Write a business letter in which you do one of the following:

1. Request the circulation manager of a newspaper to send your paper to a new address.
2. Ask the manager of a New York City hotel to reserve a room for you.
3. Call the attention of your representative in the city government to some needed repairs in a street near your home.
4. Explain to your employer why you must resign from your position at the end of the year.
5. Request the permission of a former employer to use his or her name as a reference in applying for a new position.

Glossary of Grammatical Terms

The following glossary presents brief explanations of grammatical terms frequently used by students of the language. References to further treatment of most of the terms in this glossary, as well as to a number of terms not listed, may be found in the index.

absolute construction   A parenthetical phrase which qualifies a whole clause or the rest of the sentence but which is not grammatically related to it by a connective. Its basic pattern is usually NOUN + PARTICIPLE. (This construction is often called a *nominative absolute,* a *sentence modifier,* or simply an *adverbial phrase.*)

> The expressway *jammed with rush-hour traffic,* we were delayed two hours.
> We will have our book sale in front of the library, *weather permitting.*

See also **12d(3)**.

abstract noun   See **noun**.

active voice   See **voice**.

adjectival   Like an adjective. Any word or word group used as an adjective. The limiting adjectives (articles, demonstratives, and so on) are often classified as adjectivals.

> *the* desk   *that* map   *Noah's* ark   *third* base
> The man *on third base* stumbled.   [A phrase modifying *man*]
> The dog *that barks* may bite.   [A clause modifying *dog*]

423

grt

adjective A part of speech regularly used to modify (describe or limit) a noun or a pronoun.

cloudy sky	*good* food	*finer* homes	[Descriptive]
those keys	*an* apple	*few* players	[Limiting]
Irish humour	a *Christlike* figure		[Proper—capitalized]

A *predicate adjective* is used with a linking verb and modifies the subject.

The shirts were *inexpensive*.   How *busy* is he?

See also Section **4**.

adjective clause A subordinate clause used adjectivally.

Velasquez, *whose work influenced the French Impressionists,* was a famous Spanish realist. [The adjective clause modifies the noun *Velasquez*.]

See also pages 20–21.

adverb A part of speech regularly used to modify (qualify, describe, or limit) a verb or verbal, an adjective, another adverb, or even the rest of the sentence.

Mildred owns an *extremely* old clock, which runs *very quietly*. [*Extremely* modifies the adjective *old; quietly* modifies the verb *runs; very* modifies the adverb *quietly*.]

See also **adverbial** and Section **4**.

adverb clause A subordinate clause used adverbially. According to meaning, it may be classified as an adverb clause of time, place, manner, cause, purpose, condition, concession, comparison, or result.

The common mole is valuable *because it eats insects.*
Although it is only fifty-six kilometres long, the Niagara is one of the world's most famous rivers.
Cartoonists make at least eighteen drawings *so that Woody Woodpecker can laugh victoriously.*

See also pages 20–21 and **12b**.

adverbial Like an adverb. Any word, phrase, or clause which is used as an adverb.

> Gerard went *home.* [Adverbial of place]
> He can speak *without stuttering.* [Adverbial of manner]
> The team plays best *after the two-minute warning is given.*
> [Adverbial of time]

agreement The correspondence in form of one word with another (for example, a verb with its subject or a pronoun with its antecedent) to indicate number: see Section **6**.

antecedent The name given to a word or group of words to which a pronoun refers.

> Before *Ron* left, *he* paid the *man* and *woman who* delivered
> the firewood. [*Ron* is the antecedent of the personal
> pronoun *he; man* and *woman* are the antecedents of the
> relative pronoun *who.*]

appositive A noun or noun substitute set beside another noun or noun substitute and identifying or explaining it.

> Davis, our *guide,* did not see the grizzly. [*Guide* is in appo-
> sition with *Davis.*]

See also **12d(2)**.

article *A, an,* and *the,* often called *determiners* or *adjectivals* because of their position and function before a noun.

> *a* bus   *an* apple   *the* long movie

auxiliary verb A verb (like *be, have, do*) used with a main verb in a verb phrase. An auxiliary regularly indicates tense but may also indicate voice, mood, person, number.

> *are* eating   *will be* eating   *was* eaten
> *has* eaten   *Do* eat with us.   *have been* eaten

Modal auxiliaries (such as *will, would, shall, should, may, might, must, can, could*) do not take such inflectional endings as *-s, -ing,* or *-en.*
See also **1a** and Section **7**.

case The inflectional form of a pronoun, or a possessive noun, which shows the function of the word in the sentence. A subject of a verb or a subject complement is in the *subjective,* or *nominative,* case (*we, they*). A possessive pronoun or noun used adjectivally is in the *possessive,* or *genitive,* case (*our* ideas, *their* car, *nobody's* fault, *Leslie's* camera). Possessive pronouns may take the noun position (*ours, theirs*). And an object of a verb (or verbal) or of a preposition is in the *objective* case (*us, them*).

See also **inflection,** Section **5,** and **15a.**

clause A group of related words that contains both a subject and a predicate and that functions as a part of a sentence. A clause may be *main* (*independent, principal*) or *subordinate* (*dependent*). A main clause can stand by itself as a simple sentence; a subordinate clause cannot. Subordinate clauses are used as nouns, adjectives, or adverbs: see **1d(3)** and **1d(4).**

MAIN	*The moon rose,* and *the stars came out.* [Two main clauses, either of which could be written as a separate sentence]
SUBORDINATE	*That he will run for office* is doubtful. [Noun clause: a subordinate clause used as the subject of the sentence]

collective noun A word (like *crowd, herd,* or *orchestra*) which is singular in form but which may be singular or plural in meaning: see **6a(7).**

colloquial Appropriate for conversation and informal writing but usually inappropriate for formal writing.

common noun See **noun.**

comparison The change in the form of an adjective or adverb to indicate degrees in quality, quantity, or manner. There are three degrees: *positive, comparative,* and *superlative.*

Positive	Comparative	Superlative
good, well	better	best
high	higher	highest
quickly	more quickly	most quickly
active	less active	least active

See also **inflection** and **4c.**

complement A word or words used to complete the sense of the verb and structure of the predicate (*direct* and *indirect objects*), the subject (*subject complements*), or the object (*object complements*).

OBJECTS (with transitive verbs)

William lent *Susan* his *book.* [*Book* is the direct object; *Susan* is the indirect object.]

SUBJECT COMPLEMENTS (with linking verbs)

The boy is *obedient.* [*Obedient,* a predicate adjective, modifies the subject *boy.*]

Samuel is a good *child.* [*Child,* a predicate noun, refers to the subject *Samuel.*]

OBJECT COMPLEMENTS (with verbs like *name, elect, make,* and *paint*)

He appointed Bruce *treasurer.* [The noun *treasurer* refers to *Bruce,* the direct object.]

Jacqueline painted the garage *blue.* [The adjective *blue* modifies the direct object *garage.*]

complete predicate See **predicate.**

complete subject See **subject.**

complex sentence See **sentence.**

compound A word or word group with two or more parts that function as a unit.

COMPOUND NOUNS dropout, hunger strike, sister-in-law

COMPOUND SUBJECT *Postal workers, policemen,* and *telephone operators* are all out on strike.

COMPOUND PREDICATE Kate *has tried* but *has* not *succeeded.*

See also **sentence.**

compound-complex sentence See **sentence.**

compound sentence See **sentence.**

concrete noun See **noun.**

conjugation A list of the inflected forms of a verb that indicate tense, person, number, voice, and mood. A shortened form of the traditional conjugation of *see* follows:

PRINCIPAL PARTS

see   saw   seen

Active voice	*Passive voice*

INDICATIVE MOOD

PRESENT TENSE

I / you / we / they *see*
he / she / it *sees*

I *am seen*
he / she / it *is seen*
you / we / they *are seen*

PAST TENSE

I / he / you / we / they *saw*

I / he *was seen*
you / we / they *were seen*

FUTURE TENSE

I / he / you / we / they *will*
(OR *shall*) *see*

I / he / you / we / they *will*
(OR *shall*) *be seen*

PRESENT PERFECT TENSE

I / you / we / they *have seen*
he *has seen*

I / you / we / they *have been seen*
he *has been seen*

PAST PERFECT TENSE

I / he / you / we / they *had seen*

I / he / you / we / they *had been seen*

FUTURE PERFECT TENSE

I / he / you / we / they *will*
(OR *shall*) *have seen*

I / he / you / we / they *will*
(OR *shall*) *have been seen*

SUBJUNCTIVE MOOD

PRESENT TENSE

that he / I / you / we / they
see

that he / I / you / we / they *be
seen*

PAST TENSE

that he / I / you / we / they
saw

that he / I / you / we / they
were seen

PRESENT PERFECT TENSE

that he / I / you / we / they
have seen

that he / I / you / we / they
have been seen

PAST PERFECT TENSE

(same as the indicative)

IMPERATIVE MOOD

PRESENT TENSE

see

be seen

See page 64 for a synopsis of the progressive forms.

conjunction A part of speech used to connect and relate words, phrases, clauses, or sentences. There are two kinds of conjunctions: coordinating and subordinating.

Coordinating conjunctions connect words and word groups of equal grammatical rank: *and, but, or, nor, for.*

Subordinating conjunctions mark a dependent clause and connect it with a main clause: *after, although, as, as if, because, before, if, since, unless, until, when, while,* and so forth.

conjunctive adverb An adverb used to connect or relate main clauses: *accordingly, also, anyhow, besides, consequently, furthermore, hence, henceforth, however, indeed, instead, likewise, meanwhile, moreover, nevertheless, otherwise, still, then, therefore, thus,* and so on.

429

connective A word or phrase (such as *and, because, however, so, yet, also, finally, on the contrary*) which links and relates words, phrases, clauses, or sentences. See also **31b(4)**.

constituent A layer of a construction or a sentence element having a specific function—such as a subject or a predicate, a modifier, or a subordinate clause. The smallest meaningful element of a word is also called a constituent: *un | friend | ly, teach | er | s.*

construction The arrangement of related words in a phrase, a clause, or a sentence.

content word See **vocabulary word**.

correlatives Coordinating conjunctions used in pairs: *both . . . and; either . . . or; neither . . . nor; not only . . . but also; whether . . . or.* See also **26c**.

declension A list of the inflected forms of a noun or a pronoun: see **inflection**.

demonstrative pronoun One of the four pronouns that point out: *this, that, these, those.* These words often function in sentences as adjectives.

> *This* brand is as good as *that.*

dependent clause A subordinate clause: see **clause**.

descriptive adjective See **adjective**.

determiner A word (such as *a, an, the, my, their,* or *our*) which signals the approach of a noun.

diagramming A graphic means of showing relationships within the sentence. Various forms are used; any form is serviceable if it helps the student to understand the sentence. Illustrations of three kinds of diagrams follow:

The dark clouds on the horizon had appeared suddenly.

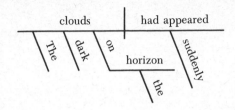

The key to the diagram:

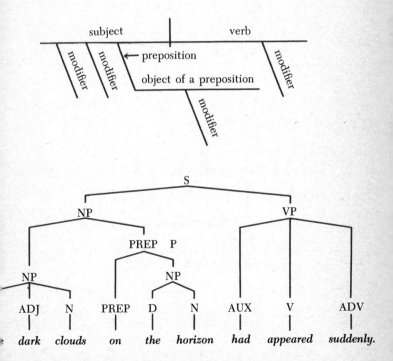

grt

The key to the abbreviations:

ADJ	Adjective
ADV	Adverb
AUX	Auxiliary
D	Determiner
N	Noun
NP	Noun Phrase
PREP	Preposition
PREP P	Prepositional Phrase
S	Sentence
V	Verb
VP	Verb Phrase

A key to the diagram below (which shows the layers of structure) is not provided. Terminology is left to the analyst's choice. (For example, one analyst could write *complete subject* on the line connecting *on the horizon* with *The dark clouds*, but another might prefer *noun phrase*.)

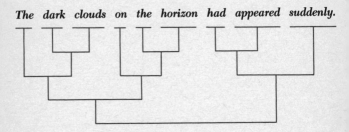

direct object See **object**.

direct quotation The exact spoken or written words of others.

> DIRECT QUOTATION John asked, "Why haven't you joined the group, Martha?"
> INDIRECT QUOTATION John asked Martha why she had not joined the group.

See also **16a**.

432

double negative A nonstandard construction containing two negatives and having a negative meaning, such as *I didn't have no change with me.* See **not . . . no**, page 200.

elliptical construction A construction in which words are omitted but clearly understood.

> The drapes are newer than the carpet [is].
> When [it is] possible, get a full night's sleep.
> His hair is black; his face [is] deeply tanned.

expletive The word *there* or *it* used as a structural filler and not adding to the meaning of the sentence.

> *There* were only a few ballet tickets left. [Compare "Only a few ballet tickets were left."]
> *It* is obvious that they do not like us. [Compare "That they do not like us is obvious."]

finite verb The principal verb of a sentence or a clause. A finite verb can serve as the only verb of a sentence. Verb forms classified as gerunds, infinitives, and participles (verbals) are not finite verbs.

> One prisoner *escaped.*   Clyde *will read* the book.

form change See **inflection**.

function words Words (such as prepositions, conjunctions, auxiliaries, and articles) that indicate the functions of other words (*vocabulary words*) in a sentence and the grammatical relationships between them. See also **vocabulary words**.

gerund A nonfinite verb that ends in *-ing* and functions as a noun. Gerunds may take objects, complements, or modifiers.

> He escaped by *swimming rapidly.* [The gerund *swimming* is the object of the preposition *by* and is modified by the adverb *rapidly.*]
> *Borrowing money* is a mistake. [The gerund phrase—the gerund *borrowing* and its object, *money*—serves as the subject of the sentence.]

A possessive noun or pronoun before a gerund may be classified either as an adjectival (modifying the noun element of the gerund) or as the subject of the verbal.

> *His borrowing* money is a mistake. [Compare *"his* action" and *"He borrowed* the money."]

headword (head) The key word in a phrase or the nucleus of a cluster of words—such as a noun apart from its modifiers or the main verb separated from auxiliaries, objects, and modifiers. (The line in the example below divides two clusters of words.)

> The battered old *furniture* in the attic | should have been *sold* years ago. [The simple subject, *furniture,* is the headword of the complete subject (or complete noun phrase) and *sold* is the head of the predicate.]

idiom An expression in good use that is characteristic of or peculiar to a language. Perfectly acceptable idioms may seem illogical if taken literally or may violate established rules of grammar.

> He *gave himself away* by smiling.
> I have known him for *many a year.*

imperative See **mood**.

indefinite An article (*a, an*), a pronoun (*anybody, everyone,* and so on) or an adjective (*any* book, a *few* friends, *several* replies, and so on) that does not specify distinct limits.

independent clause A main clause: see **clause**.

indicative See **mood**.

indirect object See **object**.

indirect quotation See **direct quotation**.

infinitive A nonfinite verb used chiefly as a noun, less frequently as an adjective or an adverb. The infinitive is usually made up of the word *to* plus the present form of a verb (called the *stem* of the infinitive), but the *to* may be omitted after such verbs as *let, make,* and *dare.* Infinitives may have subjects, objects, complements, or modifiers.

> Hal wanted **to open** *the present.* [*Present* is the object of the infinitive *to open;* the whole infinitive phrase is the object of the verb *wanted.*]
> The work **to be done** overwhelms me. [The infinitive is used adjectivally to modify the noun *work.*]
> **To tell** *the truth,* our team almost lost. [The infinitive phrase is used adverbially to modify the rest of the sentence.]

inflection A change in the form of a word to show a specific meaning or grammatical relationship to some other word or group of words. The inflection of nouns and pronouns is called *declension;* the inflection of verbs, *conjugation;* that of adjectives and adverbs, *comparison.*

INFLECTIONS OF VERBS (indicating tense, person, number, mood)

look, looks, looking, looked
drink, drinks, drinking, drank, drunk
know, knows, knowing, knew, known
be, am, is, are, being, was, were, been

INFLECTIONS OF NOUNS (indicating number, case)

dog, dogs; dog's, dogs'
child, children; child's, children's

INFLECTIONS OF PRONOUNS (indicating person, case, number)

I, me, my, mine   we, us, our, ours
who, whom, whose   someone, someone's
This is old.   *These* are old.   *That* is older than *those.*

INFLECTIONS OF MODIFIERS (indicating comparison, number)

fast, faster, fastest   bad, worse, worst
many, more, most   little, less, least

See also **conjugation.**

grt

intensive pronoun A *-self* pronoun used to emphasize another word in the sentence.

> The president *himself* answered my letter. [The pronoun *himself* refers to and emphasizes *president*.]

interjection A part of speech used for simple exclamations: *Oh! Ouch! Whew!* When used in sentences, mild interjections are set off by commas.

intransitive See **verb**.

inversion A change in the usual word order of a sentence.

> Up go the referee's hands.
> In the middle of the lake is a small island.

irregular verb A verb that does not form its past tense and past participle in the standard way—that is, by the addition of *-d* or *-ed* to the stem of the infinitive (as with the regular verbs *hope, hoped; look, looked*). The principal parts of five common types of irregular verbs are given below.

> swim, swam, swum [Vowels changed]
> beat, beat, beaten [*-en* added]
> feel, felt, felt [Vowel changed to consonant and *-t* added]
> send, sent, sent [*-d* changed to *-t*]
> set, set, set [No change]

lexical words See **vocabulary word**.

linking verb A verb which relates the subject to the subject complement. Words commonly used as linking verbs are *become, seem, appear, feel, look, taste, smell, sound,* and the forms of the verb *be*.

> She *is* a pharmacist.   The panels *feel* rough.

main clause An independent clause: see **clause**.

modal auxiliary See **auxiliary verb**.

modifier An adjective or adverb (adjectival or adverbial), which describes, limits, or qualifies another word or word group: see Section **4**.

mood (mode) The form of the verb which indicates the manner in which the action or state is conceived. English has the indicative, imperative, and subjunctive moods.

The *indicative* is used to make statements and ask questions; the *imperative*, to give commands, make requests, and give directions. The *subjunctive* is still used to express a wish or a contrary-to-fact condition, as well as in *that* clauses of recommendation or request.

INDICATIVE	We *rented* a van. *Will* you *be* on time?
IMPERATIVE	*Rent* a van. *Turn* left.
SUBJUNCTIVE	I wish I *were* still living in Alberta.
	The committee recommended that these rules *be* changed.

nominal Like a noun. A word or word group used as a noun or taking the position of a noun.

Repairing that machine was not easy.

nominative See **absolute construction** and **case**.

nonfinite verb A verb that cannot stand as the only verb in a sentence. A nonfinite verb (a verbal) may function as a noun, an adjective, or an adverb. See also **verbal**.

nonrestrictive Nonessential to the meaning of a sentence. A phrase or clause is nonrestrictive (parenthetical) when it is not necessary to the meaning of the main clause and may be omitted: see **12d**.

The old horse, *slow but confident,* plodded on.   [Phrase]
The airplane, *now being manufactured in large numbers,* is of
   immense commercial value.   [Phrase]
The airplane, *which is now being manufactured in large numbers,* is of immense commercial value.   [Clause]

See also **restrictive**.

grt

noun A part of speech that names a person, place, thing, idea, animal, quality, or action: *Mary, Canada, apples, justice, goose, strength, departure*. A noun usually changes form to indicate the plural and the possessive case, as in *man, men; man's, men's*. See also **inflection**.

Types of nouns

COMMON	a *man*, the *cities*, some *trout*	[General classes]
PROPER	*Mr. Ford*, in *Quebec*, the *Forum*	[Capitalized, specific names]
COLLECTIVE	a *flock*, the *jury*, my *family*	[Groups]
CONCRETE	an *egg*, the *bus*, his *ear*, two *trees*	[Tangibles]
ABSTRACT	*ambition, jealousy, pity, hatred*	[Ideas, qualities]
COUNT	two *dollars*, a *fact*, many *quarrels*	[Plural or singular, numerables]
MASS	some *money*, the *information*, much *friction*	[Not used with *a* or *an*, singular in meaning]

Functions of nouns

SUBJECT OF FINITE VERB *Dogs* barked.

OBJECT OF FINITE VERB OR OF PREPOSITION He gave *Jane* the *key* to the *house*.

SUBJECT COMPLEMENT (PREDICATE NOUN) She is a *nurse*.

OBJECT COMPLEMENT They named him *Jonathan*.

SUBJECT OF NONFINITE VERB I want *Ed* to be here.

OBJECT OF NONFINITE VERB I prefer to drive a *truck*.

APPOSITIVE Moses, a *prophet*, saw the promised land.

DIRECT ADDRESS What do you think, *Angela?*

noun clause A subordinate clause used as a noun.

Whoever comes will be welcome.   [Subject]
I hope *that he will recover*.   [Direct object]
I will give *whoever comes first* the best seat.   [Indirect object]
Spend it for *whatever seems best*.   [Object of a preposition]
This is *what you need*.   [Subject complement]
I loved it, *whatever it was*.   [Appositive]
Whoever you are, show yourself!   [Direct address]

noun phrase See **phrase**.

number The inflectional form of a noun, a pronoun, a demonstrative adjective, or a verb which indicates number, either singular or plural.

> book, man, I, one, this, that [Singular]
> books, men, we, ones, these, those [Plural]

Verbs change form to indicate a third-person singular subject: see **6a**.

object A noun or noun substitute governed by a transitive active verb, by a nonfinite verb, or by a preposition.

A *direct object*, or the *object of a finite verb*, is any noun or noun substitute that answers the question *What?* or *Whom?* after a transitive active verb. A direct object frequently receives, or is in some way affected by, the action of the verb.

> William raked *leaves*.   *What* did he say?
> The Andersons do not know *where we live*.

As a rule, a direct object may be converted into a subject with a passive verb: see **voice**.

An *object of a nonfinite verb* is any noun or its equivalent that follows and completes the meaning of a participle, a gerund, or an infinitive.

> Washing a *car* takes time.   He likes to wear a *tie*.
> Following the *truck*, a bus rounded the bend.

An *indirect object* is any noun or noun substitute that states *to whom* or *for whom* (or *to what* or *for what*) something is done. An indirect object ordinarily precedes a direct object.

> He bought *her* a watch.
> I gave the *floor* a second coat of varnish.

It is usually possible to substitute a prepositional phrase beginning with *to* or *for* for the indirect object.

> He bought a watch for her.

An *object of a preposition* is any noun or noun substitute which a preposition relates to another word or word group.

> Cedars grow tall in these *hills*. [*Hills* is the object of *in*.]
> *What* am I responsible for? [*What* is the object of *for*.]

grt

object complement See **complement**.

objective See **case**.

paradigm An illustration of all the inflectional forms of a word, such as a verb or a pronoun.

participle A verb form that may function as part of a verb phrase (was *laughing*, had *finished*), as an adjective (the *laughing* children, the *finished* product), or as a nonfinite verb (The children, *laughing* loudly, left).

The present participle ends in *-ing* (the form also used for verbal nouns: see **gerund**). The past participle of regular verbs ends in *-d* or *-ed;* for a list of past participles of irregular verbs, see page 66.

Functioning as nonfinite verbs in *participial phrases*, participles may take objects, complements, modifiers:

> The prisoner *carrying the heaviest load* toppled forward. [The participle *carrying* takes the object *load;* the whole participial phrase modifies *prisoner.*]

> The telephone operator, *very confused by my request*, suggested that I place the call later. [The participle *confused* is modified by the adverb *very* and by the prepositional phrase *by my request;* the participial phrase modifies *telephone operator.*]

See also **absolute construction** and **verbal**.

particle with verb A phrasal unit consisting of a verb plus an uninflected word like *after, in, up, off,* or *out* and having the force of a single-word verb.

> We *ran out on* them. [Compare "We deserted them."]
> He *cut* me *off* without a cent. [Compare "He disinherited me."]

parts of speech The eight classes into which most grammarians group words according to their form changes and their position, meaning, and use in the sentence: *verbs, nouns, pronouns, adjectives, adverbs, prepositions, conjunctions,* and *interjections.* Each of these is discussed separately in this glossary. See also **1c**.

passive voice See **voice**.

person The form of a verb (like *am* or *has*) or of a pronoun (like *I* or *she*) which indicates the identity of the subject: whether it is the one speaking (*first person*), spoken to (*second person*), or spoken about (*third person*).

FIRST PERSON	*I* am	*I* think	*we* have lived
SECOND PERSON	*you* were	*you* think	*you* have lived
THIRD PERSON	*it* is	*he* thinks	*she* has lived

personal pronoun See **pronoun**.

phrase A group of related words without both a subject and a verb.

NOUN PHRASE *A young stranger* stepped forward.

VERB PHRASE All day long they *had been worrying*.

PREPOSITIONAL PHRASES *By seven o'clock*, the lines stretched *from the box office to the corner*.

GERUND PHRASE *Building a sun deck* can be fun.

INFINITIVE PHRASE Do you want *to use your time that way?*

PARTICIPIAL PHRASE My friends *travelling in Italy* felt the earthquake.

possessive See **case**.

predicate A basic grammatical division of a sentence. A predicate is the part of the sentence comprising what is said about the subject. The *complete predicate* consists of the main verb along with its auxiliaries (the *simple predicate*) and any complements and modifiers.

The town ***used** a unity theme for its annual fair that year.* [*Used* is the simple predicate, the headword of the complete predicate.]

predicate adjective An adjective functioning as a subject complement: see **complement**.

predicate noun A noun functioning as a subject complement: see **complement**.

preposition A part of speech (often called a *function word*) that is used to show the relation of a noun or noun equivalent (the *object of the preposition*) to some other word in the sentence. Words commonly used as prepositions include *across, after, as, at, because of, before, between, by, for, from, in, in front of, in regard to, like, near, of, on, over, through, to, together with, under, until, up,* and *with.*

> The portrait hung *in* the hall. [The preposition *in* shows the relationship of its object *hall* to the verb *hung.*]

See also **1c**

prepositional phrase See **phrase**.

principal clause A main clause: see **clause**.

principal parts The forms of any verb from which the various tenses are derived: the present infinitive (*take, laugh*), the past (*took, laughed*), and the past participle (*taken, laughed*).

See also Section **7**.

progressive verb A verb phrase consisting of a present participle (ending in *-ing*) used with a form of *be* and denoting continuous action.

> I *have been playing* tennis all afternoon.

See also pages 63–64.

pronoun A part of speech, one of a small closed class of words, often considered a subgroup of nouns. Pronouns take the position of nouns or of noun phrases and function as nouns do.

> NOUNS The old *house* was sold to *Fred's cousins.*
> PRONOUNS *It* was sold to *his* cousins. OR *It* was sold to *them.*

Types of pronouns

> PERSONAL *You* and *I* will see *him.*
> INTERROGATIVE *Who* is he? *Which* is it? *What* was that?
> RELATIVE The boy *who* served us is the one *that* I tipped.

DEMONSTRATIVE	*This* is better than *that*.
INDEFINITE	*Each* of you should help *someone*.
RECIPROCAL	Help *each other*. They like *one another*.
REFLEXIVE	Carl blames *himself*. Did you injure *yourself*?
INTENSIVE	We need a vacation *ourselves*. I *myself* saw the crash.

See also **inflection** and Sections **5** and **6**.

proper adjective A capitalized adjective formed from a proper noun, as *Spanish* from *Spain*. See also **adjective**.

proper noun See **noun**.

quotation See **direct quotation**.

reciprocal pronoun See **pronoun**.

reflexive pronoun A *-self* pronoun used as an object or a complement and referring to the individual or individuals named by the subject.

They denied *themselves* nothing.   I am not *myself* today.

regular verb A verb that forms its past tense and past participle by adding *-d* or *-ed* to the stem of the infinitive: *love, loved; laugh, laughed.*

relative pronoun One of a small group of noun substitutes (*who, whom, whose, that, which, what, whoever, whomever, whichever, whatever*) used to introduce subordinate clauses; sometimes called a *subordinate-clause marker*.

He has a son *who is a genius*. [Adjective clause introduced by the relative pronoun *who*]
Whoever wins the prize must have talent. [Noun clause introduced by the relative pronoun *whoever*]

restrictive Essential to sentence meaning. A phrase or clause is restrictive when it is necessary to the meaning of the main clause and cannot be omitted: see **12d**.

Every drug *condemned by doctors* should be taken off the
market. [Phrase]

Every drug *that doctors condemn* should be taken off the
market. [Clause]

See also **nonrestrictive**.

sentence An independent unit of expression. A simple sentence
follows the pattern **SUBJECT—PREDICATE**. Sentences are often
classified according to structure as *simple, compound, complex,* or
compound-complex.

SIMPLE We won. [Subject—predicate]

COMPOUND They outplayed us, but we won. [Two main
clauses]

COMPLEX Although we did win, they outplayed us. [Subor-
dinate clause, main clause]

COMPOUND-COMPLEX I know that they outplayed us, but we
did win. [Two main clauses, with one containing a subordinate clause]

sentence modifier A word or word group that modifies the rest
of the sentence in which it appears.

Yes, the train will be on time.
Generally speaking, Americans are a friendly people.

subject A basic grammatical division of a sentence. The subject
is a noun or noun substitute about which something is asserted or
asked in the predicate. It usually precedes the predicate. (Imperative sentences have subjects that are not stated but are implied.)
The *complete subject* consists of the *simple subject* and the words
associated with it.

*The small **dog** in the hot car* needed air. [*Dog* is the simple
subject, the headword of the complete subject.]

See also **1b**.

subject complement See **complement**.

subjective See **case**.

subjunctive See **mood**.

subordinate clause A dependent clause: see **clause**.

subordinator A word that marks a dependent, or subordinate, clause: see page 19.

suffix An inflectional or a derivational ending added to a word.

the play*s*	walk*ed*	the tall*est*	[Inflectional]
dark*ness*	legal*ize*	accident*al*	[Derivational]

See also **inflection** and **1c.**

syntax Sentence structure. The grammatical arrangement of words, phrases, and clauses.

tense The form of the verb which indicates its relation to time. Inflection (*eat, eats, eating, ate, eaten*) and the use of auxiliaries (*will* eat, *have* eaten, *had* eaten, *will have* eaten, and so on) show the tense of a verb. See also **inflection** and Section **7**.

transformation A construction that is derived by converting a kernel sentence (simple, affirmative, and declarative, with a subject preceding a verb in the indicative mood, active voice) to another structure according to specific rules. Below are three examples.

John locked the office.
The office was locked by John.
  [Active voice changed to passive]

A stranger stood at the door.
At the door stood a stranger.   [Shift in word order]

Honey is in the bread.
There is honey in the bread.   [The expletive *there* added]

transitive See **verb**.

verb A part of speech denoting action, occurrence, or existence (state of being). Inflections indicate tense (and sometimes person and number) and mood of a verb: see **inflection, mood, voice,** and Section **7**.

A *transitive verb* is a verb that requires an object to complete its meaning. Transitive verbs can usually be changed from the active to the passive voice: see **object** and **voice**.

> Sid *laid* a wreath on the tomb.   [Direct object: *wreath*]

An *intransitive verb* is a verb (such as *go* or *sit*) that does not have an object to complete its meaning. Linking verbs, which take subject complements, are intransitive.

> She *has been waiting* patiently for hours.
> I *was* sick last Christmas.

The same verb may be transitive in one sentence and intransitive in another.

> TRANSITIVE   Lydia *reads* novels.   [Direct object: *novels*]
> INTRANSITIVE   Lydia *reads* well.

verb phrase See **phrase**.

verbal Having the characteristics of a verb. A verb form used as a noun, an adjective, or an adverb. Like verbs, verbals may take objects, complements, modifiers, and sometimes subjects.

> Cars **parked** *in the loading zone* will be towed away. [*Parked,* a participle, modifies *cars.*]
>
> **Studying** *dialects in our area* was fun. [*Studying,* a gerund, heads the phrase that is the subject of the verb *was.*]
>
> **To summarize,** the problem is so complex that there is no simple solution. [*To summarize,* an infinitive, is an adverbial, a sentence modifier.]

See also **gerund, infinitive, participle**.

vocabulary (content, lexical) word Nouns, verbs, and most modifiers—those words found in vocabulary-building lists. See also **function words**.

voice Transitive verbs have voice. A verb with a direct object is in the *active voice*. When the direct object is converted into a subject, as is done in the sentences below, the verb is in the *passive voice*. A passive verb is always a verb phrase consisting of a form of the verb *be* (or sometimes *get*) followed by a past participle.

ACTIVE VOICE

Priscilla *chose* John.
Ed *must learn* that.
Lacy *fired* Merle.

PASSIVE VOICE

John *was chosen* by Priscilla.
That *must be learned*.
Merle *got fired*.

word order The arrangement of words in sentences. Because of lost inflections, modern English depends heavily on word order to convey meaning.

Nancy gave Henry $14,000.
Henry gave Nancy $14,000.

Tony had built a barbecue pit.
Tony had a barbecue pit built.

Index

Index

Numbers in **boldface** refer to rules; other numbers refer to pages. A colon is used after each boldface number to indicate that the following pages refer to the rule or the part of the rule concerned. The **boldface** rule is given in detail—**9a(4)** or **20a(3)**, for example—in order to pinpoint a needed correction, but a less detailed reference (**9** or **9a**) will usually be sufficient for the student.